*The site of the original Prince Frederick Church. Only the mysterious
tangled graveyard left.*

Inscription on the Slate Tomb Stone.

Here lys the Bodys of
WILLIAM BROWN
*Who departed this Life
the 18 of Nov. 1749
Aged 34 Years
and HESTER BROWN His Wife
Who also departed this Life
the 27 of Sept. 1788*

*Our Savior shall our Lives restore
And raise us from our dark Abode
Our Flesh and Souls shall part no More
But dwell forever near our Lord.*

This stone is of slate and quite unimpaired by time. March 1916.

"Waiting in a holy stillness, Wrapt in sleep."

THE REGISTER BOOK

FOR THE

PARISH PRINCE FREDERICK WINYAW

ANN: DOM: 1713

PUBLISHED BY

THE NATIONAL SOCIETY OF
THE COLONIAL DAMES OF AMERICA

1916
WILLIAMS & WILKINS COMPANY
BALTIMORE

Please direct all correspondence and orders to:

www.southernhistoricalpress.com
or
SOUTHERN HISTORICAL PRESS, Inc.
PO BOX 1267
375 West Broad Street
Greenville, SC   29601
southernhistoricalpress@gmail.com

Originally published: Baltimore, MD. 1916
Reprinted by:
Southern Historical Press, Inc.
Greenville, SC
ISBN #0-89308-299-6
All rights Reserved.
Printed in the United States of America

FOREWORD

In 1682 it was found necessary to divide the inhabited parts of the Province of South Carolina into Counties, of which three were laid out, Berkeley, embracing Charleston, and the space around the capital, "extending from Sewee on the north to Stono Creek on the South; beyond this to the North-ward was Craven County; and to the Southward Colleton County, all extending within the land to a distance of thirty-five miles from the Sea-coast." (Rivers History of South Carolina, p. 134.)

Shortly afterwards Carteret county was added to the number. "These counties were subdivided into squares of 12,000 acres each, for the several shares of the proprietors, land-graves, and cassiques." Oldmixon in Carroll's vol. 2. Craven, formerly denominated Clarendon county, embraced in its subsequent extensions a much larger territory than the other counties. From Berkeley on the south, it reached towards the Cape Fear on the north, and with North Carolina for one boundary on the north, and north-west, and the Santee and its branches on the other sides, it extended through a wide belt of country from the sea-coast to the mountains. . . . It took its name from William, Earl of Craven, one of the first lord proprietors, and long retained it. . . . This county embraced the region of the Pedee throughout its course, from the North Carolina line southward.

The first parochial organization in Craven County was under an Act of Assembly of 1706, commonly called the Church Act, passed for the establishment of religious worship according to the Church of England, and for erecting churches. It divided the Province into ten parishes, of which Craven County constituted one, by the name of St. James Santee.—In 1721 the Parish of Prince George, Winyah, was established,—bounded on the S. W. by Santee River, on the N. E. by the Cape Fear River, on the East by the Ocean, and on the West "as far as it shall be inhabited by his Majesty's subjects." "Statutes" vol. 3, p. 171. In 1734, a further division took place; the Parish of Prince Frederick being established, and taken from that of Prince George, Winyah, embracing, according to the Act, the region of the Upper Pedee on the West. (Statutes, vol. 3, p. 374.) Dissatisfaction still continued to exist as to the dividing line between the two Parishes. It had been decided that the line was to extend due North over the Pedee River to the utmost bounds of the Province, it being provided "that the tract of land to the East of the said line, between that and the Sea, should be deemed as part of the Parish of Prince George, Winyah and on the other side of the line to the West, a part of the Parish of Prince Frederick." The following letter of Colonel George Pawley brought the matter to the notice of Council:—

July 7th 1739.

Please your Honour.—I think it my duty to inform your Honour that the dividing line of Prince George and Prince Frederick's Parishes is not yet finished according to the additional Act made, which was to cross Pedee River, and continue a North course till it touch the Provincial line; which, if it is done, will, in my humble opinion, break that small company as is of late erected on that Neck lying between Great Pedee and Little Pedee Rivers also it will cross some part of Queensborough Township which is a Parish of itself. Therefore if your Honour pleases to think on it, I doubt not but you will be of the opinion to have Great Pedee the boundary of the Parish upward from where the line is marked and strikes the said River; for as it now stands, there is a confusion among the Inhabitants, not knowing in what Parish they belong; also, the Surveyors know not how to certify their Plots some for one Parish and some for the other. There if the river be the Bounds the work is done, and no charge to the Publick; and that your Honour may have a better idea, I have drawn a small Draft of the Rivers in these Parts; so I beg your Honour will be so good as to forgive, if I have done amiss, for it is not my intent so to do, but the hearty desire for the good of the place. So beg leave to subscribe myself your Honour's most obedient, humble servant to command, "George Pawley."

To the Hon. Wm. Bull. (Council Journal, No. 7.)

Whereupon, it was "Ordered, that the Clerk do draw out two copies of Mr. George Pawley's letter, with the draft of the Rivers, one of them to be sent to the Parish of Prince Frederick's, the other to be sent to the Parish of Prince George to know whether they have any objection to make to the proposals contained in the said letter, for settling the Boundary of these Parishes, and to return an answer." The matter having thus been referred to the inhabitants, action was taken by them; and on the 25th January 1742, a Petition from sundry inhabitants of Prince George was laid before Council praying that the Great Pedee might be made the dividing line between the Parishes; . . . . This petition was signed by George Pawley, John Woodbury, David Cherrey and thirty-eight others.

A counter petition was at the same time presented by John Avant, and nineteen others, inhabitants of Prince Frederick's praying the line should not be so run:

"1st. Because the Inhabitants residing between the said rivers are twelve miles and upwards nearer to our Parish Church than to George-town.

2nd. The major part of the above-said Inhabitants must go through our Parish and pass by our Church to public worship, and other religious duties and other officers to George-town.

3rd. Because the said Inhabitants humbly pray to be included in the River.

4th. Because the Town-ship of Queensborough is laid on both sides of the Pedee River; and

5th. That whenever the Legislature shall to erect the Township of Queensborough and Williamsburg into separate Parishes, this of Prince Frederick's being the oldest Parish (from which Prince George was divided,) will be confined to narrow limits, and consequently for ever remain one of the smallest, if not poorest, Parishes in the Province, if so valuable a branch as that of Pedee be taken from it."

"We further presume to acquaint your Honrs that the North line appointed by Act of Assembly to be run from John Bogg's plantation, on Black River, was supposed and intended (by our

Representatives) to make Pedee River at or below the plantation Euhaney, belonging to Mr. Percival Pawley, about 18 miles distant from said Bogg's plantation; but we now find that a North course excludes from this Parish sundry families residing on Pedee River, who constantly attend divine service in this Parish, being about twelve miles distant from our Church, and at least twenty-two miles from George-town."

("Council Journal," No. 8, pp. 454–5.)

"We therefore pray your Hon^{rss}

to relieve the Inhabitants by ordering the dividing line to be run a straight course, which shall be done on our own proper Charges."

. . . . The Petitions were ordered to lie on the table.

"Council Journal" No. 8, p. 455.

These extracts from public documents will show how the two parishes bearing the names of Princes instead of Saints were established; in reading the records it almost seems as though their un-saintly names had influenced their early career; but what must strike this generation with wonder is the great importance they attached to their churchly duties, and the long journeys they made to attend Divine Service, even when ministered to by very earthly humans; their constant provision for the poor of the Parish must excite our admiration, in the midst of much which does not, to say the least. The present church of Prince Frederick is situated near the Great Pee Dee River, (which runs through North Carolina almost to the border of Virginia, under the name of Yadkin, and takes it rise in a spring at Blowing Rock.) There is a little wooden summer chapel in the village of Plantersville, where service is held every Sunday. The parish was named after that Prince of Wales, Frederic, who the father of George III, and son of George II., was himself never King; it was after his daughter the Princess Augusta, that the town of Augusta, Georgia, was named.

The first church building of this parish, as far as we know, was built on a high beautifully situated bluff, overlooking the Black River, about twenty miles south-west of the present building. An expedition to the spot, to take some photographs of it was made late in March. Nothing could have been more beautiful and peaceful that this God's Acre, lying high above the fast-flowing river, shaded by stately water-oaks, rejoicing in their glistening new foliage, and the white marble monuments, peeping through a tangle of wild azalea, dogwood, and honeysuckle, every open space covered with wild violets, purple and white, while the tiny perfect blossoms of the housetonia delighted the eye and spirit, for they are simply little wild for-get-me-nots. The photos were not very successful, but were the best that could be made in the deep shadows of the sacred spot. There is no fence or enclosure around the graveyard which must cover two acres of space, but there are private brick enclosures with locked gates, and the marble monuments within are well kept and cared for.

It was in this higher region that the first settlers fixed their homes, for indigo grew wild around and that was their first farming industry. Fortunes were made rapidly by its cultivation, and we are told that at one time it brought from four to five dollars a pound. In 1754 the amount of indigo shipped from South Carolina was 216,924 pounds (?). (Ramsay's History S. C., vol. II, p. 138.) Its cultivation ceased about the close of the century or soon after. It was then that the settlers moved away nearer to the coast and began the cultivation of Rice on the lower banks of the Pee Dee River and the church on the high bluff over-looking the short but very deep Black River, was left without a congregation. There is no record for many years, but "In 1827, Monday April 9th at the Universal Church on Pee Dee, (a church built by the neighbours of Pee Dee of all denominations as a place of worship for all denominations) to take into consideration the best means of erecting an Episcopal church, between Dr. William Allston's plantation and Black River Ferry." (Extract from the records of vestry of Prince Frederick Parish from April 1827, to March 29th, 1880.) Apparently the vestry could not agree on a suitable place for the Church, for though the money was raised and a building Committee appointed, nothing was done. The next record is date Jany 28th. 1855. The Revd Hugh Fraser in the Chair. . . . The following persons were appointed a Building Committee, viz, D. McDowell, R. F. Allston, and Francis Weston, with power to contract for and build a church of conven-

ient dimensions on a bit of land given by the Revd Hugh Fraser.
. . . The following gentlemen are requested to act as Vestry
men—viz,

> Capt. John Allston,
> D^r W^m. Allston,
> Francis Weston,
> Benj. F. Dunkin,

and Joel R. Poinsett

> As Wardens,
> R. F. W. Allston,
> D. M^c. Dowell

> As delegates to the Convention,
> Rev^d. M. H. Lance,
> B. F. Dunkin,
> J. R. Poinsett.

The building was completed the ensuing Spring, and Service
held in the Chapel.—The land liberally granted by the Rev^d.
Hugh Fraser, together with a space of fifteen feet wide on his
North line down to the River with Public Landing, was surveyed
by R. F. W. Allston, the grant recorded, and the Chapel con-
secrated by the Right Rev^d, Nathaniel Bowen, D.D. who also
preached.—Rev^d. Hugh Fraser read the sentence of Consecration,
& the Rev^d. M. H. Lance read the Morning Prayer, the Rev^d. P.
Trapier Keith, and Rev^d. Alex^r Glennie were also present. . . ."

The minutes of the Vestry meetings continue without anything
of great interest, they purchased several hundred acres of Glebe.
also erected a comfortable and commodious Winter parsonage,
for the Rector of the Chapel, and also a very comfortable summer
parsonage in the little pine-land settlement of Plantersville, and
the Parish flourished but they seemed content with the wooden
Chapel until the Easter Meeting of 1857, when we read, "The
want of sufficient accommodation for the congregation was then
discussed" and it was decided to erect a new edifice of brick,
suitable for the present and future wants of the Parish." A list
was opened and most liberal sums subscribed. The contract
was given to Mr. Louis Barbot, Architect, and is a beautiful
building, costing $12,650. . . . There were many delays;
the Contractor Glenn died; the furnishings and finishings which

were ordered abroad, were lost running the Blockade, the war having been declared before the building was quite finished, and it remained an unfinished ruin almost until 1876, when by the generosity of John Earl Allston of Brooklyn, N. Y., the building was repaired and completed. As soon as this was accomplished the wooden Church built in 1836 was moved to the summer settlement of Plantersville where it is still used for service every Sunday by the faithful few, within reach, often literally a scriptural quorum.

The writer first became interested in the publication of these records when it became necessary to repair the brick church which had been damaged by storms and was not thought safe, so that service had not been held there for a great many years. Being appointed on the Committee for raising funds for its repair, it was suggested that the publication of the Church Record by subscription, would be a means of adding to the fund; this idea was eagerly adopted and a long list of people whose family records were in the old manuscript, which was kept in a box in the Bank, being in a very frail and tattered condition, put their names down for a volume at five dollars. Then came the terrible European War, and no money was forthcoming, and the publication had to be given up. It was then that the National Society of the Colonial Dames of America came forward and through its "Committee for the Preservation of Existing Records," with great generosity gave the whole amount needed for the publication of the old Register. To them our heart-felt thanks are offered.

I would also desire to return thanks to Mr S. A. Graham of Heineman, S. C. who gave me a type-written copy of the Register, which he had made for his own use; also my warm thanks to Mr D. E. Huger Smith, of Charleston, for his great assistance in verifying the copy with the original; also to D^r. Joseph S. Ames, of Johns Hopkins University, for his most valuable aid in making the index, as well as for his advice, and support in the matter when I was cast down and discouraged, seeing no prospect of getting the money to accomplish the work in which I had become so deeply interested.

ELIZABETH W. ALLSTON PRINGLE.

Chicora Wood, April 17th, 1916.
Georgetown, S. C.

A CATALOGUE OF PERSONS NAMES BORN AND BAPTIZED IN THIS PLACE CALLED BLACK RIVER WINYAW BEFORE THE SAME WAS CONSTITUTED INTO A DISTINCT PARISH

Peter Son of John Lane and of Sarah his Wife was Born Nov^{br} ye 5th 1713

Tabitha Daughter of John Lane and of Sarah his Wife was Born 8^{br} ye 1st 1716.

James Son of John Lane and of Sarah his Wife was Born 8^{br} ye 19th 1719.

John Son of John Bell and of Martha his Wife was Born Feb^{ry} ye 28th 1716/7

Marmaduke Son of John Bell and of Martha his Wife was Born 8^{br} ye 10th 1719.

Mary Daughter of John Bell and of Martha his Wife was Born May ye 24th 1722.

William Son of John Bell and of Martha his Wife was Born Decem^{br} ye 4th 1724.

Christopher Son of Christopher Butler and of Abigail his Wife was Born Feb^{ry} ye 27th 1723/4

Sarah Daughter of John Lane and of Sarah his Wife was Born Jan^{ry} ye 15th 1722/3

Zechariah Exal Son of Peter Sanders and of Susannah his Wife was Born March ye 11th 1716/7

Peter Son of Peter Sanders and of Susannah his Wife was Born Dec^{br} ye 17th 1718

Lydia Daughter of Peter Sanders and of Susannah his Wife was Born Jan^{ry} ye 1st 1720/1

William Son of Peter Sanders and of Susannah his Wife was Born May ye 31st 1723

Sarah Daughter of Peter Sanders and of Susannah his Wife was Born Feb^{ry} ye 15th 1724/5

Gennett Daughter of Daniel Shaw and of Mary his Wife was Born May ye 8th 1724

Bartholomew Son of Edwd Butler and of Mary his Wife was
      Baptized Feb^{ry} ye 21st 1724/5
Sarah Daughter of Thomas Jenkins and of Mary his Wife was
      Born 8^{br} ye 15th 1724

REGISTER OF SUNDRY ADULT PERSONS BAPTIZED BY THE REVEREND MR MORRIT[T (rubbed off)]

Susannah the Wife of Peter Sanders was Baptized on Decem^{br} ye 25th 1726

Hannah the Wife of John Avant was Baptized on Decem^{br} ye 25th 1726

Mary the Wife of Caleb Avant was Baptized on Jan^{ry} ye 2^d 1726/7

Richard Son of Samuel Miller and of Mary his Wife was Baptized Feb^{ry} ye 28th 1724/5

Lydia Daughter of John Avant and of Hannah his Wife was Born December the 18th 1718 and was Baptized Feb^{ry} ye 25th 1724/5

Avant Francis the Son of John Avant and of Hannah his Wife was Born July the 29th 1722 and was Baptized Feb^{ry} ye 25th 1724/5

Avant Hannah The Daughter of John Avant and of Hannah his Wife was Born Decemb^r ye 28th 1725 and was baptized the Sunday following

Avant Rebecca the Daughter of John Avant and of Hannah his Wife was Born Feb^{ry} ye 27th 1728/9 and was baptized April ye 27th ensuing

Thompson Deborah the Daughter of John Thompson and of Martha his Wife was Born ye 3^d of Janu^{ry} 1724/5

Thompson Margaret the Daughter of John Thompson and of Martha his Wife was Born ye 15th of September 1726

Thompson Sarah Wigfall the daughter of John Thompson Junr and of Anna his Wife was Born ye 22^d of August 1728

Beech Mary the Daughter of Joseph Beech and of Mary his Wife was Born the 10th of February 1729/30

Hughes Meredith the Son of Meredith Hughes Esqr and of Elizabeth his Wife was Born March ye 23^d 1724/5 Baptized Decemb^r. 26th 1726

Shaw Amos Son of Daniel Shaw and of Mary his Wife was Born July ye 8th 1726

Sanders Samuel Son of Peter Sanders and of Susannah his Wife
was Born 8ʙʳ yᵉ 10ᵗʰ 1726

Atkinson George Son of Anthony Atkinson and of Mary his Wife
was Baptized on Decemᵇʳ yᵉ 25ᵗʰ 1726 was Born October
18th 1725

Hughes William Son of Meredith Hughes Esqʳ and of Elizabeth
his Wife was Born Novᵇʳ yᵉ 12ᵗʰ 1726 Baptized December
26ᵗʰ 1726

White Mary Daughter of Anthony White and of Mary his Wife
was Baptized on Decemᵇʳ yᵉ 26ᵗʰ 1726

Hoddy Hannah Daughter of John Hoddy and of Hannah his
Wife was Born 8ʙʳ yᵉ 18ᵗʰ 1724

Butler Henrietta Daughter of Christopher Butler and of Abigail
his Wife was Born 8ʙʳ yᵉ 19ᵗʰ 1725

Allen Susannah Daughter of Joseph Allen and of Susannah his
Wife was Baptized Janʳʸ yᵉ 1ˢᵗ 1726/7

Oldham John Son of John Oldham and of Priscilla his Wife was
Baptized Janʳʸ 5ᵗʰ 1726/7

Green John Son of John Green and of Elizabeth his Wife was
Born Decemᵇʳ yᵉ 28ᵗʰ 1726

Avant Aaron Son of Benjamin Avant and of Mary his Wife was
Baptized Sepᵗʳ yᵉ 3ᵈ 1727

Avant Agnes Daughter of Caleb Avant and of Mary his Wife was
Baptized Sepᵗʳ yᵉ 3ᵈ 1727

Port Joseph Son of Joseph Port and of Anne his Wife was Born
August yᵉ 25ᵗʰ 1726

Bell Anne Daughter of John Bell and of Martha his Wife was
Born Augˢᵗ yᵉ 16ᵗʰ 1727

Butler Samuel Son of Christopher Butler and of Abigail his Wife
was Born Sepᵗʳ yᵉ 11ᵗʰ 1727

White Hannah Daughter of Anthony White and of Mary his Wife
was Born Sepᵗʳ yᵉ 13ᵗʰ 1727

Roberts James Son of Benjamin Roberts and Abigail his Wife was
Born Janʳʸ yᵉ 20ᵗʰ 1724/5

Roberts Josiah Son of Benjamin Roberts and Abigail his Wife
was Born Novᵇʳ yᵉ 30ᵗʰ 1726

Brunson Abigail Daughter of John Brunson and Anne his Wife
was Born Sepᵗʳ yᵉ 6ᵗʰ 1727

Jenkins James Son of Thomas Jenkins and of Mary his Wife was Born Nov^br ye 18th 1726

Sanders Susannah Daughter of Peter Sanders and of Susannah his Wife was Born March ye 27th 1729

Brown Elizabeth Daughter of Jonathan Brown and of Margaret his Wife was Born May ye 11th 1726

Brown Frances Daughter of Jonathan Brown and of Margaret his Wife was Born Feb^ry ye 28th 1728/9

Thompson Anna Daughter of John Thompson & of Anna his Wife was Born April ye 29th 1730

Clark George the Son of Joseph Clark and of Anna his Wife was Born Feb^ry ye 4th 1728/9

Jenkins Samuel the Son of Thomas Jenkins and Mary his Wife was Born   and Baptized August ye 25th 1730

Johnson Deborah the Daughter of Peter Johnson Junr and Deborah his Wife was Born   and Baptized August ye 25th 1730

Mackintosh Mary the Daughter of John Mackintosh and Mary his Wife was born   and Baptized August ye 25th 1730

Allen Joseph the Son of Joseph Allen and of Susannah his Wife was Born August ye 7th and Baptized September ye 13th 1730

Crib John the Son of John Crib and of Elizabeth his Wife Was Born December ye 10th 1729 and baptized ye 27th of September ensuing

Shaw Mary the Daughter of Daniel Shaw and Mary his Wife was Born the 8th of May 1728 and baptized ye 5th of August ensuing

Shaw Isabel the Daughter of Daniel Shaw and of Mary his Wife was Born the 9th of February 1729/30 and Baptized ye 22^d of March ensuing

Marbeuff William the Son of Joseph Marbeuff and of Elizabeth his Wife was Born August ye 2^d and Baptized ye 28th of February ensuing 1730/1

Bonnell Daniel the Son of John Bonnell and of Honora his Wife was Born August ye 8th and Baptized ye 11th of April ensuing 1731

Brown Jonathan the Son of Jonathan Brown and of Margret his Wife was born ye 20th of March and Baptized ye 18th of April ensuing 1731

White Anthony Martin the Son of Anth^o White and of Mary his Wife was Born September 23^d and Christned ye 1st of October ensuing

Brown Hannah the Daughter of James Brown and of Hannah his Wife was Born May ye 7th and Christned ye 10th of June ensuing 1727

Bell Jean Daughter of John Bell and of Martha his Wife was Born Sep^{tr} ye 17th 1729

Bond Mary Daughter of Abraham Bond and of Abigail his Wife was Born Decem 3^d 1730

Allstone John the Son of William Allstone and of Hester his Wife was Baptized July 8 1731

Foster Blanch the Daughter of Arthur Foster and Mary his Wife was Born March and Baptized May ye 9th 1731

Clegg Lydia Daughter of Sam^{el} Clegg and Mehittobell his Wife was Born September 9th 1731 and Baptized October 17th 1731

Lewis Mary Daughter of Henry & Hester Lewis Baptized Febry 27th 1731/2

Cribb Thomas the Son of Thomas and Elizabeth Cribb Born Octob^r 25th 1731 Baptized Janry 16th & Inducted March 5th 1731/2

Hughes Henry Son of Meredith Hughes and Mary his Wife was Born January 19th 1735 and Baptized June 6th 1736

BAPTIZED BY THE REVrd Mr JOHN FORDYCE

Benjamin Avant Son of Benjamin Avant & Mary his Wife Born February 24th 1735 Baptized November 14th 1736

Staples Abraham Son of Abraham Staples & Sarah his Wife Born August 24th 1735 Baptized November 14th 1736

Ball Bartholomew Son of Bartholomew Ball & Elizabeth his Wife Born June 11th 1736 and Baptized December 12th 1736

Fordyce Thomas Son of the Rev^rd Mr John Fordyce & Elizabeth his spouse Born January 24th 1736/7 Baptized February 23rd 1736/7

Stephens Oliver Son of William Stephens & Sarah his Wife Baptized April 10th 1737

Maiden Ann Daughter of John Maiden & Unity his Wife Baptized April 17th 1737

Kemp Sarah Daughter of William Kemp & Elizabeth his Wife Born February 22^d 1736 Baptized May 1st 1737

Barton John Son of John Barton & Elizabeth his Wife Born July 16th 1736 Baptized May 8th 1737

Skinner William Son of John Skinner & Mary his Wife Born February 8th 1736 Baptized May 8th 1737

Chinnars Mary Daughter of Isaac Chinnars & Rebecca his Wife Born April 28th 1737 Baptized May ye 9th 1737

Henning Ursilla Daughter of John Henning & Grace his Wife Born March 1737 Baptized May 15th 1737

Smith Catherine Daughter of William Smith & Mary his Wife Born November 26th 1735 Baptized May 17th 1737

Willis, William Son of Widow Willis Baptized November 12th 1736

Bonnell, Hannah Daughter of John Bonnell & Honora his Wife Baptized June 5th 1737

Hughes, John Son of Meredith Hughes & Mary his Wife Born June 5th Baptized July 10th 1737

White, Catherine, Daughter of John White & of Sarah his Wife Born March 7th 1736 Baptized July 10th 1737

Buckholts, Elizabeth, adult Baptized August 2^d 1737

Roberts, John, Son of Benjamin Roberts & of Abigail his Wife Born March 6th 1736 Baptized October 16th 1737

Colt, Sarah, Daughter of William Colt and of Rebecca Anne his Wife Born October 8th Baptized November 12th 1737

Hughes, Peter, Son of William Hughes & of Eleonora his Wife Born March 27th 1736 Bapt^d Novemb^r 27th 1737

Windham, Mary, Daughter of Charles Windham and of Mary his Wife Born Septemb^r 7th 1735 Bapt^d Decemb^r 8th 1737

Minnikin, Moses, Son of Moses Minnikin & of Mary his Wife Born April 4th Baptized Decemb^r 25th 1737

Saunders, Ann, Daughter of George Saunders & of Hannah his Wife Born November 5th 1736 Baptized Decemb^r 25th 1737

Burtley, Sarah, Daughter of Richard Burtley & of Sarah his Wife
Born March 23ᵈ 1735 Baptized February 12ᵗʰ 1737

Burtley, Margret, Daughter of Richard Burtley & of Sarah his
Wife Born Decembʳ 30ᵗʰ Baptᵈ February 12ᵗʰ 1737

Lane, Peter, Son of Peter Lane & of Sarah his Wife Born December
16ᵗʰ Baptized March 12ᵗʰ 1737

Tamplet, Joseph, Son of Peter Tamplet & of Isabel his Wife Born
April 1ˢᵗ Baptized May 14ᵗʰ 1738

Jenkins, Patience, Daughter of Thomas Jenkins & of Mary his
Wife Born March 2ᵈ 1737 Baptized May 14ᵗʰ 1738

Hendlin, Benjamin, Son of John Hendlin & of Margret his Wife
Born May 27ᵗʰ 1737 Baptized May 18ᵗʰ 1738

Martha Mary Skipper, natural Daughter of Henry Overstreet and
of Mary Skipper Born February 20ᵗʰ 1735 Baptd July
1ˢᵗ 1738

Gardner, William, Son of William Gardner & of Sarah his Wife
Born June 26ᵗʰ Baptized July 14ᵗʰ 1738

Blake, John, Son of John Blake & of Ann his Wife Baptᵈ July 30ᵗʰ
1738

McGinney, Ann, Adult Baptized August 4ᵗʰ 1738

Harrington, Mary, Daughter of Thomas Harrington & of Hannah
his Wife Born July 15ᵗʰ 1736 Baptized December 24ᵗʰ
1738

Dupree, John, Son of Josias Garnier Dupree & of Ann his Wife
Baptized December 24ᵗʰ 1738

Staples, Joannah, Daughter of Abraham Staples & of Sarah his
Wife Born November 12ᵗʰ 1737 Baptized January 21ˢᵗ
1738

Barton, Joannah, Daughter of William Barton and of Mary his
Wife Born November 14ᵗʰ Baptized January 21ˢᵗ 1738

Stephens, James, Son of William Stephens & of Sarah his Wife
Born August 25ᵗʰ Baptized February 5ᵗʰ 1738

Cain, John, Son of John Cain & of Ann His Wife Born May 7ᵗʰ
Baptized February 4ᵗʰ 1738

Farewell, Henry, Son of Thomas Farewell & of Mary his Wife
Born April 25ᵗʰ Baptized February 4ᵗʰ 1738

Bonnell, Elizabeth, Daughter of John Bonnell & of Honora his
Wife Born Decʳ 24ᵗʰ Baptized March 4ᵗʰ 1738

Hughes, Ann, Daughter of Meredith Hughes & of Mary his Wife Born January 20th Baptized March 7th 1738

Senior, Sarah, Daughter of George Senior And of Mary his Wife Baptized March 11th 1738

Port, Benjamin, Son of Joseph Port and of Ann his Wife Born Septemb^r 4th Baptized March 24th 1738

Harrington, Sarah Whitmel, Daughter of Thomas Harrington and of Hannah his Wife Born Octob^r 21st Bapt^d March 24th 1738

Hall, Edward, Son of Thomas Hall and of Grace his Wife Born Novemb^r 2^d 1738 Baptized June 24th 1739

Plowden, Katherine, Daughter of Edward Plowden and of Susannah his Wife born September 18th 1737 Baptized June 24th 1739

Saunders, Sarah, Daughter of George Saunders and of Hannah his Wife Born February 18th 1738 Baptized September 15th 1739

Lanning, Ann, Daughter of James Lanning and of Sarah his wife Born February 21st 1738 Baptized July 15th 1739

Avant, Hannah, Daughter of Benjamin Avant and of Mary his Wife Dec^d Born August 8th 1737 Baptized October 28th 1739

Keen, Andrew, Son of John Keen and of Elizabeth his Wife Born October 2^d 1739 Baptized October 28th 1739

June, Elizabeth, Daughter of John June and of Ann his Wife Born August 2^d 1739 Baptized November 7th 1739

Goodyear, John, Son of Jacob Goodyear and of Mary his Wife Born July 23^d 1739 Baptized November 11th 1739

Roberts, David, Son of Benjamin Roberts and of Abigail his Wife Born July 9th 1739 Baptized November 11th 1739

Windham, Daniel, Son of Charles Windham and of Mary his Wife Born September 1st 1738 Baptized February 5th 1739

Outerbridge, Leonard, Son of Leonard Outerbridge and Ann his Wife Born December 6th 1739 Baptized February 15th 1739

Godbolt, John, (alias John Hains) natural Son of John Godbolt and Elizabeth Hains Born July 24th 1739. Baptized April 24th 1740. N B The s^d Godbolt & Hains Married the same day

Tamplet, Christian Mary, Daughter of Peter and Isabell Tamplet Born January 31st 1739 Baptized May 24th 1740

Blake, John, Son of John Blake and of Ann his Wife Baptized June 15th 1740

Cain, Sarah, Daughter of John Cain and of Ann his Wife Born December 25th 1739 Baptized July 20th 1740

Plowden, Coulen, Son of Edward Plowden and of Susannah his Wife Born January 20th 1739 Baptized August 10th 1740

Dial, Mary, Daughter of Thomas Dial and of Katherine his Wife Born December 21st 1739 Baptized August 10th 1740

King, Priscilla, Daughter of Charles King and of Mary his Wife Born July 5th 1740 Baptized August 11th 1740

Collins, Sarah, Daughter of Andrew Collins and of Sarah his Wife Born September 3d 1738 Baptized October 26th 1740

Fordyce, Elizabeth, Daughter of the Revrd John Fordyce and of Elizabeth his spouse Born July 25th 1740 Baptized August 24th 1740

Goodall, Mary, Daughter of William Goodall and of Elizabeth his Wife Born December 25th 1739 Baptized October 26th 1740

Lewis, Judith, Daughter of Henry Lewis and of Hester his Wife Born August 18th 1740 Baptized October 31st 1740

Lane, Tabitha, Daughter of Peter Lane and of Sarah his Wife Born November 9th 1740 Baptized December 14th 1740

Booth, Abigail, Daughter of John Booth and of Margaret his Wife Born September 5th 1740 Baptized February 22d 1740

Dupree, John Elders, Son of Josias Garnier Dupree and of Ann his Wife Born February 17th 1740 Baptized February 27th 1740

Collins, Andrew, Son of Andrew Collins and of Sarah his Wife Born February 18th 1740 Baptized March 20th 1740

Bonnell, Anthony, Son of John Bonnell and of Honora his Wife Born March 3d 1740 Baptized April 19th 1741

Tamplet, Elisha, Son of Peter Tamplet and of Isabel his Wife Born February 9th 1740 Baptized April 23d 1741

Barton, Sarah, Daughter of William Barton and of Mary his Wife Born April 2d 1741 Baptized May 17th 1741

Staples, Hannah, Daughter of Abraham Staples and of Sarah his Wife Born April 22d 1740 Baptized May 24th 1741

Blake, Ann, Daughter of Richard Blake and of Elizabeth his
Wife Born February 9th 1740 Baptized June 7th 1741

Colt, William Saxby, Colt Son of William Colt and of Rebecca
his Wife Born April 10th 1741 Baptized July 6th 1741

Outerbridge, Joseph, Son of Leonard Outerbridge and of Ann his
Wife Born July 23d 1741 Baptized August 23d 1741

Gardner, Mary, Daughter of William Gardner and of Sarah his
Wife Born March 8th 1740 Baptized September 3d 1741

White, William, Son of John White and of Sarah his Wife Decd
Born August 17th 1741 Baptized September 10th 1741

Evans, Rebecca, Wife of John Evans aged 25 years Baptized
October 2d 1741

Evans, John, Son of John Evans and of the above said Rebecca
his Wife Born July 29th 1741 Baptized October 2d 1741

Kemp, Stephen, Son of William Kemp and of Elizabeth his Wife
Born July 26th 1741 Baptized October 18th 1741

Ball, Elizabeth, Daughter of Robert Ball and of Mercy his Wife
about 18 years of age Baptized December 14th 1741

Millikin, Rachel, Daughter of Moses Millikin and of Mary his
Wife Born October 5th 1741 Baptized January 3d 1741

Saunders, Nathaniel, Son of George Saunders and of Hannah his
Wife Born March 15th 1740 Baptized February 7th 1741

Heatley, William, Son of William Heatley and of Mary his Wife
Born August 8th 1741 Baptized March 9th 1741

Heatley, Elizabeth, Daughter of William Heatley and of Mary his
Wife Born June 5th 1740 Baptized March 9th 1741

Green, John, Son of William Green and of Lydia his Wife Born
February 14th 1741 Baptized March 21st 1741

Thomas, Samson, Adult, Aged about 34 years Baptized March
26th 1741

Cain, Hannah, Daughter of John Cain and of Ann his Wife Born
November 7th 1741 Baptized April 11th 1742

Ford, Susannah, Daughter of James Ford and of Sarah his Wife
Born December 28th 1741 Baptised May 27th 1742

Hemsworth, William, Son of William Hemsworth and of Naomi his
Wife Born December 15th 1741 Baptized June 13th 1742

Plowden, Elizabeth, Daughter of Edward Plowden and of Susannah
his Wife Born December 5th 1741 Baptised June 13th 1742

Dyal, Catherine, Daughter of Thomas Dyal Jun[r] and of Catherine his Wife Born November 3[d] 1741 Baptised June 13th 1742

Turbevill, Obedience, Daughter of William Turbevill & of Margaret his Wife Born May 30th 1741 Baptised June 13th 1742

Robertson, Alexander, Son of Born June 4th 1739 Baptised June 13th 1742

Robertson, Eleonar, Daughter of Born March 15th 1741 Baptised June 13th 1742

Rhodas, Nathaniel Son of Born January 18th 1735 Baptised June 13th 1742

Rhodas, Joseph Born February 2[d] 1737 Baptised June 13th 1742

Rhodas, Solomon Born February 18th 1739 Baptised June 13th 1742

Rhodas, Isabell Born January 23[d] 1741 Baptised June 13th 1742

Fox, Temperance, Daughter of Henry Fox and of Martha his Wife Born March 19th 1741 Baptised June 17th 1742

Mack Girt, Sarah, Daughter of James Mack Girt and of Priscilla his Wife Born December 24th 1741 Baptised June 17th 1742

Elizabeth, Hainsworth, alias Hesse, natural Daughter of Richard Hainsworth and of Elizabeth Hesse, Born January 8th 1741. Baptized June 17th 1742.

John, Saunders, alias Kelly, natural Son of George Saunders and of Agnes Kelly, Born August 1st 1741. Baptized June 17th 1742

Richardson, Richard, Son of Richard Richardson & of Mary his Wife Born March 4th 1741 Baptised June 17th 1742

Fraser, Philip, Son of Fraser and of Elizabeth his Wife aged about 10 years Baptised June 17th 1742

Ballantine, Catherine, Daughter of William Ballantine and of Eleoner his Wife Born September 5th 1737 Baptised June 17th 1742

Griffin, John, Son of Joseph Griffin and of Joyce his Wife Born October 8th 1719 Baptized June 17th 1742

Ryland, William, aged about 18 years Baptised June 18th 1742

Canty, Martha, Daughter of Joseph Canty and of Mary his Wife Born April 12th 1742 Baptised June 18th 1742

Canty, William, Son of Samuel Canty and of Ann his Wife Born
     July 21st 1733 Baptised June 18th 1742
Canty, Joseph, Son of Samuel Canty and of Ann his Wife Born
     January 26th 1735 Baptised June 18th 1742
Canty, Jane, Daughter of Samuel Canty and of Ann his Wife
     Born March 19th 1740 Baptised June 18th 1742
Snow, Jacob, Son of William Snow and of Mary his Wife Born
     February 22d 1735 Baptised June 19th 1742
Snow, William, Son of William Snow and of Mary his Wife Born
     April 22d 1738 Baptised June 19th 1742
Snow, Mary, Daughter of William Snow and of Mary his Wife
     Born February 20th 1739 Baptised June 19th 1842
Snow, Ann, Daughter of William Snow and of Mary his Wife
     Born March 1st 1741 Baptised June 19th 1742
Abigail, Mineally, Natural Daughter of Thomas Wright and of
     Sarah Mineally Baptised June 19th 1742
Elizabeth, Mineally, natural daughter of Edward Chambers and
     of Mary Mineally Baptised June 19th 1742
Brown, Hester, Daughter of William Brown and of Hester his
     Wife Born January 7th 1741 Baptised June 20th 1742
Oliver, Hannah, Daughter of Robert Oliver and of Mary his Wife
     Born April 14th 1742 Baptised June 20th 1742
Michew, William, Son of Abraham Michew and of Lydia his Wife
     Born May 5th 1742 Baptised June 23d 1742
Henning, Joseph, Son of John Henning and of Grace his Wife
     Born June 4th 1742 Baptised July 29th 1742
Barton, Honora, Daughter of John Barton and of Honora his Wife
     Born July 17th 1742 Baptised July 29th 1742
Blake, Richard, Son of Richard Blake and of Elizabeth his Wife
     Born June 11th 1742 Baptised August 9th 1742
Metcalfe, Ann, Daughter of William Metcalf and of Sarah his
     Wife Born January 25th 1741 Baptised August 10th 1742
Avant, Ann, Daughter of Benjamin Avant and of Ann his Wife
     Born June 27th 1742 Baptised September 1st 1742
Ford, Jane, Aged About 16 or 17 years Baptised September 10th
     17—
Murphy, Maurice, Son of Michael Murphy and of Mary his Wife
     Born August 28th 1740 Baptised October—1742

Cromwell, Oliver Ireton, Son of Thomas Ireton Cromwell & of
      Mary his Wife Born October 26th 1737 Baptised October
      28th 1742

Hughes, Elijah, Son of Solomon Hughes & of Judith, natural Son
      Born December 4th 1740 Baptised October 31st 1742

Blake, Elisabeth, Daughter of John Blake and of Ann his Wife
      Born March 5th 1741 Baptised December 4th 1742

King, Sarah Berrisford, Daughter of Charles King and of Mary
      his Wife Born July 24th 1742 Baptised December 12th
      1742

Dupre, Richard, Son of Josias Garnier Dupre and of Ann his Wife
      Born December 7th 1742 Baptised December 17th 1742

M^cpharson, Daniel, Son of James M^cpharson & of Elizabeth his
      Wife Born November 14th 1742 Baptised December 19th
      1742

Onion, George, Son of John Onion and of Martha his Wife Born
      September 1st 1741 Baptised December 21st 1742

Mary Harrington Daughter of Whitmell Harrington and Janit his
      Wife Born December 12th 1742 Baptised January 9th
      1742/3

John McDowell Son of John McDowell and Lucretia his Wife
      Born November 7th 1742 Baptised April 10th 1743

Charity Crawford Daughter of James Crawford and Cassia his
      Wife Born June 4th 1742 Baptised 15th Day of April,
      1743

Sarah Noland Daughter of George Noland and Rebeccah his Wife
      Born October 12th 1740 Baptised April 24th 1743

Anne Outerbridge Daughter of Leonard Outerbridge and Anne his
      Wife Born and Baptised August 10th 1743

Mary Hickman Daughter of Isaac Hickman and Elizabeth his Wife
      Born December 7th 1740 Baptised August 14th 1743

Sarah Hickman Daughter of Isaac Hickman and Elisabeth his
      Wife Born February 7th 1742/3 Baptised August 14th
      1743

George Chekin Son of William Chekin and Elisabeth his Wife
      Born April 6th 1743 Baptised August 21st 1743

Elisabeth Hall Daughter of John Hall and Mary his Wife Born
      April 8th 1741 Baptised October 8th 1743

Mary Spencer Daughter of John Spencer and Judith his Wife
Born September 17th 1743 Baptised October 9th 1743

William Gibson Son of Gideon Gibson and Mary his Wife Born
September 15th 1743 Baptised October 9th 1743

Thomas Walley Son of Thomas Walley and Jemima his Wife
Born June 24th 1743 Baptised October 9th 1743

Hannah Saunders Daughter of George Saunders and Hannah his
Wife Born June 19th 1743 Baptised October 8th 1743

Malachy Murphey Son of Michael Murphey and Mary his Wife
Born August 24th 1743 Baptised October 9th 1743

James Woold Son of John Michael Woold and Frances his Wife
Born March 29th 1743 Baptised October 9th 1743

John Freeman Son of Thomas Freeman and Mary his Wife Born
September 20th 1741 Baptised October 10th 1743

David Perkins Son of John Perkins and Mary his Wife Born July
15th 1743 Baptised 11th October 1743

Peter Megee Son of William Megee and Elisabeth his Wife Born
September 17th 1742 Baptised October 12th 1743

Elisabeth Crutchley Daughter of Jonathan Crutchley Deceas'd
and Elizabeth Megee Born January 10th 1739 Baptised
October 12th 1743

Arthur Bowers Son of Giles Bowers and Martha his Wife Born
February 15th 1741/2 Baptised October 12th 1743

David Jones Son of James Jones and Elisabeth his Wife Born May
5th 1743 Baptised October 16th 1743

Judith Elleby Daughter of Thomas Elleby and Martha his Wife
Born October 3d 1740 Baptised October 16th 1743

Thomas Elleby Son of Thomas Elleby and Martha his Wife Born
March 20th 1742/3 Baptised October 16th 1743

Hester Young Daughter of Fransis Young and Obedience his Wife
Born November 9th 1741 Baptised October 16th 1743

Hester Carter Daughter of John Carter and Martha his Wife Born
January 21st 1742/3 Baptised October 16th 1743

Mary Hix Daughter of John Hix and Obedience his Wife Born
August 31st 1741 Baptised October 16th 1743

Frances Hix Daughter of John Hix and Obedience his Wife Born
August 6th 1739 Baptised October 16th 1743

John Wilson Prentice to John Evans Born April 1736 Baptised
     October 17th 1743

Susannah Groom Daughter of William Groom and Judith his
     Wife Born September 6th 1741 Baptised October 21st 1743

Sarah Groom Daughter of William Groom and Judith his Wife
     Born September 7th 1743 Baptised October 21st 1743

Thomas Smith Natural Son of William Thornwel and Elizabeth
     Smith Born 1743 Baptised October 21st 1743

Amos Windham Son of Charles Windham and Mary his Wife
     Born November 11th 1741 Baptis'd October 23d 1743

George Myars Son of John Myars and Anne his Wife Born January 16th 1739/40 Baptised October 23d 1743

John Myars Son of John Myars and Anne his Wife Born November
     2d 1742 Baptized October 23d 1743

John Smith Son of Benjamin Smith and Elizabeth his Wife Born
     January the 29th 1743 Baptized October 23d 1743

Hester Barton Daughter of William Barton and Mary his Wife
     Born July the 1743 Baptized November 6th 1743

Marcy Handlen Daughter of Edward Handlen and Mary his Wife
     Born April 23d 1729 Baptized November 18th 1743

Edward Handlen Son of Edward Handlen & Mary his Wife born
     September the 3d 1733 Baptized November 18th 1743

Robert Handlen Son of Edward Handlen & Mary his Wife born
     June 28th 1735 Baptized November 18th 1743

Champinion Handlen Son of Edward Handlen & Mary his Wife
     born March 3d 1737 Baptized November 18th 1743

Parmenas Handlen Son of Edward Handlen and Mary his Wife
     born September 13th 1742 Baptized November 18th 1743

Helenor Roberts Daughter of Robert Roberts & Jane his Wife
     born October the 26th 1743 Baptized November 27th 1743

William Robertson Son of John Robertson & Mary his Wife born
     March 23d 1742 Baptized November 27th 1743

Aaron Fryerston Son of John Fryerston & Sarah his Wife born
     April the   1743 Baptized November 27th 1743

Catherine Rawlins, Daughter of Thomas Rawlins &   his
     Wife born   Baptized November 27th 1743

Susannah Rawlins Daughter of Thomas Rawlins &   his
     Wife born   Baptized November 27th 1743

George Fox Son of Samuel Fox & Willoby his Wife born February
the 24th 1741 Baptized November 27th 1743

Anne Obryen Daughter of Timothy Obryen & Anne his Wife born
November 24th 1743 Baptized December 26th 1743

Mary Hester Stewart Daughter of John Stewart deceased &
Frances his Wife born October 25th 1743 Baptized January 8th 1743

John Alexander Cromwell Son of Thomas Ireton Cromwell &
& Mary his Wife born May the 27th 1743 Baptized January 29th 1743

Samuel Worth Son of John Worth & Martha his Wife born January 9th 1743 Baptized February 15th 1743

Mary Foord Daughter of James Foord & Sarah his Wife born
January the 9th 1743 Baptized February 19th 1743

Sarah Staples Daughter of Abraham Staples & Sarah his Wife
born July 26th 1743 Baptized March 4th 1743

Jane Brown Daughter of William Brown & Hester his Wife born
February the 24th 1743 Baptized March 21st 1743

William Witten Son of Thomas Witten and Mary his Wife born
August 6th 1740 Baptized April 12th 1744

Thomas Witten Son of Thomas Witten & Mary his Wife born
October the 18th 1742 Baptized April 12th 1744

Sarah Burdell Daughter of Thomas Burdell & Mary his Wife
born July the 17th 1742 Baptized April 12th 1744

Thomas Bennet Son of Henry Bennet & Rebekah his Wife born
July the 11th 1743 Baptized April 12th 1744

Hester Michau Daughter of Abraham Michau & Lydia his Wife
born January the 17th 1743 Baptized April 12th 1744

Julian Michau Daughter of Abraham Michau & Charlotte his Wife
born January the 18th 1721 and Baptized by the Revd
Mr Poudroux Minister of St James Santee April 22d 1722

Abraham Michau Son of Abraham Michau & Charlotte his Wife
born November the 20th 1723 and Baptized by the Revd
Mr Poudroux Minister of St James Santee March 21st 1723

Peter Michau Son of Abraham Michau & Charlotte his Wife born
March the 6th 1725 and Baptized by the Revd Mr Poudroux Minister of St. James Santee May the 3d 1725

Daniel Michau Son of Abraham Michau & Lydia his Wife born
June 20th 1733 and Baptized by the Revd Mr Morritt
Minister of this Parish in the same year.

Noah Michau Son of Abraham Michau & Lydia his Wife born
April the 26th 1735 and Baptized by the Revd Mr Benany
Minister June 13th 1735

Paul Michau Son of Abraham Michau & Lydia his Wife Born
November the 15th 1736 and Baptized by the Revd Mr
Duplessis Minister of St James Santee December 7th
1736

Lydia Michau Daughter of Abraham Michau & Lydia his Wife
born January the 7th 1738 and Baptized by the Revd Mr
Duplessis Minister of St James Santee June 10th 1739

Thomas Nolan Son of George Nolan & Rebekah is Wife born
January the 25th 1743 Baptized April 29th 1744

Mary Goodyer Daughter of Jacob Goodyer & Mary his Wife
born July the 16th 1741 Baptized May 6th 1744

Jacob Goodyer Son of Jacob Goodyer & Mary his Wife born
August the 6th 1743 Baptized May 6th 1744

Susannah McDaniel Daughter of Daniel McDaniel & Mary his
Wife born June 11th 1744 Baptized July 1st 1744

John Christmas Son of Jonathan Christmas & Easther his Wife
born January 10th 1743/4 Baptized July the 1st 1744

Sarah Dyal Daughter of Thomas Dyal & Cathorine his Wife born
January the 3d 1743/4 Baptized July the 1st 1744

Thomas Snow Son of William Snow & Mary his Wife born April
30th 1744 Baptized July the 1st 1744

Mary Conners Daughter of John Conners and Mary his Wife born
February the 10th 1743/4 Baptized July the 1st 1744

Edward Plowden Son of Edward Plowden & Susannah his Wife
born June 17th 1744 Baptized July the 1st 1744

Hannah Thomas Natural Daughter of Thomas Wright and Susannah Thomas born June 30th 1744 Baptized July 29th
1744 Dead Since

Peter Wiggins Son of Edmund Wiggins & Olive his Wife born
February 26th 1743/4 Baptized August 27th 1744

John Cathridge Son of Edmund Cathridge & Elizabeth his Wife
Born September 1744 Baptized October 4th 1744

Sarah Bonnel Daughter of John Bonnel & Honnorah his Wife
Born August 27th 1744 Baptized October the 5th 1744
Dead Since

Elizabeth Keen Daughter of Thomas Keen and Mary his Wife
Born November the 8th 1742 Baptized October the 6th
1744

Lewis Dupre Son of Josiah Dupre & Ann his wife Born October
the 20th 1744 Baptized November 8th 1744

Jannet Harrington daughter of Whitmell Harrington & Jannet
his Wife Born October the 27th 1744 Baptized December
the 25th 1744

Anna Avant daughter of Francis Avant and Sarah Wigfall Avant
his Wife Born March the 1st 1744/5 and departed this
Life March the 2^{d} 1744/5

Elizabeth Lane daughter of Peter Lane & Sarah Lane his Wife
Born January the 12th 1744/5 & Baptized Jan^{ry} the 24th
1744/5

Jannet McPharson daughter of James McPharson & Elizabeth
his Wife born March the 17th 1744/5 Baptized April the
7th 1746

Hester Newman daughter of Robart Newman and Julian his Wife
Born June 12th 1744 Baptized April the 18th 1745

Margaret Jaudon daughter of Paul Jaudon and Margaret his Wife
Born Nov^{br} the 8th 1744 Baptized April the 18th 1745

Anne Moor daughter of James Moor & Elizabeth his Wife Born
June the 10th 1744 Baptized April the 18th 1743

John June Son of John June & Lucretia his Wife Born November
the 13th 1744 Baptized April the 18th 1745

Daniel Roders Son of Joseph Roders & Anne his Wife Born March
the 6th 1743/4 Baptized April the 18th 1745

John Leger Son of John Leger & Anne his Wife Born February
the 17th 1745/5 Baptized the 18th April 1745

William McDowal Son of John McDowal & Lucretia his Wife
Born March the 7th 1744/5 Baptized August the 4th 1745

Jonathan Palmer Son of William Palmer & Agnes his Wife Born
July 1745 Baptized August the 4th 1745

James Foord Son of James Foord & Sarah his Wife Born April the
19th 1745 Baptized August the 4th 1745

Samuel Wright Son of Thomas Wright & Elizabeth his Wife & Thomas Wright Son also of the Said Tho[s] & Elizabeth Both Born the 27th of August 1745 Baptized the 2[d] September 1745 both dec[d]

Margaret Millikin daughter of Moses Millikin & Mary his Wife Born March the 30th 1744 Baptized Sep[tr] the 8th 1745

Joseph Graves Son of Joseph Graves & Mary his Wife Born February the 9th 1743/4 Baptized the 15th Sep[tr] 1745

William Forbes Son of William Forbes & Charity his Wife Born August the 18th 1745 Baptized the 25th Sep[tr] 1745

Alexander Cole Son of William Cole & Rachel his Wife Born June the 13th 1745 Baptized Oct[tr] the 20th 1745

Jonathan Lacey Son of William Lacey & Sarah his Wife Born May the 1st 1744 Baptized October the 20th 1745

William Hickman Son of Isaac Hickman & Elizabeth his Wife Born March the 14th 1744/5 Baptized the 20th October 1745

Sarah Gibson daughter of Gideon Gibson & Martha his Wife Born July the 19[th] 1744/5 Baptized Oct[r] the 20[th] 1745

Elizabeth Sullivan daughter of Timothy Sullivan & Mercy his Wife Born March the 20[th] 1738/9 Baptized Oct[r] the 21[st] 1745

Mary Sullivan daughter of Said Timothy & Mer[c]y his Wife Born Nov[br] the 15[th] 1742 Baptized Oct[r] the 21[st] 1745

James Sullivan Son of the Said Timothy Sullivan & Mercy his Wife Born Sep[r] 1745 Baptized October the 20[th] 1745

John Bowers Son of Giles Bowers & Martha his Wife Born May the 26[th] 1744 Baptized Oct[r] the 23[d] 1745

Eade Walston daughter of William Walston & Elizabeth his Wife Born Dec[m] the 29th 1744 Baptized the 23[d] Oct[r] 1745

Jonathan Evans, Son of John Evans & Rebeccah his Wife Born January the 12th 1743/4 Baptized Oct[r] the 27th 1745

Abraham Paul Son of Abraham Paul & Amey his Wife Born March the 8th 1742/3 Baptized Oct[r] the 27th 1745

Mary Paul daughter of Said Parents Born January the 12th 1744/5 Baptized the 27th Oct[r] 1745

Burlingham Rudd Son of Burlingham Rudd & Elizabeth his Wife Born October the 13th 1741 Baptized the 27th Oct[r] 1745

The Present Church

Walter Rudd Son of Said Parents Born March 20th 1743/4 Baptized the 27th October 1745

Martha Rudd daughter of Said Parents Born March 1st 1738/9 Baptized the 27th October 1745

John Booth Son of John Booth & Margaret his Wife Born Novr the 26th 1743 Baptized October the 27th 1745

Isaac Johnston Son of Martin Johnston & Sarah his Wife Born May the 11th 1738 Baptized Octr 27th 1745

Jacob Johnston Son of Said Parents Born Feb the 23^d 1740/1

William Johnston Son of Said Parents Born Jany 8th 1744/5

Martha Johnston daughter of the Said Parents Born Jany the 8th 1742/3 All Baptized the 27th Day of October 1745

Arthur Councill Son of Hardy Councill & Beatrix his Wife Born Novr the 6th 1739

James Councill Son of Said Parents Born October 20th 1742

Sarah Councill daughter of Said Parents Born July 5th 1745 All Baptized the 27th Day of October 1745

Anne Griffin daughter of James Griffin and Elizabeth his Wife Born January the 20th 1743/4 Baptized the 27th Octr 1745

Elisabeth Short daughter of Daniel Short & Elianor his Wife Born January the 5th 1743/4 Baptized the 27th Octr 1745

Thomas Kusu [?] Johnston Son of Harmon Johnston and Elis his Wife Born May 15th 1743 Baptized the 27th Octr 1745

William Duke Son of Benjamine Duke and Mary his Wife Born Sepr 27th 1745 Baptized the 29th Octr 1745

Edward Ball Son of Bartholomew Ball and Elisabeth his Wife Born February 1744/5 Baptized the 29th Octr 1745 _

Elisabeth Thornhill daughter of Joseph Thornhill and Elisabeth his Wife Born April the 23^d 1745 Baptized Octr the 29th 1745

Anne Isbell daughter of Henry Isbell and Elizabeth his Wife Born Sepr the 13th 1744 Baptized Octr the 30th 1745

Mary Goodyear daughter of Jacob Goodyear and Mary his Wife Born July the 16th 1741 Baptized May the 6th 1744

Jacob Goodyear Son of Jacob Goodyear and Mary his Wife Baptized May the 6th 1744

Susannah McDaniel daughter of Dan^{el} McDaniel and Mary his Wife Born June 11th 1744 Baptized July 1st 1744

John Christmas, Son of Jonathan Christmas and Hester his Wife
  Born Jany the 10th 1743/4 Baptized July the 1st 1744

Sarah Dyall daughter of Thomas Dyall and Katharine his Wife
  Born Jany the 3rd 1743/4 Baptized the 1st July 1744

Thomas Snow, Son of William Snow & Mary his Wife Born April
  the 30th 1744 Baptized July the 1st 1744

Mary Conyers daughter of John Conyears and Anne his Wife
  Born Feby the 10th 1743/4 Baptized the 1st July 1744

Edward Plowden Son of Edward Plowden and Susannah his Wife
  Born June the 17th 1744 Baptized July the 1st 1744

Peter Wiggins Son of Edmund Wiggins and Olive his Wife Born
  Feby the 26th 1743/4 Baptized August the 27th 1744

John Cartlidge Son of Edmund Cartlidge and Elisabeth his Wife
  Born Sepr the 5th 1744 Baptized Octr the 4th 1744

Sarah Bonnell daughter of John Bonnell and Honorah his Wife
  Born August the 27th 1744 Baptized the 5th Octr 1744

Ruth Wally daughter of Thomas Wally and Jemima his Wife
  Born Novr the 28th 1744 Baptized Octr the 30th 1745

Elisabeth Wool daughter of Muhall Wool and Frances his Wife
  Born June the 26th 1745 Baptized Octr the 30th 1745

Thomas Harrington Son of Thos Harrington and Hannah his Wife
  Born March the 24th 1741/2

Hannah Harrington daughter of Said Parents Born 22^d Sepr 1745
  Both Baptized the 30th October 1745

William Dewitt Son of Charles Dewitt and Sarah his Wife Born
  March the 26th 1744 Baptized the 30th Octr 1745

Frances Whitington daughter of Francies Whittington and Martha
  his Wife Born Novr the 19th 1744 Baptized the 30th Oct^r
  1745

James Wilkinson Son of Wm Wilkinson & Sarah his Wife Born
  Novr the 3^d 1744 Baptized the 30th Octr 1745

Mercy Crawford daughter of James Crawford and Cassia his Wife
  Born March the 27th 1745 Baptized the 30th Octr 1745

Anne Leith daughter of John Leith & Elizabeth his Wife Born
  Jany the 25th 1744/5 baptized 30th Octr 1745

Anne Huges Adult natural daughters of Sollomon Huges & Judith
  Haughton Widow Born Feby the 8th 1724/5 Baptized the
  30th Octr 1745

Richard Kennedy Son of Bryan Kennedy and Mary his Wife
Born August the 10th 1742

Mary Kennedy Daughter of Said Parents Born March the 29th
1740

James Kennedy Son of Said Parents Born Sepr the 21st 1744 Baptized the 31st Octr 1745

Susannah Man daughter of John Man & Susannah his Wife Born
April the 6th 1745 Baptized Novr the 30tth 1745

Isaac Fordyce Son of Rev^r John Fordyce and Elisabeth his Wife
Born Decr the 30th 1745 Baptized Jany 26th 1745/6

Hannah White daughter of Anthoney White Junr & Mary his
Wife Born November 25/1745 Baptized the 26th Jan^y
1745/6

Amos Worth Son of John Worth and Martha his Wife Born Dec^r
the 30th 1745/6 Baptized Feby the 6th 1754/6

Archibald Glen Son of John Glen and Anne his Wife Born Jan^y
the 5th 1745/6 Baptized Feby the 16th 1745

Mary, Hannah, Cain, Daughter of John Cain & Anne his wife
Born Jany the 28th 1745/6 Baptized the 28th March 1745/6

Hester Brown daughter of William Brown & Hester his Wife
Born Jany the 10th 1745/6 Baptized the 1st April 1746

Mary Brown daughter of Alex Brown by Mary his Wife Born May
the 7th 1746 Baptized May the 18th 1746 N. B. The Said
Mrs Mary Brown departed this Life the 19th instant &
was Intered the 20th

Sarah White, Dau^r of Leonrd White & Hannah his Wife Born May
4th 1746, & Baptized the 29th June 1746

Elizabeth Cribb, Dau^r of Thomas Cribb & Elizabeth his Wife
Born Decr 30th 1745 Baptized August 10th 1746

James Brown, Son of Saml Brown, & Sarah his Wife, Born, Feb^y
5th 1727/8 Baptized Augt 16th 1746

Sarah, Wigfall, Avant, Daw^r of Francis Avant & Sarah Wigfall
his Wife Born Octr 5th 1746 Baptized Novr 16th 1746

Frances Goodyear, Daw^r of Jacob Goodyear, & Mary his Wife,
Born   Baptized Novr 27th 1746

Margaret Summers, Daw^r of James Summers, & Anne his Wife,
Born Octr 29th 1746 & Baptized the 4th Decr 1746

John Connor, Son of John Connor, & Anne his Wife, Born March
    14th 1745/6 Baptized, Decr 25th 1746

Mary Anne, Noland, Dawr of George Noland, & Rebeccah his
    Wife, Born Septr 31st 1746, Baptized Decr 28th 1746.

Daniel Myars, Son of John Myars, & Anne his Wife, Born July
    4th 1745.   Baptized Janry 24th 1746/7.

Anne Collins, Dawr Wm Collins & Elizabeth his Wife, born   Day
    of Febry 1745/6, Bap: Feby the 11th 1746/7

Thomas Wright, Son of Thomas Wright, & Isbelle his Wife,
    born, March 2d 1746/7, & Baptized April 12th 1747.

Nathaniel Snow, Son of William Snow, & Mary his Wife, was
    Born February the 8th 1746/7 & Baptized the 12th April
    1747

1747.   ⎱ James Mcpharson, Son of James Mcpharson & Eliza-
May 31st ⎰ beth, his Wife, was Born May the 11th 1747, & Bap-
    tized, date on the Margin.

Elizabeth Dupont, Dawr of Alexr Dupont, & Anne his Wife born
    Sepr 4th 1746, Baptized April 23d 1747.

Peter June, Son of John June, & Lucretia his Wife, Born August
    23d 1746 & Baptized April 24th 1747.

George Newman, Son of Saml Newman & Katharine his Wife,
    Born May 7th 1746, & Baptiz'd May 6th 1747

Daniel Leger, Son of John Leger, & Anne his Wife born Febry 1st
    1746/7, & Baptized May 6th 1747.

Thomas Burdell, Son of Thomas Burdell, & Mary his Wife, Born
    Janry 18th 1745/6.   Baptized May 6th 1747.

Robert Newman, Son of Robert Newman, & Julian his Wife,
    Born May 27th 1746, Baptized May 6th 1747.

1747   Baptiz'd as per Date on the Margin

May 6.   Hester Jaudon, Dawr of Paul Jaudon, & Margaret his
    Wife, Born Septr 21st 1746, Baptized as in the Margin.

June 7.   Samuel Duprè, Son of Josias Garnier Duprè & Anne his
    wife, Born April 24th 1747 Baptized Date in the Margin.

    14.   Jemima Cromwell Dawr of Thomas Ireton Cromwell,
    & Mary his Wife, Born Novr 2d 1746.

July 19 Edmund Cartlidge, Son of Edm^d. Cartlidge & Elizabeth his Wife, Born Novr 10th 1746.

July 26. Grace Forbes, Daw^r of William Forbes, & Charity his Wife, Born March 2^d 1746/7.

Septr 20. Benjamine Brunstone, Son of John Brunstone Junr, & Mary his Wife, Born April 3^d 1747.

Elisabeth Robertson, Daw^r of John Robertson and Mary his Wife Born the 2^d of may 1745 & Baptized the 21st Day of Said Month by John Fordyce.

Octr 4. Moses Fryerstone, Son of John Fryerstone, & Sarah his Wife, Born May 21st 1747.

Do   4. Anne Rhodes, Daw^r of Joseph Rhodes, & Anne his Wife, Born the 25th Decbr 1746.

4. Thomas Dyall, Son of Thomas Dyal, & Katharine his Wife, Born July the 14th 1746.

4. Mary Courtis, Daw^r of Henry Courtis, & Margaret his Wife, Born Novr 14th 1746

4. William Wright, Son of Wm Wright, & Sarah his Wife, Born July 21st 1747.

Turn Over

1747/8   Baptisms Continu'd Date as pr Margine.

July 12. Sarah Brown, Daw^r of Alex^r Brown, & Mary his Wife, Born Novr 25th 1747.

17. John Glen, Son of John Glen & Anna his Wife Born Decr 20th 1727.

26. Lydia White, Daw^r of Anth^y White Senr, & Mary his Wife, Born May 29th 1747.

Febry ⎫ William Naylor Barton, Son of William Barton, & Mary
14th ⎭ his Wife, born Janry 5th 1747/8.

April 17th Hannah Brown, Daw^r of Wm Brown & Hester his Wife, Born Jany 10th 1747/8.

May 8th Isaac Staples, Son of Abram Staples, & Sarah his Wife, Born Augst 16th 1745.

31. Mary Man, Daw^r of Doctor John Man Esqr, & Susannah his Wife, born May 12th 1748.

June 7th Elianor Lindly, Daw^r of Robert Lindly, & Anne his Wife, born Febry 3^d 1746/7.

June 16th Elisabeth Burdell, Daw^r of Thomas Burdell, and Margaret his Wife, Born Decr 1st 1747.

July 1st Katharine Chicken, Daw^r of Thomas Chicken, & Margaret his Wife, born Augt 2^d 1747.

24th Hester White, Daw^r of Leonard White & Hannah his Wife, born

Augst 24 Meridith Hughes, Son of Wm Hughes & Sarah his Wife, Born March 18th 1747/8.

1748   Baptisms continu'd, Date as pr Margine

Augt 28th John Bosier, Son of John Bosier, & Mary his Wife, Born May 3^d 1747.

Septr 11 Josiah Evans, Son of John Evans, & Rebeccah his Wife, Born Decr 16th 1745.

Idem Die } Theophilus Evans, Son of Said Parents, Born July
Septr   } 30th 1748, both Baptized by Mr Keith.

Novr 9. Daniel, George, Williams, Son of John Williams, & Mary his Wife, born March 8th 1738

Decr 4 Blake, Lea White, Son of John White, & Mary his Wife, Born Augst 20th 1748.

Decr 13th Elizabeth Pyat, Daw^r of John Pyat, & Hannah his Wife, Born, Septr 13th 1748.

17th Nathaniel Ford, Son of James Ford, & Sarah his Wife, Born March 18th 1747/8.

1748/9   } Samuel Wright, Son of Thomas Wright, & Isabell his
Janry 29. } Wife, Born Septr 28th 1748.

Febry. 14th Anthony White, Son of Anth^y White, & Mary his Wife, Born Decr 30th 1748.

March 31st Dorothy Dupont, Daw^r of Alex^r Dupont, & Ann his Wife, Born, Decr 5th 1748.

April 14. Katharine June, Daw^r of John June, & Lucretia his Wife, Born Octr 2^d 1748.

May 7th John Worth, Son of John Worth, & Martha his Wife Born Septr 9th 1748.

Do   7th   Elizabeth Jenner, Daw^r of James Jenner, & Frances his
          Wife, Born Jan^{ry} 30th 1748/9.

June 2^d   Elias McPharson Son of James McPharson & Elisabeth
          his Wife Born April 26th 1749.

1749   Baptisms continued, Date as pr Margine

June 25th   Hannah Avant Daw^r of Francis Avant, & Sarah Wigfall
          his Wife, Born May 24th 1749.

Augt 12th   Elizabeth Leger, Daw^r of John Leger, & Ann his Wife,
          Born May the 22^d 1749.

Augt 12   Elizabeth Newman, Daw^r of Saml Newman & Kath-
          arine his Wife, born Novr 25th 1748.

Do 12   Susannah Michau, Daw^r of Abraham Michau Junr &
          Susannah his Wife, Born April 5th 1749.

Septr 3^d   Sarah Jamison, Daw^r of John Jamison, & Isabella his
          Wife, born July 3^d 1748.

Octr 5th   John Crawford, Son of James Crawford, & Cassiah his
          Wife, born Feb^{ry} 16th 1746/7.

Do 5.   James Crawford, Son of Ditto Parents, born Janry 1st
          1748/9

Novr 5th   Susannah Simpson, Daw^r Thomas James Simpson &
          Martha his Wife, born Augt 28th 1749.

     12th   Peter Keighly Son of John Keighly & Jane his Wife,
          born April 18. 1749.

{ Baptiz'd by the Revrd Mr Alex^r Keith of Prince George Parish }
{ the following Children Augt 15th 1746. }

          Elisabeth Graves Daw^r of Joseph Graves & Mary his Wife,
          born Janry 12th 1745.

          Mary Graves Daw^r of Do Parents, born Novr 27th.

Decr 28   John Popperwell, Son of John Popperwell, & Mary his
          Wife, born Sept. 28th 1749.

1749/50   Baptisms continu'd Date as p^r Margine

Feby 4th   Stephen Peak, Son of Stephen Peak, & Abigael his
          Wife Born 25th Jany 1748/9.

March 3ᵈ Lydia, Jane, Glen, Dawʳ of John Glen, & his Wife, Born the Same 3ʳᵈ Day of March

April 1ˢᵗ Bryan Kennedy, Son of Bryan Kennedy, & Mary his Wife, Born Septʳ 11ᵗʰ 1749.

Stewart Robert Son of Robert Stewart & of Hannah his Wife Born June 9ᵗʰ 1734. Baptᵈ Same year Omitted being Registerd.

Stewart Rebecca Daughter of Robert Stewart & of Hannah his Wife Born March 25 1739 Baptd Same year Omitted being Regisᵈ

Pyatt John Son of John Pyatt & of Hannah his Wife Born June 20ᵗʰ 1750 Baptized August 8ᵗʰ 1750.

Atkinson Hannah and Mary Twin Daughters of George Atkinson and Mary his Wife Born August 10ᵗʰ 1750 Baptized Octobʳ 29ᵗʰ 1750

Carr Elizabeth Daughter of Isaac Carr and of Abigaill his Wife May 4ᵗʰ 1742 Baptized December 13ᵗʰ 1752.

Carr Isaac Son of Isaac Carr and of Abigaill his Wife Born March 24ᵗʰ 1743 & Baptᵈ May 20ᵗʰ 1743.

Carr Ester Daughter of Isaac Carr and of Abigaill his Wife Born March 16ᵗʰ 1745 Baptizᵈ Febʸ 9ᵗʰ 1745

Carr Edmund Son of Isaac Carr and of Abigaill his Wife May 2ᵈ 1748 Baptizᵈ Septembʳ 25ᵗʰ 1748.

Carr Abigaill Daughter of Isaac Carr & of Abigaill his Wife Born Septemʳ 27ᵗʰ 1750 Baptᵈ same Year.

Carr Abigaill Daughter of Isaac Carr & Abigaill his Wife Baptized Februʸ yᵉ 8ᵗʰ 1753 being then 2 years & 4 Months & 12 days old.

Pew Martha Daughter of Richard Pew & Brigit his Wife Born January 5ᵗʰ 1751/2 Baptiz'd Janʳʸ 20ᵗʰ 1754

Barns Mary Daughter of John Barns and Mary his Wife Born July 12ᵗʰ 1752 Baptizᵈ June 16ᵗʰ 1754

Lane Hannah Daughter of Peter Lane and Sarah his Wife Born 29ᵗʰ Octobʳ 1752 Baptizᵈ 8ᵗʰ July 1753

Futhy John Son of Harthy Futhy and Elizᵗʰ his Wife Born 22ᵈ June 1753 Baptzᵈ Jany 20ᵗʰ 1754

Largent Sarah Daughter of Richd Largent and Sarah his Wife Born September 17ᵗʰ 1753 Baptizᵈ 25ᵗʰ Decembʳ

Atkinson George Son of George Atkinson & Mary his Wife Born
    December 19th 1753 Baptiz'd March 29th 1754
Walker William Son of William Walker & Elizabeth his Wife
    Born December 20th 1753 Baptiz'd Same year
McCormack Sarah Daughter of Thomas McCormack & of Mary
    his Wife Baptiz'd March 29th 1754 aged then abt 15
    years
Barton Hannah Daughter of William Barton & Mary his Wife
    Born March 19th 1755 Baptiz'd Same year
Palmer Son of William Palmer & Agness his Wife Born January
    19th 1750/1 Baptiz'd Decembr 24th 1752
Avant Fransis Son of Frans Avant & Sarah Wigfall his Wife Born
    January 8th 1752 Baptizd Decembr 24th
Green William Son of William Green and Lydia his Wife Born
    December 14th 1743 Baptized same year
Green Fransis Son of William Green & Lydia his Wife Born Aprill
    ye 26th 1746 and Baptized
Green Tabitha Daughter of William Green & Lydia his Wife
    Born Decemr 27th 1748 Baptizd —
Green John Thomson Son of William Green & Jane his Wife
    Born July 15th 1753. Baptizd —
Green Ann Daughter of William Green & Jane his Wife Born
    February 1st 1755. Baptized —
Newman Martha Daughter of John Newman & Elizth his Wife
    Aged then 14 Years old
Newman Thomas Aged then 12 Years Son of Said Parents
Newman Elizabeth Aged 11 years Daughter of Said Parents
Newman Catherine Aged 5 Years Daughter of Said Parents
Newman William Aged 3 years Son of Said Parents
Newman Susannah Born January 30th 1753
    N B The above Children were Baptized May ye 29th 1753
Duboie Isaac & Elizabeth Twin Son and Daughter of John Duboie
    and Mary his Wife Born November 5th 1742 Baptd 29
    May 1753
Duboie Joseph Son of John Duboie and Mary his Wife Born
    October 10th 1745 Baptized May 29th 1753
Duboie Rebecca Daughter of John Duboie and Mary his Wife
    Born Novemr 8th 1752 Baptized May 29th 1753

Sparrow Martha Daughter of Henry Sparrow and Mary his Wife
 Born December y^r 24th 1749 Baptized May 29th 1753
Sparrow Mary Daughter of Henry Sparrow and Mary his Wife
 Born August ye 7th 1752 Baptized May 29th 1753
Warren John Son of John Warren and Martha his Wife Born
 December 18th 1752 Baptized May 29th 1753
Lewis Charlot Daughter of Robert Lewis and Susanna his Wife
 Born May ye 7th 1753 Baptized 29th May
Fryerston Catherine Daughter of John Fryerston and Sarah his
 Wife Born August 12th 1749 Baptized May 29th 1753
Fryerston John Son of John Fryerston and Sarah his Wife Born
October 15th 1752 Baptized May 29th 1753
Newman Aann Daughter of Edmund Newman and Martha his
 Wife Born November 11th 1752 Baptized May 29th 1753
Newman Mathew Son of Edmund Newman and Martha his Wife
 Born ye 30th of February 1753 Baptized May 29th 1753
Phillips James Son of Anthony and Ann Phillips Born May 30th
 1751 Baptized May 29th 1753
Peek Sarah Daughter of William Peek and Mary his Wife Born
 May 22^d 1752 Baptized May 29th 1753
Wally William Son of Thomas Wally and Jamina his Wife Born
 November 18th 1751 Baptized May 29th 1753
Bennet Jacob Naturall son of Bennet and Christian Loyd Born
 January 16th 1750 Baptized May 29th 1753
Bennet Bennet Son of Bennett Born January 3^d 1751
Bennet John Naturall Sons of Bennet and Christian Loyd Born
 December 23^d 1752 Baptized May 29th 1753
McLendan Isaac Son of Jacob McLendan and Martha his Wife
. Born Aprill ye 25th 1750 Baptized May 29th 1753
McLendan Jamima Daughter of Jacob McLendan and Martha his
 Wife Born October ye 13th 1752 Baptized 29th May
 1753
Field Mary Daughter of William Field and Tabitha his Wife
 Born June ye 5th 1751 Baptized May 29th 1753
Field Elizabeth Daughter of William Field and Tabitha his Wife
 Born Aprill 1753 and Baptized May 29th 1753
Crosby Charity Daughter of William Crosby and Jamima his
 Wife Born February 9th 1749 Baptized May 29th 1753

Crosby Jerman Son of William Crosby and Jamima his Wife Born
June 9th 1752 Baptized May 29th 1753

Shibbs William Son of John Shibbs and Rebecca his Wife Born
January ye 19^{sh} 1750 Baptized May 29th 1753

Shibbs Susanna Daughter of John Shibbs and Rebecca his Wife
Born May ye 12th 1752 Baptized May 29th 1753

Knee Elizabeth Daughter of John Knee and Elinor his Wife Born
January 17th 1752 Baptized May 29th 1753

Carter Price Son of John Carter and Martha his Wife Born July
8th 1750 Baptized May 29th 1753

Carter Elizabeth Daughter of John Carter and Elinor his Wife
Born August 1st 1752 Baptized May 29th 1753

Smith Mary Daughter of John Smith and Mary his Wife Born
September 19th 1750 Baptized May 29th 1753

Smith Sarah Daughter of John Smith and Mary his Wife Born
December 2^d 1751 Baptized May 29th 1753

Smith Samuel Son of John Smith and Mary his Wife Born May
1st 1753 Baptized May 29th 1753

Jones Frederick Son of Frederick Jones and Martha his Wife Born
December ye 27th 1749 Baptized May 29th 1753

Jones James Son of Frederick Jones and Martha his Wife Born
February 28th 1751 Baptized May 25th 1753

Crawford Hepsabeth Daughter of James Crawford and Kessiah
his Wife Born April 1st 1752 Baptized May 29th 1753

Buckston Sarah Daughter of Samuel Buckston and Ann his Wife
Born December ye 27th 1751 Baptized May 29th 1751

Campble Mary Daughter of Alexander Campble and Priscilla his
Wife Born January 8th 1751 Baptized May 29th 1751

Campble John Son of Alexander Campble and Priscilla his Wife
Born January ye 9th 1753 Baptized May 29th 1753

Hughes Abaham Son of Solamon Hughes and Mary his Wife
Born July 27th 1751 Baptized May 29th 1753

Bell George Son of Samuel Bell and Ann his Wife Born Aprill
2^d 1749 Baptized May 29th 1753

Bell Ann Daughter of Samuel Bell and Ann his Wife Born May
ye 19th 1752 Baptized May 29th 1753

Fellows John Son of Joseph Fellows and Sarah His Wife Born
Aprill ye 9th 1752 Baptized May 29th 1753

Kelly Agnes Daughter of John Kelly and Elizabith his Wife Born October 8th 1752 Baptized May 29th 1753

Gibson Ruben Son of Giddian Gibson and Martha his Wife Born November ye 29th 1751 Baptized May 29th 1753

Groom Catherine Daughter of William Groom and Judith his Wife Born September 1st 1751 Baptized May ye 29th 1753

Teel [?]Sarah Daughter of Edward Teel and Mary his Wife Born June ye 10th 1752 Baptized May 29th 1753

Mixon William Son of Michael Mixon and Catherine his Wife Born March 8th 1753 Baptized May ye 29th 1753

Michael Moses Son of George Michael and Sarah his Wife Born June ye 1st 1753 Baptized May ye 29th 1753

Chisholm John Son of John Chisholm and Mary his Wife Born May ye 10th 1753 Baptized May ye 29th 1753

McDonald William Son of John McDonald and Elizabith his Wife Born August Y^e 4th 1751 Baptized May ye 29th 1753

McDonald Zachariah Son of John McDonald and Elizbth his Wife Born September ye 24th 1752 Baptized May ye 29th 1753

Michael Massay Daughter of John Michael and Francis his Wife Born December 16th 1751 Baptized May ye 29th 1753

Knight James Son of James Knight and Catherine his Wife Born November ye 12th 1751 Baptized May ye 29th 1753

Knight Ann Daught of James Knight and Catherine his Wife Born Aprill 21st 1753 Baptized May 29th 1753

Knight Thomas James Son of John Knight and Sarah his Wife Born May ye 12th 1752 Baptized May ye 29th 1753

Sanders Massay Daughter of George Sanders and Hannah his Wife Born September ye 10th 1751 Baptized May ye 29th 1753

Stewart Sarah Daughter of Thomas Stewart and Sarah his Wife Born June ye 15th 1750 Baptized May ye 29th 1753

Stewart Rebecca Daughter of Thomas Stewart and Sarah his Wife Born December ye 7th 1752 Baptized May ye 29th 1753

Evans John Son of Nathan Evans and Catherine his Wife Born February ye 14th 1748 Baptized May ye 29th 1753

Evans Catherine Daughter of Nathan Evans and Sarah his Wife
    Born December ye 30th 1749 Baptized May ye 29th 1753
Evans Nathan Son of Nathan Evans and Sarah his Wife Born
    May ye 24th 1751 Baptized May ye 29th 1753
Walston Mary Daughter of William Walston and Elizabith his
    Wife Born March ye 5th 1751 Baptized May ye 29th 1753
Hewet John Vachel Son of John Hewet and Mary his Wife Born
    January ye 15th 1749 Baptized May ye 29th 1753
Gibson Gibson Son of John Gibson and Jamima his Wife Born
    February ye 25th 1749 Baptized May ye 29th 1753
Gibson John Son of John Gibson and Jamima his Wife Born
    February ye 23^d 1751 Baptized May ye 29th 1753
Oquin Ann Daughter of John Oquin and Jane his Wife Born
    January 6th 1753 Baptized May ye 29th 1753
Johnson Susanna Daughter of William Johnson & Susanna his
    Wife Born June ye 5th 1750 Baptized May 29th 1753
Johnson William Son of William Johnson and Susanna his Wife
    Born January ye 16th 1753 Baptized May ye 29th 1753
Williams James Son of John Williams and Martha his Wife Born
    March ye 22^d 1751 Baptized May ye 29th 1753
Drury Lane Son of Christopher Lane and Mary his Wife Born
    September 15th 1751 Baptized May ye 29th 1753
Grant Ann Daughter of Duncan Grant and Martha his Wife
    Born July 6th 1752 Baptized May ye 29th 1753
Keathly Mary Daughter of John Keathly and Jane his Wife
    Born January ye 6th 1752 Baptized May ye 29th 1753
Troublefield Soloman Son of Charles Troublefield and Susanna
    his Wife Born Septem ye 11th 1751 Baptized May y^e
    29th 1753
Crew Penelope Daughter of Joseph Crew and Charity his Wife
    Born March ye 17th 1749 Baptized May ye 29th 1753
Crew Lucretia Daughter of Joseph Crew and Charity his Wife
    Born October ye 22^d 1752 Baptized May ye 29th 1753
Renalds Frederick Son of George and Mary Renanlds Born May
    ye 12th 1752 Baptized May ye 29th 1753
Herring Judith Daughter of William Herring and Rachel his
    Wife Born March ye 9th 1748 Baptized May ye 29th
    1753

Herring William Son of William Herring and Rachel his Wife
    Born November ye 28th 1749 Baptized May ye 29th 1753
Herring Hardy Son of William Herring and Rachel his Wife
    Born October ye 15th 1752 Baptized May ye 29th 1753
Buckel Mary Daughter of Abraham and Elizabith Buckel Born
    February 2^d 1753 Baptized June ye 2^d 1753
Jones Susanna Daughter of John Jones and Alice his Wife Born
    January ye 8th 1753 Baptized June ye 2^d 1753
Jones Priscilla Daughter of John Jones and Alice his Wife Born
    May ye 8th 1750 Baptized June ye 2^d 1753
Jones John Son of John Jones and Alice his Wife Born October
    ye 1st 1751 Baptized June 2^d 1753
Gibson Gidion Son of Gidion Gibson and Martha his Wife Born
    March ye 12th 1750 Baptized June ye 2^d 1753
Gibson Mary Daughter of Gidion Gibson and Martha his Wife
    Born October ye 2^d 1752 Baptized June ye 2^d 1753
Dewet Caty Daughter of John Dewet and Catherine his Wife
    Born January 15th 1752 Baptized June ye 2^d 1753
Cross William Son of Richard Cross and Mary his Wife Born
    Aprill ye 7th 1752 Baptized June ye 2^d 1753
Fletcher George Son of William Fletcher and Elizabith his Wife
    Born December 28th 1752 Baptized June ye 2^d 1753
Jenkins Charles Son of Thomas Jenkins and Dorathy his Wife
    Born June ye 10th 1749 Baptized June 2^d 1753
Jenkins John Son of Thomas Jenkins and Dorathy his Wife Born
    November ye 12th 1751 Baptized June ye 2^d 1753
Crosby Jacob Son of Thomas Crosby and Mary his Wife Born
    May ye 7th 1750 Baptized June ye 2^d 1753
Lowry Hannah Daughter of Henry Lowry and Uzilla his Wife
    Born July ye 16th 1737 Baptized June ye 2^d 1753
Glisby Frances Daughter of Daniel Glisby and Elizabith his Wife
    Born January ye 3^d 1753 [sic] Baptized June ye 2^d 1753
Glisby William Son of Daniel Glisby and Elizabith his Wife
    Born Aprill ye 3^d 1753 [sic] Baptized June ye 2^d 1753
Panper Mary Daughter of William Panper and Lucy his Wife
    Born February ye 2^d 1752 Baptized June ye 2^d 1753
Popperwell George Son of John Popperwell and Mary his Wife
    Born October ye 12th 1752 Baptized June ye 2^d 1753

Loftin Phebe Daughter of John Loftin and Hannah his Wife Born July ye 11th 1750 Baptized June ye 2^d 1753

Loftin John Son of John Loftin and Hannah his Wife Born July ye 2^d 1752 Baptized June ye 2^d 1753

Jones James Son of Richard Jones and Elizabeth his Wife Born June ye 15th 1740 Baptized June ye 2^d 1753

George Sarah Daughter of John George and Mary his Wife Aged 13 years Baptized June 2^d 1753

Scofuld Sarah Daughter of Philip Scofuld and Rachel his Wife Born June ye 3^d 1750 Baptized June ye 2^d 1753

Scofuld Elizabeth Daughter of Philip Scofuld and Rachel his Wife Born Aprill ye 26th 1752 Baptized June ye 2^d 1753

Moor Sarah Daughter of Arthur Moor and Mary his Wife Born February 13th 1749 Baptized June ye 2^d 1753

Moor James Son of Arthur Moor and Mary his Wife Born Novemb^r 17th 1752 Baptized June ye 2^d 1753

Holland Elizabeth Daughter of Joseph Holland & Mary his Wife Born April ye 22^d 1752 Baptized June ye 2^d 1753

Williams Jessy Son of John Williams and Elizabeth his Wife Born April ye 21st 1753 Baptized June ye 2^d 1753

Crosby Jacob Son of Jacob Crosby and Ann his Wife Born Aprill ye 11th 1746 Baptized June ye 2^d 1753

Crosby Winny Son of Jacob Crosby and Ann his Wife Born October ye 3^d 1750 Baptized June ye 2^d 1753

Crosby Willis Son of Jacob Crosby and Ann his Wife Born March ye 28th 1753 Baptized June ye 2^d 1753

Dewet Thomas Son of Charles Dewet and Sarah his Wife Born November ye 28th 1748 Baptized June ye 2^d 1753

Dewet Charles Son of Charles Dewet and Sarah his Wife Born Aprill ye 24th 1751 Baptized June ye 2^d 1753

Turbivil Lavina Daughter of John Turbivil and Philadelphia his Wife Born Decem^r ye 27th 1751 Baptized June ye 2^d 1753

Teel Elizabeth Daughter of John Teel and Docas his Wife Born March ye 1st 1753 Baptized June ye 2^d 1753

Lee David Son of John Lee and Margaret his Wife Born November ye 13th 1751 Baptized June ye 2^d 1753

Rogers Charity Daughter of Abraham Rogers & Mary his Wife Baptized November ye 2^d 1753 being then 13 Months Old

Dyal John Son of Thomas Dyal and Catherine his Wife Baptized
    November ye 27th 1753 being thin 4 Months & 5 Days Old
Perkin James Son of Rice Perkin and Elizabith his Wife Bap-
    tized Novem^r ye 27th 1753 being thin 2 yrs & 20 Days Old
Perkin John Son of Rice Perkin and Elizabith his Wife Baptized
    Novemb^r ye 27th 1753 being then 2 Months & 8 Days Old
Griggs Mary Daughter of William and Mary Griggs Baptized
    November ye 27th 1753 being then 6 Months & 1 Day Old
Bonnel John Son of John Bonnel and Patience his Wife Baptized
    November ye 29th 1753 Being then 3 years & 1 Month Old
Bonnel Elias Son of John Bonnel and Patience his Wife Bap-
    tized Novemb^r ye 27th 1753 Being then 9 Months Old
Thistlewood Elizabeth Daughter of Samuel Thistlewood and
    Susanna his Wife Baptized Novem^r ye 27th 1753 Being
    then 4 Years Old
Morgan Susanna Daughter of John Morgan and Susanna his
    Wife Baptized Novem^r ye 27th 1753 Being then 3 Months
    Old
Dubuz Dorcas Daughter of Stephen Dubuz and Elizabeth his
    Wife Baptized Novem^r ye 27th 1753 Being then 9 Years
    Old
Dubuz William Son of Stephen Dubuz and Elizabeth his Wife
    Baptized Novem^r ye 27th 1753 Being then 4 Years Old
Blawick Annabthe Daughter of John Blawick & Sarah his Wife
    Baptized Decem^r ye 2^d 1753 Being 2 years Old ye 26th
    Jany Next
Lucas Harrison the Son of Thomas Lucas and of Ann his Wife
    Baptized December ye 2^d 1753 Being then 4 Years Old
Lucas Mildre^{a}d Son of Thomas Lucas and of Ann his Wife Born
    Aprill ye 23^d 1753 Baptized December 2^d 1753
McClandon Zilpha Girk [?] Daughter of Denis McClandon and
    Martha his Wife Born ye 28th 1749 Baptized December
    ye 2^d 1753
McClandon Francis Son of Denis McClandon and Martha his
    Wife Baptized Decem^r 2^d 1753 Being then 8 years Old
    Last Aprill
McClandon Enoch Son of Denis McClandon and Martha his Wife
    Baptized Decemb^r 2^d 1753 Being 1 Year Old the 28th
    Day of December

Buxton George Son of Samuel Buxton Junr and Ann his Wife
 Born ye 10th October 1753 Baptized December 2^d 1753
Jones Thaieth [?] Daughter of James Jones and Sarah his Wife
 Born the 6th of Aprill 1751 Baptized Decemb^r 2^d 1753
Murry James Son of William Murry and Elizabeth his Wife
 Born ye 26th Aprill 1750 Baptized December ye 2^d 1753
Murry Alixander the Son of William Murry and Elizth his Wife
 Baptized Decem^{br} 2^d 1753 Being 10 Months Old y^e
 10th of November
Hitchbouk Mildred Daughter of William Hitchbouk and Elizth
 his Wife Born Aprill 30th 1751 Baptized Decem^{br} 2^d 1753
McClandon, Joil Jesse Son of Joil McClandon and Thamar his
 Wife Born ye 12th June 1753 Baptized December 2^d 1753
Cumbers Susanna Daughter of Peter Cumbers and Lucretia his
 Wife Born ye 5th March 1753 Baptized December 2^d 1753
Keaten Mary Daughter of John Keaten and Hannah his Wife
 Baptized Decem^r 2^d 1753 Being then 17 years Old
Keaton Sarah Daughter of John Keaton and Hannah his Wife
 Baptized Decemb^r 2^d 1753 Being then 12 years Old
Foly James Son of Walter Foly and Elizabeth his Wife Baptized
 December 2^d 1753 Being then 8 years old
Foly Isaac Son of Walter Foly and Elizabeth his Wife Baptized
 Decem^{br} ye 2^d 1753 Being then 6 years Old
Foly Margaret Daughter of Walter Foly and Elizabeth his Wife
 Baptized Decemb^r 2^d 1753 Being then 2½ years Old
Downer Moses Son of John Downer and Martha his Wife Bap-
 tized Decem^{br} ye 2^d 1753 Being then 10 Weeks Old P9–
Hodges Richard Son of John Hodges and Rebecca his Wife Bap-
 tized December 2^d 1753 Being then 3 Weeks Old
Downer Alixander Son of Joseph Downer and Hannah his Wife
 Baptized Decem^r 2^d 1753 Being then 8 Months Old
Gardnar Isom Son of William Gardnar and Mary his Wife Bap-
 tized December 2^d 1753 Being then 19 Months Old
Gardnar Ann Daughter of William Gardnar and Mary his Wife
 Baptized Decem^r 2^d 1753 Being then 8 Months Old
Shingleton Frances Daughter of John Shingleton & Mary his
 Wife Baptized Decemb^r 2^d 1753 Being then 20 Months
 Old P 90 [?]

Hicks Betty Daughter of George Hicks and Frances his Wife
    Baptized Decem^r 2^d 1753 Being then 8 Months Old

Wall Benjamin Son of John Wall and Ann his Wife Baptized
    Decem^r 2^d 1753 Being then 11 Days Old

Canty Mary Daughter of John Canty and Mary his Wife Baptized
    Decem^r 2^d 1753 Being then 4 Years Old

Canty Sarah Daughter of John Canty and Mary his Wife Bap-
    tized Decem^r ye 2^d 1753 Being then 11 Months Old

Turner Lucy Daughter of Drury Turner and Margaret his Wife
    Baptized Decem^r ye 1st 1753 Being then 4 Months Old

Omitted in

Windham William Son of William Windham & Sarah his Wife
    Baptized Decem^r 1st 1753 Being then 1 Year & 7 Months
    Old

Windham Mary Daughter of William Windham and Sarah his
    Wife Baptized December 1st 1753 Being then 4 Months
    Old

Windham Mary Daughter of Charles Windham and Ann his
    Wife Baptized Decemb^r 1st 1753 Being then 1 Year &
    7 Months Old

Pervis Nancy Daughter of William Pervis and Sarah his Wife
    Baptized Decem^r 1st 1753 Being then 6 Months Old

Oliver James Son of Thomas Oliver and Diana his Wife Baptized
    Decemb^r 1st 1753 Being then 1 Year Old

Stanbridge Jane Daughter of William Stanbridge & Jane his Wife
    Baptized Decem^r 1st 1753 Being then 1 Year & 11 Months
    Old

Pigman Charles Son of Charles Pigman and Mary his Wife Bap-
    tized Decem^r 1st 1753 Being then 4 Months Old

Irby Becca Daughter of Edmond Irby and Elizabeth his Wife
    Baptized Decem^r ye 5th 1753 Being then 2 Months Old

Forbes Ann Daughter of William Forbes and Charity his Wife
    Baptized December ye 5th 1753 Being then 2 Years 3/4
    Old

Forbes Thomas Son of William Forbes and Charity his Wife
    Baptized Decem^r ye 5th 1753 Being then 9 Months Old

Dunnin William Son of John Dunnin and Constance his Wife
    Baptized Decemb^r ye 5th 1753 Being then 2 years Old

Clark Elizabeth Daughter of James Clark and Elizabeth his
    Wife Baptized Decemb^r ye 5th 1753 Being then 11 Years
    Old

Clark Thomas Son of James Clark and Elizabeth his Wife Bap-
    tized Decemb^r ye 5th 1753 Being then 8 Years Old

Clark Dorcas Daughter of James Clark and Elizabeth his Wife
    Baptized Decem^r ye 5th 1753 Being then 6 Years Old

Clark James Son of James Clark and Elizabeth his Wife Bap-
    tized Decem^r ye 5th 1753 Being then 5 Years Old

Clark Sarah Daughter of James Clark and Eliz^h his Wife Bap-
    tized Decem^r ye 5th 1753 Being then 2 Years Old

Maple Thomas Son of Thomas Maple and Mary his Wife Bap-
    tized Decemb^r ye 5th 1753 Being then 3 Years Old

Maple Mary Daughter of Thomas Maple and Mary his Wife
    Baptized Decemb^r ye 5th 1753 Being then 13 Months Old

McPahaphy Mary Daughter of Oliver M^cpahaphy and Phibi
    his Wife Baptized Decem^r ye 5th 1753 Being then 3
    Years Old

M^cpahaphy Sarah Daughter of Oliver M^cpahaphy and Phibi
    his Wife Baptized Decemb^r ye 5th 1753 Being then 1
    Year Old

Canty John Son of William Canty and Elizabeth his Wife Bap-
    tized Decem^r 5th 1753 Being then 5 Years & 1/2 Old

Canty Jona Son of William Canty and Elizabeth his Wife Bap-
    tized Decem^r ye 5th 1753 Being then 3 Years 1/4 Old

Canty George Son of William Canty and Elizabeth his Wife
    Baptized Decem^r ye 5th 1753 Being then 11 Months Old

Scott John Son of John Scott and Arabella his Wife Baptized
    Decem^r ye 5th 1753 Being then 3 Years & 1/4 Old

Scott Josia Son of John Scott and Arabella his Wife Baptized
    Decem^r ye 5th 1753 Being then 18 Months Old

Stewart Elinor Daughter of Robert Stewart and Catherine his
    Wife Baptized Decem^r ye 5th 1753 Being then 8 Years Old

Stewart Alice Daughter of Robert Stewart and Catherine his
    Wife Baptized Decem^r ye 5th 1753 Being then 5 Years
    and 1/4 Old

Stewart Randal Son of Robert Stewart and Catherine his Wife
    Baptized Decemb^r ye 5th 1753 Being then 3 Years and
    1/4 Old

Stewart Mary Daughter of Robert Stewart and Catherine his Wife Baptized Decem^r ye 5th 1753 Being then 11 Months Old

Sanders James Son of George Sanders and Agness his Wife Baptized Decem^r ye 5th 1753 Being then 7 Years & 11 Months Old.

Sanders William Son of George Sanders and Agness his Wife Baptized Decem^r ye 5th 1753 Being then 5 Years & 1/4 Old

Sanders David Son of George Sanders and Agness his Wife Baptized Decem^r ye 5th 1753 Being then 2 Years Old

Faulkenberg Susana Daughter of John Faulkenberg and Jane his Wife Baptized Decem^r 5th 1753 Being then 2 Years Old

Killy Gerrard Son of William Killy and Emme his Wife Baptized Decem^r ye 9th 1753 Being then 2 Years Old

Killy Kizziah Son of William Killy and Emme his Wife Baptized Decem^r ye 9th 1753 Being then 1 Year Old

Hudson Mary Daughter of Lodowick Hudson and Ann his Wife Born Decem^r ye 8th 1753 Baptized Decem^r ye 9th 1753

Harrison William Son of James Harrison and Ann his Wife Baptized Decem^r ye 9th 1753 Being then 6 Months Old

Scrug Mary Magdaline Daughter of William Scrug & Mary Magdaline his Wife Baptized Decem^r ye 9th 1753 Being then 18 Months Old

McKinney Michael Son of Benj^a McKinney and Mary his Wife Baptized Decem^r ye 9th 1753 Being then 2 Years Old

McKinney Christian—of McKinney Benj^a & Mary his Wife Baptized Decem^r ye 9th 1753 Being then 7 Months Old

Harrison James Son of William Harrison and Ann his Wife Baptized Decem^r ye 9th 1753 Being then 1 Year Old

Harrison Sarah Daughter of William Harrison and Ann his Wife Baptized Decem^r ye 9th 1753 Being then 6 Months Old

Collins Margaret Daughter of William Collins and Elizabeth his Wife Baptized Decem^r ye 9th 1753 Being then 16 Months Old

Cook Thomas Son of John Cook and Elizabith his Wife Baptized Decem^r ye 9th 1753 Being then 2 Years Old

Belton Jonathan Son of Robert Belton and Sarah his Wife Baptized Decem^r ye 9th 1753 Being then 1 Month Old

Pirant Rachel Daughter of Isaac Pirant and Frances his Wife Baptized Decem^r ye 9th 1753 Being then 3 Years Old

Pirant Mary Daughter of Isaac Pirant and Frances his Wife Baptized Decem^r ye 9th 1753 Being then 3 Months Old

Dunworth Henry Son of Henry Dunworth and Ann his Wife Baptized Decem^r ye 9th 1753 Being then 2 Months Old

Rogers Sarah Daughter of Robert Rogers and Sarah his Wife Baptized Decem^r ye 9th 1753 Being then 5 Months Old

Brown Rebecca Daughter of Geofry Brown and Rachel his Wife Baptized Decem^r ye 9th 1753 Being then 6 Years Old

Brown Messer Daughter of Geofry Brown and Rachel his Wife Baptized Decem^r ye 9th 1753 Being then 4 Years Old

Brown Cathrine Daughter of Geofry Brown and Rachel his Wife Baptized Decem^r ye 9th 1753 Being then 2 Years Old

Chrismass Margaret Daughter of Jonathan & Rither Chrismass Baptized Decem^r ye 9th 1753 Being 6 Weeks Old

Bently Elizabeth Daughter of Edmond Bently and Mary his Wife Baptized Decem^r ye 9th 1753 Being then 12 Years Old

Bently Charles Son of Edmond Bently and Mary his Wife Baptized Decem^r ye 9th 1753 Being then 7 Years Old

Bently George Son of Edmond Bently and Mary his Wife Baptized Decem^r ye 9th 1753 Being then 4 Years Old

Crawford Elizabeth Daughter of Thomas and Lucretia Crawford Baptized Decem^r ye 11th 1753 Being then 11 Years Old

Crawford Margaret Daughter of Thomas Crawford and Lucretia his wife Baptized Decem^r ye 11th 1753 Being then 9 Years Old

Crawford Thomas Son of Thomas Crawford and Lucretia his Wife Baptized Decem^r ye 11th 1753 Being then 7 Years Old

Crawford William Son of Thomas Crawford and Lucretia his Wife Baptized Decem^r ye 11th 1753 Being then 4 Years Old

Moses Betty Daughter of John Moses and Jane his Wife Baptized Decem^r 11th 1753 Being then 11 Years Old

Moses Sarah Daughter of John Moses and Jane his Wife Baptized Decem[r] y[e] 11th 1753 Being then 9 Years Old

Moses John Son of John Moses and Jane his Wife Baptized Decem[r] y[e] 11th 1753 Being then 7 Years Old

Moses Joshua Son of John Moses and Jane his Wife Baptized Decem[r] y[e] 11th 1753 Being then 3 Years Old

Moses Samuel Son of John Moses and Jane his Wife Baptized Decem[r] y[e] 11th 1753 Being then 7 Months Old

William Sweat Natural Son of William Sweat and Martha Cawze Baptized Decem[r] y[e] 11th 1735 Being then 3 Years Old

Roders John Son of Joseph Roders and Ann his Wife Baptized Decem[r] y[e] 11th 1753 Being then 5 Years Old

Roders Patience Daughter of Joseph Roders and Ann his Wife Baptized Decem[r] y[e] 11th 1753 Being then 4 Years Old

Michau Abraham Son of Abraham Michau and Sarah his Wife Baptized Decem[r] y[e] 11th 1753 Being then 11 Months Old

John Lane Son of James Lane and Ursula his Wife

1758.   Born October the 29th 1757 and Baptized 12th March 1758 By the Revrn[d] M[r] John Fairweather

Elezibeth McGinney Daughter of Daniell McGinney and Susannah his Wife Born the 4 March 1757 Baptized the 20th August 1757 by the Revern'd M[r] Fairweather

Lane Hester Daught[r] of Peter Lane and Sarah his Wife Born the 16th day of August 1747 . . . . . . .Omitted in Corse of time

Lane Sarah Daught[r] of Peter Lane and Sarah his Wife Born the 14th Day of April 1750 . . . . . . .Alsoe Omitted

Lane Mary Daughter of Peter Lane and Sarah his Wife Born the 3[d] Day of Febr[y] 1755 . . . . .Omitted

James, the Son of Daniel M'Ginney and Susanna his Wife was Baptized May y[e] 6th 1759 & Born'd March 21st 1759

Sarah, y[e] Daughter of James Lane and Ursula his Wife was Baptiz'd on y[e] 6[th] Day of May 1759. Born'd Jan[y] y[e] 6[th] 1759

The two aforesaid Children was Baptiz d by y[e] Rev[d] Mr Samuel Fenner Warren of St James Santee

Green Richard the Son of William Green and Jane his Wife Born the 27 April 1757 Baptz[d] y[e] Sept 1757 by the Rev[r]nd M[r] Sam[el] Fairweather

Green Sarah the Daughter of William Green and Jane his Wife Born the 30th March 1759 Baptized ye 27th May 1759 by the Rev^rn d Mr Sam^{el} Fairweather

White John the Son of Anth^y and Deborah his Wife Born the 29th of May 1760 Baptiz'd by the Rever'd Saml Fayerweather

Carr Samuel Son of Isaac & Abigale his Wife Born November 12th 1754 Baptized February 14th 1755 by ye Revd Mr Smith

Carr Charles Son of Isaac & Abigale his Wife Born Oct 17 1760 and Baptiz'd June the —— 1761 by the Revd James Dormer

Green Samuel Son of William and Jane his Wife Born the 10th of March 1763 Baptiz^d the 10th of April 1763 by the Rever'd George Skene

Walker George Son of Richard & Elizabeth his Wife Born March 17th and Baptized June the 28th 1761 By the Revd James Dormer

Lane James Son of James and Ursilla his Wife Born November ye 13th & Baptized June 28 1761 By the Revd James Dormer

Minniss Catherine Daughter of James & Susanna Born Jan^ry 23 1761 and Baptiz^d June the 28 by the Revd James Dormer

McGinney Richard Son of Daniel & Susanna Born March 18 1761 and Baptiz^d June the 28 By the Reverend James Dormer

Dulany William Son of William &—— Born October 23 1760 & Baptiz^d July 19th 1761 By the Reverend James Dormer

Crawford Samuel Son of Samuel & —— Born Octo^r 14th 1760 & Baptized July 19th 1761 By the Reverend James Dormer

Wilson Thomas Son of Charles and Mary Born March 5th 1761 & Baptized August 2^d By the Revd James Dormer

Wilson Sarah Shaw Daughter of William & Jannet Born May 19 1760 & Baptized July 29th 1761 By the Revd James Dormer

Norvell Eleanor, Daughter of James & Isabella his Wife Born May 4th & Baptized July 31st 1761 By the Revd James Dormer

White John Son of Anthony & Deborah his Wife Born June 13th
and Baptized August 9th 1761 By the Revd James Dormer

Kemp Jno Son of Jno & Elizabh his Wife Born June 24 1756 &
Baptized Octobr 12 1761 By the Reverend James Dormer

Kemp Elizabeth Daughter of Jno & Elizabth his Wife Born 8
of March 1761 and Baptized Octor 12 1761 by the Reverend James Dormer

Perkins Reas Adult Baptized Octor 22d 1761 by the Reverend
James Dormer

Perkins Elizabeth Daughter of Rease & Elizth his Wife Born
April 3d 1758 Baptized Octor 22d 1761 By the Reverend
James Dormer

Perkins Sarah Daughter of Rease & Elizath his Wife Born March
11 1760 Baptized Octor 22d 1761 By the Revd James
Dormer

Brown Son of Abraham and Sarah his Wife 4 Years Old 14th
June 1761 Baptized Octor 22d 1761 by the Reverend
James Dormer

Brown Alpheus Son of Abraham & Sarah his Wife Born July
1st 1760 and Baptized Octor 22d 1761 by the Revd James
Dormer

Brown Zaccheus Son of Abrahm & Sarah his Wife Born July 1st
1761 Baptized October 22d 1761 by the Revd James
Dormer

Snow David Son of George Baptized Octor 1761

Snow Hannah Daughter of Do Do

Snow { Mary Ann Daughter of Nathl Do as above
{ Tyzby Daughter   Do
{ Lydia Dean Do

Snow Nath Son of Nathl Do as above

Williams McDaniell George Son of John & Mary his Wife Born
March ye 8th 1737

Williams Samuel Son of John & Mary his Wife Born July 30th 1744

Williams Benjamin Son of John & Mary his Wife Born July 7th 1755

McGinney Thomas Son of Daniel & Susanna Born March 31
1768 Baptized the 2 Day June by the Revnd George Skeen

Drinnan John Son of David & Mary Born Febry 26 1764 Baptized by the Revnd George Skeen

Lane Thomas Son of James & Ursilla his Wife Born June 21 1764
Baptized Oct 9th By the Reved George Skeen

Scott John Son of Thos Gwillim Scott and Elezbeth Born 14
March 1760 and Baptized by the Revd Mr Skeen

Scott Thomas Son of Thomas Gwillim Scott Born 17 October
1762 and Baptized by the Revd George Skeen

Green Lidya Daughter of William & Jane was Born December
ye 17th 1764 and Baptizd Janry ye 19th 1765 by ye Revd
George Skeen

Samll Gourdin Son of Theodore &   his Wife/Baptized by the
Revd George Skeen/ Born 5th January.......1760

Benjamin Harrinton Godfrey Son of John and Mary his Wife
Born 19th May 1762 Chrisned by the Revd James Dormer

Amos Shaw Tabb/Son of Edward and Sarah his Wife Baptized
by the Revd James Dormer/Born May 1st 1756

Tabitha Daughter of James and Ursilla Lane born Augst 3d 1766
and Baptized December 14th by the Revd Ofspring Pears

William Son of Anthony and Maryan White Born Decr 20th 1766
and Baptis'd 1st March 1767 By The Revd Ofspring
Pierce his Shurety's William Bartonsenr & Wm Barton
Junr & Mary Barton

Bossard John Son of Henry & Clarey his Wife Born March 7th
1761 Baptized by the Revd Mr Garden

Susannah Daughter of Henty Bossard & Clarey his Wife Born
Novr 23d 1762 Baptis'd by the Revd Ofspring Pierce

Elizabeth Daughter of Henry Bossard & Clarey his Wife Born
Apll 23d 1764 Baptis'd by the Revd George Skeen

Ann Daughter of Henry Bossard & Clarey his Wife Born Febry
14'h 1766 Baptized by the Revd Ofspring Pierce

Wilson Wilson Son of William and Jannett his Wife Baptized in
Geo-Town by the Revd Mr Alexr Keith and Born 18th
Decr 17—

Wilson Thomas Son of William and Jannet his Wife Baptiz'd
in George Town/Born Novr 28th 17—

Williams George John/Son of Danll Williams and Sarah his
Wife Born March 18th 1760 Baptis'd by the Revd James
Causgrieve

Williams Danll Son of the Above Couple Born 17th Jany 1763
and Baptis'd by the Revd Causgrieve

Williams Sarah Daughter of the Above Couple Born 19th Augst 1767

Green Benjamin Son of William Green & Jane his Wife Born Decr 26th 1766 Baptiz'd by the Revd James Fowles/ A Traveling Minister

John McDowell Son of William McDowell and Ann his Wife Born Septr 28th 1767

Gouge John Son of John Goudge and Mary his Wife Born Feby 12th 1768

Clarke Elizabeth Daughter of Bartley Clarke & Rebecah his Wife Born Jany 5th 1760

Chapple Jarusha Daughter of James & Rachel Chapple Born 9th June 1769 and Baptized by the Revd Mr Thomas Streaker

Hannah Green Daughter of William & Jane Green Born Apr^{ll} 27th 1769 and Baptized by the Revd Thomas Streaker Traveling Minister

White Joanna Daughter of Anthony & Maryan White Born 29th July 1769 Baptized by the Revd Thos Streaker

William Paulling Son of William Paulling and Mary his Wife/ was born Tuesday July 23^d 1765 Baptised by the Revd George Skein

Robert Paulling Son of William Paulling & Mary his Wife was Born 17th Feby 1768 Baptized by the Revd George Spencer

Godfrey Harrinton the first Son of John & Mary Godfrey Born March 3^d 1765 Died

Godfrey Harrinton the Second Son of the above Born April 7th 1767

Godfrey Mary the Wife of John Died March 16th 1771

Green Elizibeth Daughter of William Green & Jane his Wife Born 14th Ap^{ll} 1771 & Baptised by the Revd James Foulis

Godfrey Thomas Wilson Son of John Godfrey & Mary his Wife Born Feby 4th 1771 & Baptised by the Revd John Villette

Joulee Mary Daughter of James Joules & Mary his Wife Born 22^d Augst 1770

Colhoon Elizabeth Daughter of James Colhoon & Mary his Wife Born Novr 8th 1770

White Mary Daughter of Anthony White Junr & Hannah his Wife Born Novr 23^d 1771 & Baptized by the Rev^d Mr John Vilette

Whitworth Mary Daughter of Abraham Whitworth & Martha his
Wife Born The 5th Augst 1769 & Baptised By the Revd
John Villette

Brown Martha Also Baptized by the Revd John Villette & Born
20th June 1771

Allston Peter Son of Peter Allston & Mary his Wife Born 30th
June 1770 And Baptised by the Revd John Villette

Allston Samuel Son of Peter & Mary Allston Born 17th March
1772 And Baptised by the Revd John Villette

Britton Abraham Son of Daniel & Mary Britton Born 15th June
1771 and Baptized by the Revd John Villette

Worrell Patience Daughter of William & Pennine Worrell Born
Jan 29th 1772 And Baptized By the Revd John Villette

Davis Ruth Daughter of Adam and Mary Ann Davis Born 4th
Sep 1771 And Baptized by the Revd John Villette

Phillips William Son of Anthony & Ann Phillips Born Feby 9th
1765 And Baptized by the Revd John Villette

Hodges Elizebeth Barge, Daughter of Joshua & Ann Hodges
Born Apll 17th 1771 And Baptised By the Revd John
Villette

Keith James, Son of Benjamin & Sarah Keith Born 17th May
1760 And Baptised by the Revd John Villette

Keith William, Son of Benjamin & Sarah Keith Born 21st May 1770

Keith Benjamin, Son of Benjamin & Sarah Keith Born 11th March
1772 & Baptised by The Revd John Villette

And his   William Baptised by the Revd John Villette

Dozer Leonard Son of John & Elizebeth Dozer Born 2 Decemr
1771 And Baptised By The Revd John Villette

Dawsey John an Adult, Baptise By The Revd James Dormer
Augst 20th 1772

White, Joseph, Barton, Son of Anthony White Senr & Mary Ann
his Wife Born 27th Octr 1772 & Baptised By The Revd
Mr. James Stewart

McDowell Fargus, Son of William McDowell & Susannah his
Wife Born Decr 4th 1772 & Baptised By The Revd Mr
James Stewart

Green Jane Born 27th Feby 1774 Baptised By The Revd Mr James
Stewart Being the Daughter of William Green & Jane
His Wife

Glen William, Son of John Glen & Elizebeth his Wife/Born Dec^r
    4th 1773 & Baptised By The Revd James Stewart

Wadringham Ann, Daughter of Sam^{ll} Wadringham & Rebeccah
    his Wife Born 8th Jany 1774 & Baptized By The Rev^d
    Mr Stewart

White Esther, Daughter of Anthony White Junr & Hannah his
    Wife Born March 21st 1775 & Baptized By The Rev^d
    James Stewart

Thomson William, Son of William Thomson & Jannet his Wife
    Born The 1st Feby 1771 Baptised By the Revd James
    Fowles

Thomson Alex^r Son of William Thomson & Jannet his Wife Born
    Octr 16th 1772 Baptised By the Revd James Stewart

Wilson Willm Son of Thos Wilson & Jane his Wife Born 20th
    July 1775 Bapt^d By the Revd James Stewart

Green Jane Daughter of William & Jane Green Born 27th Febru-
    ary 1774 and Baptised By the Revd James Stewart

Barton Sarah, Daughter of William & Jane Barton Born 7th
    Feby 1775 Baptised By the Revd James Stewart/dec^d/
    The 26th Augst 1776 & was Ent^d 27th

Barton Sarah Daughter of William & Jane Barton Born the 21st
    Septr 1776 & Baptized By the Revd James Stewart

Wilson Jannett Daughter of Thos Wilson & Jane His Wife Born
    Sepr 20th 1777 & Baptized By the Revd James Stewart

North Hester Daughter of Thos North & Rose his Wife Born
    Jan^{ry} 23^d 1772 at 55 Minutes after 11 at Night And
    Baptized By the Revd John Villette

North McIver John Son of Thos North & Rose his Wife Born
    July 1773 & Baptized By the Revd John Warond

North William Son of Thos North & Rose his Wife Born Feb^{ry}
    23^d 1777 And Baptized By the Revd James Stewart

Cribb Elizabeth Daughter of Thomas Cribb & Ann his Wife
    Born Jan^{ry} 26th 1761

Cribb Ann Born November 13 1763

Cribb Thomas Born May 20th 1766

Cribb Charity Born October 23rd 1768

Cribb Richard Born December 26 1771

Cribb John Born June 1st 1775

Cribb Frances Born March 22nd 1778

Gouge Rebecca Born June 7th 1779

Carr Elizbeth Daughter of Edmond Carr & Mary his Wife Born December 12 1777

Elizabeth Sarah Daughter of William & Sarah Stewart Born September the 2^d 1775 & Baptiz'd By the Revd James Stuart in George Town

Barton Mary Ann Daughter to William Barton & Jane his Wife was born the 24 July 1778 & was baptiz'd Thursday July 1779

Barton William, Son of William & Jane Barton was born the 12 of April 1781 & was baptiz'd 8th July 1782. both of them By The Rev^d Mr Warren of St James Santee. William Son of W^m & Jane Barton departed this Life the 7 October 1782 & was Ent^d the 9 Instant

Barton Jane, daughter of William Barton & Jane his Wife was born the 7th Day of November 1784 & baptiz'd the 28th Day of Said Month

Barton Esther Daughter of William Barton & Sarah his Wife was Born the 28th Day of Feby 1788 & Baptized the May following by the Revd Mr Jas Twifoot

Anth^y White and Hannah his Wife was married August 30th 1770

Esther White Daughter to Anth^y White & Hannah his Wife was born March 21st 1775 & baptis'd By the Revd James Stewart

Anth^y White Son of Anth^y and Hannah White his Wife Born January 21st 1779 & baptised by the Rev^d Mr Hill

Lydia White Daughter to Anth^y & Hannah White his Wife was born October 23^d 1781 baptised by the Rev^d Mr Warrin

Leonard White Son of Anth^y & Hannah White his Wife born February 20th 1784 & baptized by the Revd Mr Twifoot Elizabeth White Daughter of Anth^y & Hannah White his Wife was born October 22^d 1786 & baptized by the Revd Mr Twifoot

John Barton White Son of Anth^y & Hannah White his Wife Born April 3^d Day 1789 & was baptized July 1789 by The Revd Mr White

William White Son of Anth^y White & Hannah his Wife was Born December 19th 1791 & was Baptized by the Rev^d Mr McCulley in June '92

White Thomas William, Son of Anthony White Senr & Mary Ann his Wife born 3^d February 1778 and baptized by the Rever^d William Knox

Hamlin Mary Ann Daughter of John Hamlin & Joanna his Wife born 8th October 1786 & Baptised by the Reverend James Twifoot

Thomas Barton, Son of John Hamlin & Joanna his Wife Born 15th October 1788 & Baptised by the Reverend William Knox

Anthony, Son of John Hamlin & Joanna his wife born 21st January 1790 & Baptised by the Reverend William Knox

Anth^y Cribb Son of John Cribb & Ann his Wife was Born the 5th day of June 1785

Elie Cribb Son of John Cribb & Sarah his Wife Born the 20th of April 1789

Noah Cribb Born the 23^d of December 1790

Manuel Cribb Born the 3^d of July 1794

1729 Abraham Stapels and Sarah Monnalin were Married December ye 15th

Thompson John and Anna Wigfal were Married ye 23 of March 1726/7

Beech Joseph and Mary Hanley were Married ye 6th of Novem^{br}

Howard Thomas and Mary Westcoat were Married ye 9th of March 1729/30

Band Abraham and Abigail Butler Widow were married

Dantford John and Sarah Boiser were Married ye 12th of June 1730

Heatley William and Susannah Ford were Married y^e 24th of June 1730

Swinton William and Hannah Brown Widow were Married y^e 22^d of October 1730

Robinson Robert and Susannah Sanders Widow were Married Decem^{br} y^e 7th 1730

Davis John and Hannah Sibley Widdow were married December y$^:$ 26th 1730

Hughes Meredith and Mary Pyatt were married December y^e 4th 1734

MARRYED BY THE REV[nd] MR JOHN FORDYCE IN PRINCE FREDERICK PARISH AS FOLLOWETH

Richardson Richard and Mary Canty October 11th 1736
Myers Matthias and Mary Abner January 24th 1736
Lane Peter and Sarah Johnston Marry[d] Feb'[y] 24th 1736
Cain John and Ann Power Marryed April 15th 1737
Kerwon Crafton and Mary Hall Married May 16th 1737
Cratchley Jonathan and Elizabeth Buckholts Marry[d] Marry[d] Aug[st] 2[d] 1737
Conner John and Ann M[c]kdaniel Marryed August 4th 1737
Williams John and Mary M'Ginney August 18th 1737
Edwards Job and Mary Wild were Married September 10th 1737
Smith John and Abigail Commander Marry[d] Octob[r] 4th 1737
Thompson William and Margaret Nesmith Marry[d] Octob[r] 27th 1737
Boyd James and Mehitabel Clegg Wid[o] Marry[d] Nov[r] 7th 1737
Cox Job and Mary Wilden Marry[d] November 7th 1737
Noland George and Rebeccah Ellans [?] Marry[d] Decemb[r] 31st 1737
Dial Thomas and Catherine M[c]Ginney Marry[d] March 14th 1737
Howard Edward and Rebecca McKleveney Marry[d] April 25th 1738
Sinckler John and Martha Bretton Marry[d] May 15th 1738
Keen John and Elizabeth Pelleo Marry[d] July 2[d] 1738
Williams Anthony and Elizabeth Canty Wid[o] July 24th 1738
Metcalf William and Sarah Bosher Wid[o] August 3[d] 1738
George John and Mary Skipper Married August 17th 1738
Fox Henry and Martha Keen Widow Marry[d] August 20th 1738
Kolp Tinman and Beersheba Watkins Widow Decemb[r] 19th 1738
Dinkins William and Sarah Tompkins Marry[d] Feb[y] y[e] 12th 1738
Boaree Stephen and Elizabeth Headwit Wid[o] Marry[d] Feby 27th 1738
Futhy James and Margaret Glenn Marryed March 4th 1738
Smith William and Sarah Bennet Marry[d] March 22[d] 1738

Sloper William and Susannah Coshet Marry^d June 30th 1739

Swinton David and Hannah Clyatt Wid^o Marry^d Augst 1st 1739

Hughes, Thomas and Catherine Neany Married August 1st 1739

Crawford, James and Kaziah Saunders Marry^d Septr 15th 1739

Goodall, William, and Elizabeth Greenwood Married December 24th 1739

Blake, Richard, and Elizabeth Staples Married December 25th

Wort, John, and Martha Jenner......Married......March 23^d

McKants, James, and Agnes Moneally Married July ye 1st 1740

Danilly, Patrick, and Elizabeth Gracebery Marry^d Septemb^r 24th

Tellar, William and Ann Evans Married Decemb^r 8th

McPherson, James and Elizabeth Brown February 11th

Green, William of Prince George Parish and Lydia Avant of Prince Frederick Married......March 31st 1741

Britton, Moses, and Hester Jolly Married April 23^d 1741

Rutlidge, William, and Jenet Knox Married April 23^d

White, John, and Mary Drower Wid^o Married April 28th

Myars, John, and Ann Bruce Married May 15th 1741

Avant, Benjamin of Prince George Parish and Ann Brunston of this Parish } Marry^d June 3^d

Barton, John, and Honora Bonnell Married June 4th

Christmas, Jonathan, and Hester Morton Marry^d June 19th

Davis, Samuel, and Margaret Matthew Wid^o Marry^d Septr 1st

Bentley, Edmund, and Mary Wells Married Septr 15th 1741

Fryerstone, John, and Sarah Dial, Married November 22^d 1741

Boody, John, and Sarah Evans Married November 22^d

Westberry, Jonathan, and Mary Tamplet Married December 24th

Kerr, Isaac, and Abigail Hawkins Married December 31st

Harrington, Whitmill, and Jennet Shaw Married February 2^d

Carter, John, and Martha Sarten Married March 26th 1742

Buttler, Edward, and Mary Skipper Married April 13th 1742

Woolly, or Wally, Thomas, and Jemima Troublefield May 31st

Secare, Peter, and Mary Rea Married June 3^d

Stoar, Benjamin, and Mary Shields July 19th

Smith, William, and Eleonar James August 13th

McDaniel, Daniel, and Sarah Evans August 13th

Moonys, Thomas, and Rebecca Brown August 13th

Perkins, John, and Mary Graceberry September 4th

Smith, John, and Jane Ford September 10th

Davidson, Alexander, and Elisabeth Ball December 3^d

Green, George, and Mary Britt Married December 15th 1742

Minors Robert Widow & Elizabeth Leopard Widow Married
    December 23^d 1742

Burdell, Thomas, and Margaret Wright Married January the 16th
    1742

Obryen Timothy & Anne Thompson Widow Married January
    the 24th 1742

Logan George of Christ Church Parish & Elizabeth Baker of
    this Parish Married February the 3^d 17—

Goodwin John and Lydia Wilds Married April the......4th 1743

Man John of this Parish Chirurgeon &c and Susanna Laroche
    of Prince George Parish Married April 7th 1743

Graves Joseph and Mary Bennet Married April the......29th
    1743

Brunson John Widow and Susanna Robinson Widow Married
    August 13th 1743

Dewit Charles & Sarah Troublefield Married September the 15th
    1743

Whittington Francis and Martha Freeman Married October the
    8th 1743

Murphy Moses and Lucia Troublefield Married October the 9th
    1743

Dick George Practioner in Physick and Mary Allein Married
    November 12th 1743

Cartlidge Edmund and Elizabeth Keble Married December
    9th 1743

Miller Samuel and Helen Hughes Married December the......
    26th 1743

June John and Lucy Kennel Married December the......28th
    1743

Jaudon Paul and Margaret Lieubrey Married December the......
    28th 1743

Avant Francis and Sarah Wigfal Thompson Married January
    the 6th 1743

Wild Samuel and Elizabeth Jones Married March the......26th
    1744

Pyat John of this Parish & Hannah Labruce of Prince George
  Parish Married March the 28th 1744

Cromby John and Mary Tompkins Married April the......
  19th 1744

Turbevil Charles and Susannah Saunders Married May the......
  12th 1744

Turbevil William & Mary Phillips Widow Married May the 26th
  1744

Collins William and Elizabeth Smith Widows Married June the
  ......28th 1744

Bosher John & Mary Whitton Married July the 22d 1744

Jeno or Jenner James and Frances Brown Married August the
  1st 1744

Burdell John and Mary Lieubray Married August the 23d 1744

White Joseph and Susannah Smith Widow Married September
  15th 1744

Wright Thomas & Isabell Tomplet Widow Married November
  27th 1744

Conyers James and Mary Mackintosh Married December the
  18th 1744

Ball Stephen and Lydia Sanders Married January the 1st......
  1st 1744/5

White Anthony Junr and Mary King Widow Married February
  the 12th 1744/5

Douglass Daniel and Margaret Gandy Married ditto 24 1774/5

White Leonard and Hannah Brown Marryed......April......the
  2d 1745

John Glen and Anna Thompson Married April 16 1745

William Saunders of this Parish, and Sarah Franks of Prince
  George Parish, Married May 20th 1745

Thomas Mitchel of P. G. P. & Elisabeth Atkinson of this Parish
  Married, July 11th 1745

James King & Elisabeth Thompson Married Octr 19th 1745

James Walker & Elisabeth Palmer, Married Novr 6th 1745

John Bowls & Susannah Saunders Married Decr 9th 1745

William Wright & Sarah Paterson Married, Decr 26th 1745

James Summers, & Anne Morritt Daur of the Revd Mr Thomas
  Morritt & Margt his Wife, Married, Febry 1st 1745/6

Ebenezer Dunnham & Frances Commander Married February
    20th 1745/6
Godfrey Brown, & Rachel Burkitt Febry 20th 1745/6
Amos Shaw & Persis Avant March 25 1746
Thomas Hasel Junr in St Thomas's Parish & Alice Morritt Eldest
    Dawr to the Revd Mr Thomas Morritt Married April
    26 1744

1746   Marriages Continued

John Purvis and Sarah Johnson Married April 2d 1746
Stephen Peak of P. G. Parish, & Abigaill Brunston of Prince
    Frderick, Married, Mary 5th 1746
Marmaduke Bell & Mary Geurin Married May 21st 1746
Joseph Dubourdieu of P. G. P. & Mary White of this Parish,
    Married, June 24th 1746
Moses Martine, & Martha Jones Married Novemr 27th 1746
Robert Lewis & Susannah Dubusk Married Decr 8th 1746
George Pawley Junr of P. G. P. & Anne Duprè of this Parish,
    Married, Decr 23d 1746
John Dexter, & Mary Buckells Married Febry 14th 1746/7

1747

April 23d James Bellin of P. G. Parish & Mercy Hendlin of P. F.
    Parish N. B and this was the Brides Birth Day
June 2d William Hughes and Sarah Potts Married this Day
    21 Joel Whealer, & Frances Philips
    29 Thomas Hughes & Anne Hawkins
July 5 John Haynsworth & Elisabeth Davidson
    18 Joseph Allen & Mary-Anne, Taylor
Septr 6 Edward Rowse & Hannah Gidens
    7 Jonathan Brown & Mary Shaw
Octr 11th William Procter & Margaret Dyar
    Carried Forward

1747   Marriages Continued   Date as pr Margine

Octr 26 John Bryan, & Sarah Atnor

Decr 16 John Keatly, & Jane Troublefield

1747/8

Janry 26 Daniel Britton, & Elizabeth Hyrne
Feb^{ry} 8 Abraham Giles, & Elizabeth Fletcher, Widow
29th Dy Febry Thomas James Simpson & Martha Collson
March 17th William Wilson & Janet Harrington Widow Daughter
   Danll Shaw
April 9 John Hoskins, & Sarah Taylor
Sept 11th John Bryan & Sarah Margareta Finlay
Novr 3^d Michael Mixan & Sarah Britton
Dec 3^d John Bonnell & Patience Windham
Dec 21st Bryan Connore & Anne Campbell Widow
Dec 23^d Kary Keeble & Mary Kelly
Dec 27th Brewer Sinnixann & Anne Dewit Widow

1748/9

Janry 29 John Popperwell & Mary Purvis
  31st & Amy Walker
Febry 21st Benjamin Davis & Rachel Port
March 14th George Atkinson & Mary Stuart
April 25. John McDaniel & Magdalen Lenud
June 7 John Cope & Mary Burkett
July 30 Stephen Clyat & Katherine Avant

1749   Marriages continued

Septr 3^d John Arrino & Mary McDaniel
Dy 3^d James Campbell, & Judith Dwyer
 5th Thomas Handlen & Elisabeth King
Octr 3^d John Perret, & Julian Newman Widow
Novr 19^h John Turbevill & Philadelphia Isabell
  26th Elias Stallings & Hannah Vaughan
Oct^{tr} 20th 1748 The Revrd John Fordyce was Married to Mary
   Karwon Widow this Day by the Revrd Mr Alex^r Keith
   Min^r of Prince George Parish Which was omited to be
   recorded in the preceeding Page

Green William & Jane Thomson Married August ye 19th 1752

Crawford Thomas and Mary Evans were Married Decr ye 11th 1753

White Joseph and Mary Anna King Married August ye 4th 175–

Paulling William and Mary Dunlop Married December ye 29th 1761

Lane James and Ursula Henning Married february ye 3^d 1757

John Godfrey and Mary Harrinton Both P. F. P. Married By the Rev^rd James Dormer 29th July 1761

Bossard Henry and Clary Wolf Married 8th May 1760 By the Rev^rd Mr Warrin

1729

Capt James Brown Departed this Life Aug^st ye 30th 1729

Peter Sanders Departed this Life Feb^ry ye 2^d

Hughes Elizabeth Wife to Meredith Hughes Esqre Departed this Life Feb^ry ye 26th

Mary Collins Wife to Andrew Colins Departed this Life Feb^ry ye 15th

1730   Clerk Ann Wife to Joseph Clerk Departed this Life May ye 6th

Flewellen John Departed this Life February ye 22^d 1730/1

Bell John Departed this Life Feb^ry ye 23^d 1730/1

Heatley Susannah Wife to William Heatley Departed this Life Janury ye 11th 1730/1

Brunson Anne Wife to John Brunson Departed this Life March ye 6th 1730/1

Atkinson Jane Dawghter of Anthony Atkinson and of Mary his Wife Departed this Life September ye 24th 1732

Hughes Meredith Departed this Life October 2^d 1739 Buryed October 3^d 1739

Atkinson, Mary, Wife to Anthony Atkinson Departed this Life January 17th and was Buryed January 18th 1740.

Sarah White, Wife of John White Departed this Life, August 17th 1741.

John, Alex^r, White, Son of John White, and Sarah his Wife, Departed this Life, Octr 20th 1742.

Sarah White, Daw^r of John White, & Sarah his Wife Departed
    this Life, Decr 3^d 1742.

———— Swinton Departed this Life Jany ye 27th 1743/4

———— White Colon^l Anth^y White, Departed this Life Octr 14th
    1744

1746 May 19th Mary Brown, Wife of Alex^r Brown Departed this
    Life.

Hannah Avant Wife of John Avant Departed this Life Novr 3^d
    1744

1747

Augt 10 Crafton Kerwon Departed this Life

Decr 17 John Nayler Departed this Life, & Buryed the 18th

1747/8

January 21st John Avant Departed this Life

March 1st Elisabeth Fordyce, Wife of the Revrd John Fordyce
    Departed this Life, & Bury'd the 4th Aged 44 Years the
    28th Janry Last.

May 23^d Meridith Hughes Departed this Life this Day & Buryed
    the 25th Instant

1748/9

Jany 11th Elisabeth Pyat Daw^r of John Pyat & Hannah his Wife
    Departed this Life, & was Buryed the 12th

May 31st Elisabeth M^{c}pharson, Wife of James M^{c}pharson De-
    parted this Life, & Buryed June 2^d

Octr 31 Elizabeth Bonnell Departed this Life & was Buried
    Nov 2^d

Novr 10th Wm Brown Departed this Life, & was Buried Nov
    12th

Novr 26th Leon^d White Departed this Life, & was Buried the
    28th

1749/50

Jany 16th Anthony Atkinson Esqr Departed this Life, & was
   Buried Jany 19th
Lane Sarah Widow of John Lane Departed this Life Aprill 7th
   1751 and was Buried Aprill 8th 1751

1751

The Revd Mr John Fordyce Departed this Life July 21st 1751 and
   was Buried July 22^d 1751

1752

Glen Ann Wife of John Glen Departed this Life Aprill 4th 1752
   And was Buried Aprill 6th 1752
Andres John Departed this Life July 30th 1752 and was Buried
   July 31st
Mitchell Eliz^h Wife to Thomas Mitchell Departed this Life August
   11th 1752 was Buried August 13th
Dec 17 James King Departed this Life August ye 15th 1752
Green John Son of William Green and Lydia his Wife Departed
   this Life 1743
Green Lydia Wife of William Green Departed this Life 3^d Aprill
   1751
Collo^l John White Departed this Life   1760 and was Buried
White Jno Son of Antho^y & Deborah White Departed this Life
   ......1760 and was Buried
Mackpherson James Departed this Life   1760 & was Burried
McPherson Daniel Son of James McPherson &c Departed this Life
   1760 & was Burried
Thomas Gull^m Scott departed this Life   1765 and was
   Burried
Elizebeth Green Widow of John Green of P. G. P. Departed this
   Life 1766 and was Burried
Lydia Green daughter of William & Jane his Wife   Departed
   this Life and was Buryed   1766
The Rev^d Mr George Spencer departed this Life 28th June 1769

[End of Register]

RECORDS OF MEETINGS OF VESTRY
OF PRINCE FREDERICK WINYAW

"Securely shall their ashes lie, Waiting the summons from on high."

Easter Monday April

At a Meeting of the parishoners of the parish of Prince George
........The following persons were elected parish Officers for
the ensuing year

Meredith Hughes Esqr ⎤
Mr John Hayes ⎟
Mr Antho. Atkinson ⎟
Mr Jno Bell ⎬ Vestry Men
Mr Jno Lane ⎟
Mr Peter Sanders ⎟
Mr Andrew Collins ⎦

Mr Antho. White ⎤ Church Wardens
Mr John Ridley ⎦

The Same Day the under named persons being present were
Qualified into their Several Offices as the Law Directs, viz,

present The Rev Mr Morritt Rec^r
Meredith Hughes Esq ⎤
Mr John Hayes ⎟ Vestry Men
Mr Antho. Atkinson ⎟
Mr Andrew Collins ⎦

Mr Antho. White ⎤ Church Wardens
Mr John Ridley ⎦

The Same Day they chose Matthew Quash to Serve as Clerk,
Sexton, and Register who was Qualified accordingly

May the 26th 1729 being the Monday in Whitsun Week The
Vestry and Church Wardens mett at the parish Church as is
usual where were present

The Rev^d Mr Morritt Rec^tr ⎫
Meredith Hughes Esqr ⎪
Mr John Hayes ⎪
Mr Antho. Atkinson ⎪
Mr John Bell ⎬ Vestry Men
Mr John Lane ⎪
Mr Peter Sanders ⎪
Mr Andrew Collins ⎭

Mr Antho. White ⎫
Mr John Ridley ⎬ Church Wardens

Mr John Lane, Mr Peter Sanders, and Mr John Bell being absent at Easter were this Day Qualified to Serve as Vestry Men for the ensuing year

The Same day the Rev^d Mr Morritt did Declare that he had received the following number of Cattle for the use of the Parsonage and his Successors given by the Gen^le of this parish whose names are hereunto Annexed. viz.

Mr John Hayes Two Cows and Calves
Mr John Bell Two Do
Meredith Hughes Esq Two Do
Mr Abraham Staples one Do
Mr Antho: White one Do
Mr Antho: Atkinson one Do
Mr Andrew Collins one Do
Mr Francis Avant one Do
Mr John Avant one Do
Mr Daniel Shaw one Do
Mr John Lane one Do
Mr Thomas Hanley one Cow

I do hereby acknowledge to have receiv'd the above mentioned Cattel viz fourteen Cows and Calves for the use of the Parsonage to be accountable for the same and see them, delivered to the parish, in Quantity and quality either at my relinquishinsing of the Said parish or at my decease Witness my hand

The Same Day (being the 26th of May before mention'd) the Rev^d Mr Morritt having communicated to the Vestry and Church Wardens a letter he Received the Honr^ble Society appointing him Missionary of this Parish. Resolv'd that a letter of thanks be drawn up by Meredith Hughes Esqr and Mr Anthony Atkinson to be redy by Saturday next being the 31st Instant to be........ by the Rest of the Vestry and Church Wardens

At a meeting of the Vestry and Church Wardens at the parsonage house y^e .. day of June 1729 where were present all the Vestry and the Church Wardens who then and there agreed and bargain'd with Jonathan Brown for the bricks and also to build a double Chimney in the parsonage house and to under pin it with ....and to lath, plaister, and white wash the same and also to build a Kitchen Chimney, for all which work and bricks they are to pay him the Sum of one hundred and Twenty three pounds and to give him 200 lbs. weight of Meat and one Gallon of Rumm.

The same day the Vestry gave an Order to Mr Anthony White Church Warden to buy Shells and laths for the above Work.

They also ordred Capt Hughes to buy the Nails and promised to see the above charges paid.

At a meeting of the Vestry and Church Wardens of Prince George Parish march ye 30th 1730 where were present

The Rever^d Mr Morritt ⎫
Mr John Lane   ⎪
Mr Anth° Atkinson   ⎬ Vestry Men
Mr Andrew Collins   ⎪
Mr John Bell   ⎭

Mr Anth° White ⎫
Mr jn° Ridley ⎬ Church Wardens

Resolved that an Order be Drawn upon Alexander Paris Esqr Treasurer for the payment of half a years Salary from Michaelmas to Lady Day the 25th instant payable to the Rever^d Mr Morritt for Serving the said Cure, and likewise that an Order of Forty pounds be Drawn for the Parochial Charges made payable to the said Mr Morritt to be accountable to the Vestry for the Same when Received, which Said Orders were then Drawn, and Deliver'd to the Rever^d Mr Morritt accordingly.

At the Same meeting of the Vestry Resolved that Mr Wood having made Apology to the Vestry in behalf of himself and Mr Clark and Desir'd further time, it was then Resolv'd to give the said Mr Wood and Mr Clark longer time that is to meet ye Vestry and Church Wardens on the 11th of April next. And that Mr ANth° White the late Church Warden be then ordered to bring his accounts for money received and Disbursed during his office of Church Warden.

The Same Day being Easter Munday March ye 30th 1730 Several of the parishioners qualified to Choose Vestry Men for the year ensuing being present they proceeded to Election, and Chose

> Meredith Hughes Esqr
> Mr John Lane
> Mr Anth° White
> Mr John Hayes   } Vestry Men
> Mr John Bell
> Mr John Bonnell
> Mr Francis Avant

> Mr Anth° Atkinson }
> Mr Andrew Collins } Church Wardens

At the Same meeting of the Vestry the day above said the Question being put to Matt. Quash to know whether he was mindful to continue in the Office of Clerk, Sexton, and Register, who then agreed to Serve the parish the ensuing year in the Same offices, otherwise upon his relinquishing thereof Engages likewise to relinquish his right to his Salary for the time past to any other person whom the Said Vestry shall approve of

[Data obliterated by breaking of edge of page]

According to appointm^t the Vestry mett att the parsonage the day said and were Qualified as the Law Directs where were ᵖsent

The Rev Mr Morritt
Mr Meredith Hughes ⎫
Mr John Lane ⎪
Mr John Hayes ⎪
Mr John Bell ⎬ Vestry men
Mr Francis Avant ⎪
Mr Anth° White ⎭

Resolv'd that a Subscription be imdiately promoted in Order to Raise Money to enable the Vestry and Church Wardens to finish the Church, and to Beautify and Adorn the Same, and it is further Agreed that any person Subscribing the Sum of Fifteen pounds or more shall have the privilege of Building a Pew in the Said Church, and that the highest Subscriber shall have the first Choice of a place in the Church to Build their Pew on, and So in proportion

Item. Mr Wood appearing according to appointm^t and refusing to repair the Defects then found in the parsonage House, and Kitchen by Workmen indifferently Chosen, the Vestry agree'd with Mr John Gardener, and his parents to repair the Same, and Agreed to pay them. pr Diem.

At a meeting of the Vestry at the Parsonage House the 20th Day of July where were present

The Rev^d Mr Morritt ⎫
Mr John Lane ⎪
Mr John Hayes ⎪
Mr John Bell ⎬ Vestry Men
Mr Anth° White ⎪
Mr Fran: Avant ⎭

Mr Anth° Atkinson ⎫
Mr Andrew Collins ⎬ Church Wardens

The Same Day the Vestry Drew an Order on Mr John Lane for Eighty pounds payable to Jonathan Brown for work done to the Parsonage House.

Received from the Gentlemen of the Vestry of Prince George's
Parish the Summ of Eighty Pounds Currant Money in part of
Payment for Work done in the Parsonage House of the above
Said Parish.

Matt. Quash   I Say Rece^d this 20th Day of July 1730
Register   Pr Me Jonathan Brown

Item. Mr Gardner's conveniency not permitting him to repair
the Parsonage House as before mentioned this Day the Vestry and
Church Wardens agree'd with Mr. Robert Robinson and Mr Gerard
Bromley to Shingle the Parsonage House, and to put up three
Closets in the Same and also to put up Ceiling Joyce and ashlers
for the plaistering above Stairs. And to new lay the Kitchen
Floors, and to put up a Dresser and Shelves and a partition in the
Same for which they are to pay them the Sum of Forty four
pounds.

Item   Agreed with Mr Anth° Atkinson for Five Thousand Cypress
Shingles at 55 Shill^s per Thousand

At a Meeting of the Vestry the 5th day of October 1730 at the
Parish Church of Prince Georges where were present

        The Rever^d Mr Morritt

        Capt. Meredith Hughes ⎫
        Mr John Hayes   ⎪
        Mr John Bell   ⎬ Vestry Men
        Mr Anth° White   ⎪
        Mr Francis Avant   ⎭

        Mr Anth° Atkinson ⎫
        Mr Andrew Collins ⎬ Church Wardens

The Same Day Mr Atkinson undertook to furnish the above said
workmen, with Materials to finish the Parsonage House (viz)
with Nails, Locks and Hanges for which he is to give Credit for
one year after the receipt of the Same

Item. Resolv'd to give the said workmen an Order on Mr John
Lane for Forty Pound when the said work is finished, in part of
pay.

Item. The Vestry examined the Acc^{ts} of Mr Anthony White Late Church Warden and finds the Parish indebted to him the Sum of Fifty Seven pounds Fifteen Shill.^s

Item. The Vestry and Church Wardens drew an order on the Treasurer to pay to the Reverend Mr Morritt the Sum of 250 pounds due to him for serving the Cure of Prince George's Parish from the 25th of March to the 29th of Sep^{br} last past

At a Meeting of the Vestry the 25th of February 1730/1 at the Parish Church of Prince Georges where were present

> The Rever^d Mr Morritt
> Mr John Hayes ⎫
> Mr John Bell   ⎪
> Mr John Lane   ⎬ Vestry Men
> Mr Anth° White ⎪
> Mr Fran: Avant ⎭

> Mr Anth° Atkinson ⎫ Church Wardens
> Mr And^r Collins   ⎭

The Same Day the Vestry taking into consideration that the Parsonage Kitchen was too small they agreed to put a shade to the same the Length of the House. To new Shingle the Kitchen and also to build a Milk-house and a House of office on the Parsonage

Item. Mr Atkinson one of the Church Wardens undertook to furnish Clap-boards and Shingles of the above work.

Item. The Vestry wrote to Mr Hughes (one of the Vestry and then in Town) to inform himself what Answer they were like to have to a petition prefer'd to the General Assembly for some assistance of money to carry on the work of the Church and Parsonage House of this Parish. They also desir'd him to use his endeavours with the Assembly for the Loan of a Church Bible

At a meeting of the Vestry and Church Wardens at the Parish Church on Easter Munday being the 19th of Aprill 1731 where were present

The Rev^d Mr Morritt
Mr Meredith Hughes ⎫
Mr John Lane   ⎪
Mr John Hayes   ⎬ Vestry Men
Mr Anth° White   ⎪
Mr Fran^s Avant ⎭

Mr Andrew Collins   Church Warden

The Same Day the Vestry Drew an order on Coll^{el} Paris for 250 pounds payable to the Rev^d Mr Morritt for Serving the Cure of this Parish [broken out] September ye 29th to March ye 25th 1731

The Same Day the Vestry and Church Wardens drew an order on Coll^l Paris for Forty pounds to defray the Parochial Charges for the year 1730 Payable to Mr Matt. Quash or order

The Same day Several of the Parishioners Qualify'd to Elect a Vestry for the ensuing year, (being present) proceeded to an Election and Chose

Mr John Lane   ⎫
Mr John Hayes   ⎪
Mr Antho: White   ⎪
Mr Josias Dupree   ⎬ Vestry Men
Mr Arthur Foster   ⎪
Mr Francis Avant   ⎪
Mr Edward Henlin   ⎭

Mr Meredith Hughes ⎫ Church Wardens
   Antho. Atkinson ⎭

Item. The Vestry & church Wardens elected
Mr William Swinton ⎫ Overseers of ye Poor
Mr Robert Robinson ⎭

Item. The Vestry gave an order to Mr Sam^{ll} Woodward for Thirty Three pounds

Item   Drew an order on Mr John Lane payable to Messrs Robinson & Bromley for Forty four pounds
Item   Drew an order on Mr Jno Lane payable to James Lanning
for 20 pounds
Item   Gave their Promis^ry Note to James Lanning for Eighteen
pounds

At a Meeting of the Vestry on Munday August ye 2d 1731 Where
were present and then Qualify'd

> Mr John Lane
> Mr John Hayes
> Mr Antho: White } Vestry Mem
> Mr Arthur Foster
> Mr Josias Dupree

> Mr Meredith Hughes } Church Wardens
> Antho: Atkinson

This day Mr William Swinton was Qualify'd to Serve as Overseer
of the Poor.
Item   Mr Thomas Jenkins was Elected Clerk, Sexton, and Regis-
ter.
Item   The Church Commiss^rs Past their Accounts and the Ballance
remains in their favour the Sum of Three pounds.
Item   Agreed with Joseph Baily to finish the Work at the Par-
sonage House and Kitchen, agreeable to a memorandum of ye Same
Delivered by order of the Rev^d Mr Morritt for the sum of Thirty
Two pounds Ten Shill^s
Item   Ordered that the Church Wardens supply ye above Work-
men Shingles and Nales.
[Edge of page broken] . . . . Of the Vestry Munday October 1731
Where were The Rev^d Mr Morritt

> Mr Anth^o White
> Mr Arthur Foster } Vestry Men
> Mr Franc^s Avent

Antho° Atkinson   Church Warden

Item.   The same day adjourned untill Thursdy Octob^r 21st where were present

        The Rev^d Mr Thos Morritt

        Mr Jno Hayes ⎫

        Mr Arthur Foster ⎬ Vestry Men

        Mr Anth^o White

        Mr Fran^s Avant ⎭

        Antho: Atkinson   Church Warden

Item.   The same day the Vestry drew an order on Coll^{11} Pariss Treasurer payble to the Reverend Mr Morritt for 250£ for Serving the Cure of this parish from the 25th of March, to the 29th of September last.

Item.   The Same Day Rec^d a Letter from Mr Willm Swinton in answer to aspersions cast on the Rev^d Mr Morritt, which letter being a Submission from the s^d Swinton was accepted, with the resolution of the [edge of page torn] that the s^d Swinton pay or Cause to be paid unto the Rev^d Mr Morritt the Sum of Ten pounds.

Item.   An answer deliver^d to the Rev^d Mr Morritt's Letter (to ye Vestry) of date 8. . . . .[torn]

At a Meeting of the Vestry on Munday April ye 10th 1732 where were present

        The Rev Mr Thos Morritt ⎫

        Mr John Lane

        Mr John Hays ⎬ Vestry Men

        Mr Arthur Foster

        Mr Antho: White ⎭

        Antho: Atkinson   Church Warden

Item.   The Same day the Vestry drew an Order on Coll^l Paris Treasurer payble to the Reverend Mr Morritt for Serving the Cure of this parish from ye 29th of September to ye 25th of March last past.

Item.   Same day drew an order on Collo¹ Paris for Forty pounds
payble to Antho: Atkinson or order to defray the parochial Charges
for yᵉ year past.

Item   The Same day the Vestry Examined the accounts of
Anthony Atkinson and found the ballance in his favour yᵉ Sum
of [edge of page torn] and agreed to pay the Same with Interest.
[Top of page broken off]

Resolv'd that Mr Thomas [broken off]

Serveing as Clerk of this parish yᵉ year past to be paid [broken]
    (viz) By Anthʸ Atkinson part of the parochial

Charges wʰ Recᵈ   £20
By Ditto the Sum of Ten pounds for the Gentⁿ of the Vestry   10
                                                                  £30

[Broken] Letter deliver'd to the Revᵈ Mr Morritt to request his
diligence in yᵉ Discharge of his Ministerial Function &c

Same Day being Easter Munday Several of the Parisioners Qualified to Elect a Vestry for the Ensueing Year, (being present)
proceeded to an Election and Chose

Meredith Hughes Esqʳ	
Mr Jnᵒ Lane	
Mr Anthʸ White ʸ	
Mr John Hayes	Vestry Men
Anthoʸ Atkinson	
Mr Franˢ Avant	
Mr Edwᵈ Henlin	

Mr Arthur Foster	Church Wardens
Mr John Bonnel	

Mr John Thomson Junʳ	Overseers of Poor
Mr Josias Garʳ Dupre	

The above Vestry and Church Wardens Qualified.

At a Meeting of the Vestry on Saturday May yᵉ 20th 1732 where
were present

Meredith Hughes ⎫
John Lane   ⎪
John Hayes   ⎬ Vestry Men
Anthony White   ⎪
Edwd Henlin   ⎪
Anth^y Atkinson ⎭

Arthur Foster   Church Warden

Item.   The Same Day an assessment was made on the Inhabitants
to raise the Sum of 201,1,6, to Defray ye Charges of the Poor
Item.   The Same Day a Subscription by the Vestry was forwarded
towards raiseing a Sufficient Sum of money to discharge the debts
due from ye s^d Vestry and towards the Building a Pulpit &ca
Item.   Resolv'd that the highest subscriber shall have the first
Choice of a place in the East End of the Church for the building
of a Pew and that each Choice be made in proportion to Each
persons Subscription and the Several Sums which have been heretofore paid shall be deducted out of ye said subscriptions.
Item.   Examined the account of Mr John Lane and find the ballance thereof paid in full by the s^d Lane
[Top of page broken]
At a meeting of the Vestry on Tuesday June..................

John Lane   ⎫
Meredith Hughes ⎪
Anthony White   ⎬ Vestry men
Anthony Atkinson ⎪
Francis Avant   ⎭

Arthur Foster   Church Warden

A Letter sent to ye Rev^rd Mr Morritt to request his Answer to
one Letter of date ye 10th of April &ca. signed by ye above Vestry
At a meeting of the Vestry on Monday March 26th 1733 being
Easter Monday where were present

Meredith Hughes Esqr
Captn Anth^y White
Mr Fran^s Avant　　　} Vestry
Anth^y Atkinson

Mr Arthur Foster　　　Ch^h Warden

The same Day drew an order on Coll^l Paris Treasurer 250£ payble to the Rev^d Mr Morritt for serveing the Cure from the 29th Septr last to the 25th Inst^t

Item Drew an order on Col^l Paris payble to Anth^y Atkinson for 40£ to defray the Parochial Charges for the year 1732

Item Ordered that Anth^y Atkinson pay to Mr Thomas Jenkins 20£ for oficiateing as Clerk for the last Year.

The same day sev^{r}al of the parishoners Quallified to Elect Vestrymen for the Ensueing Year proceeded to an Election & Chose by a Majority of Votes

Captn Anthy White
Anth^n Atkinson
Meredith Hughes Esq
Captn Richard Smith　} Vestry
Mr Robert Stewart
Elias Horry Esq
Mr John White

Mr Fran^s Avant　　} Church Wardens
Mr Edwd Henlin

[Top of page broken off]........Church on Munday November 19th 1733........for three Vestrymen to Supply the Vacancy of Capt Richards, Elias Horry Esqr, and Mr Robert Stewart, who refused to Qualify
were Chose　Mr J^{no} Lane
　　　　　　Mr J^{no} Avant
　　　　　　Mr J^{no} Bonnell

At a meeting of the Vestry on Saturday January the 19th 1733 where were present

Meredith Hughes Esq
Captn Anth^y White
Mr John White
Mr John Lane } Vestry
Mr John Avant
Anth^y Atkinson

Mr Franc^s Avant   Ch^h Warden

Memo^m The above s^d Mr J^{no} Lane & Mr J^{no} Avant Quallify'd
Item   The Same day drew an order on Col^l Paris Treas^r for 250£ payble to the Rev^d Mr Morritt for Serveing the Cure from the 25th March to the 29th September last past.

At a meeting of the Vestry on Munday March the 5th 1733 where were present

Meredith Hughes Esq
Mr J^{no} Lane
Captn Anth^y White } Vestry
Mr John White
Mr John Avant

Mr Francis Avant   Ch. Warden

Item.   The Same day an agreement was made with Mr Thomas Landon that the s^d Landon Build a Pulpit, Pews, and Gallery, in the parish Church and find Boards & all other Materials and finish the Same as pr Artikles of agreem^t may appear)
For the Sum of 300£ & Ten pound more Conditionly.

At a meeting of the Vestry on Munday April 15th 1734 where were present

Meredith Hughes Esq
Capt Anth^y White
Mr John White } Vestry
Mr John Lane
Anth^y Atkinson

Mr Fran^s Avant   Ch^h Warden

The Same Day drew an Order on the Treasurer for 250£ payble to the Revrd Mr Morritt for Serveing the Cure of the parish from Septr 29th to March 25th 1734

Item   One Order payble to Anth^y Atkinson for 40£ paroch^l for the year 1733

Item   The Same Day being Easter Munday Several of the parisioners met at the parish Church in order to Elect Vestry Men and Church Wardens for the Ensuing Year, and Elected

Meredith Hughes Esq Capt Anth^y White Mr John Lane Mr John White Mr John Avant Mr Edwd Henlin Anth^y Atkinson	} Vestry
Mr Fran^s Avant Mr Daniel Shaw	} C^h Wardens

Item   The above Vestry & Church Wardens Quallified the Same day

Item   Mr Josias Dupre Elected Clerk of the parish for the Ensuing Year.

A meeting of the Vestry on Thursday July 18th 1734 at ye Ch^r where were present

The Revrd Mr Morritt Meredith Hughes Esq Captⁿ Anth^y White Mr John Lane Mr John White Mr John Avant Mr Edwd Henlin	} Vestry
Mr Fran^s Avant Mr Daniel Shaw	} C^h Wardens

The Rev^r Mr Morritt was desired by the above Vestry &c to declare whether he purposed to leave the parish as he had Said he Intended   In answer Mr Morritt Declared that he would take care of this parish untill the Society's pleasure is known.   That he would Preach in Georgetown only one Sunday in Every month and that he will not write to the Society without the Vestry's knowledge

At a meeting of the Vestry at ye Parish Church on Saturday Octb^r 2d where were present

Meredith Hughes Esq
Captn Anth^y White
Mr Jno White   } Vestry
Mr Jno Lane
Mr Jno Avant

Mr Fran^s Avant   Ch Warden

Resolved that the Pews should be Vallued and that the price shall be as followeth; and that the highest Subscribers shall have ye preference of Choice.

1............£22	No 7.........£22	No 13.........£12
2.............22	8..........22	14...........14
3.............16	9..........22	15...........16
4.............16	10.........20	16...........18
5.............22	11.........18	17...........20
6............£22	No 12.......£16	No 18.........£22

(15)
Item   The the Vestry should meet again on Saturday ye Second day........ next and that Advertisement should be Imediately put up in Church by ye Church Wardens to give notice to all persons Concerned to be then present to make Choice of Pews According to their respective Subscriptions

At a meeting of the Vestry at the parish Church on Saturday November ye 2d in order to proceed in the Choice of Pews agreeable to the above resolves of the Vestry

Present   Meredith Hughes Esq ⎫
             Mr Jn° Lane   ⎪
             Jn° White   ⎬ Vestry
             Jn° Avant   ⎪
             Edwd Hendlin   ⎪
             Anth^y Atkinson ⎭

             Fran^s Avant   ⎫
             Daniel Shaw   ⎬ Church Wardens

Item   The Choice was made as followeth viz

No 9 by Mr John Brown	No 5 by Meredith Hughes Esq
No 17 " Mr John Lane	No 2 " Captn Anthony White
No 10 " The Rev^d Mr Thos	No 6 " Anthony Atkinson
Morritt	No 1 " Mr John White
No 4 " Mr Jn° Thomson	No 8 " Mes^rs Laroche
Junr	No 7 " William Swinton Esq
No 11 " Mr Daniel Shaw	No 18 " Mr J^no Bonnell
No 12 " Mr Francis Avant	No 3 " Mr Josias Dupre
No 15 " John Walliss Esq	No 14 " Mr Caleb Avant
No 16 " Mr Edwd Hendlin	
No 13	

(17)

At a meeting of the Vestry at the Parish Church on Saturday
February 22d 1734

present   Meredith Hughes Esq ⎫
             Mr Jn° Lane   ⎪
             Anth White   ⎬ Vestry
             Jn° Avant   ⎪
             Anth^y Atkinson ⎭

             Fran^s Avant   Church Warden

Agreed with Mr Peter Secare to Plaster the Church at 2/6 pr y^d
to Supply him with Lime & hair and Boards for Scaffolding and
Labourers to attend &ca
also to allow him y^e Sum of Forty pounds for his Diet &ca

A Plan of the Pews &c.
in the Church

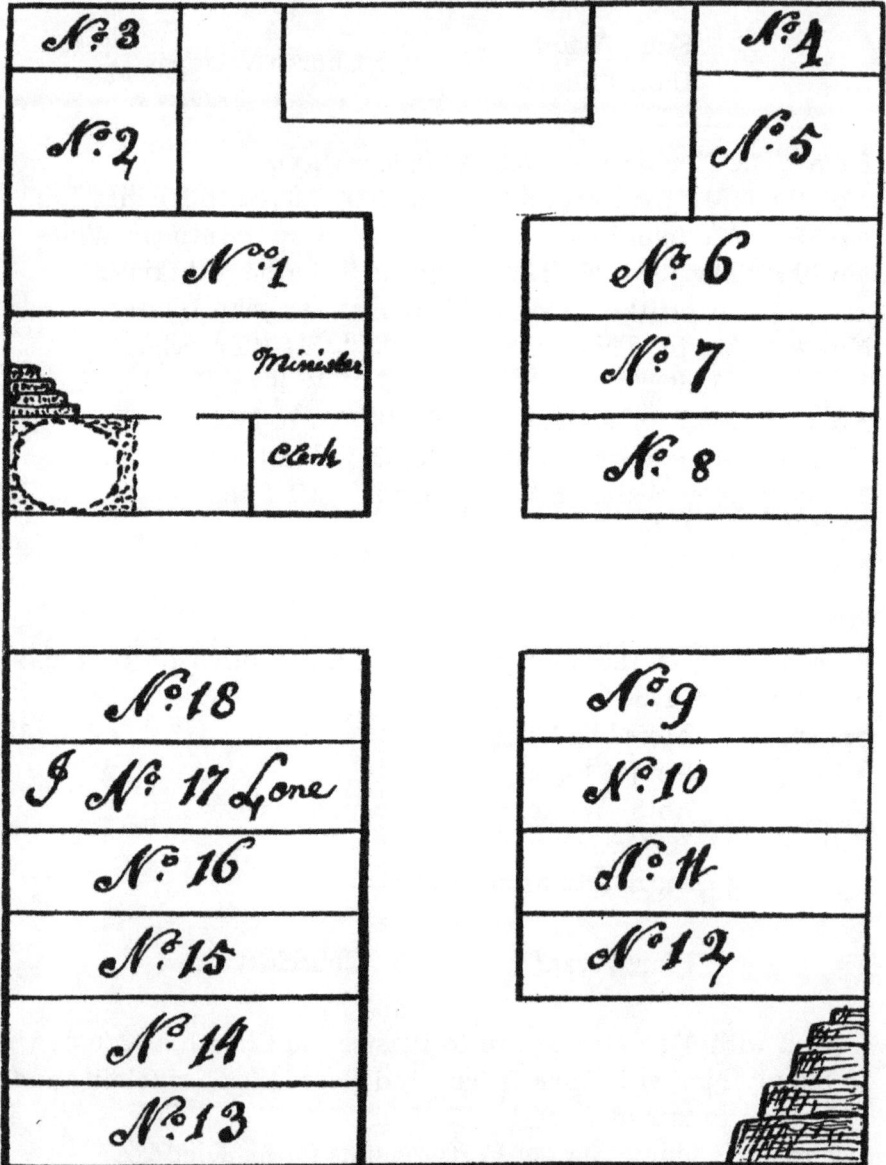

No 3

No 2

No 4

No 5

No 1

Minister

Clerk

No 6

No 7

No 8

No 18

I No 17 Lone

No 16

No 15

No 14

No 13

No 9

No 10

No 11

No 12

Item. The Same Day agreed with Mr Jn° Lane for two negroes to attend the Plasterer at $6/10^{1/2}$ per day for each Slave the s^d Mr Lane finding y^e negroes in provisions

Item. The Same Day Signed a Letter to the Society for another Minister and Inclos'd the Same in a Letter to y^e Rev^d Mr Garden

Item Delivered Sundry Titles for Pews

Viz To Mr John Brown for the Pew....................No 9
      To Mr John White for.........................No 1
      To Mr Francis Avant for......................No 12
      To Mr Edward Hendlin for.................. ......No 16
      To Mr John Bonnell for.......................No 18
      To Mr Anthony White for.....................No 2
      To Mr William Swinton for....................No 7
      To Mes^rs Daniel & Thomas Laroche............No 8
          Mr Morritts Title........................No 10

At a meeting of the Vestry at y^e Parish Church on Thursday Decr 26th 1734 Examined the Accounts of Anth^y Atkinson, & find Ball^e due to him $20£ 00,3/^{1/2}$ Examined the Acc^ts of Mr Anth^y White & find Ball^e due from him $28£, 16, 3$

At a meeting of the Vestry at the Parish Church on Munday April y^e 7th 1733

present   Meredith Hughes Esqr
              Mr Jn° Lane
              Mr Jn° White
              Mr Ant White   Vestry
              Mr Jn° Avant
              Anth^y Atkinson

           Fran^s Avant   Ch^h Warden

Signed Titles for Pews

To Meredith Hughes Esq for the Pew....................No 5
To Anthony Atkinson for............................No 6
To Mr John Thomson for............................No 4
To Mr Daniel Shaw for.............................No 11

Item. Drew an order on Gabriel Manigault Esq Treasurer payble to the Rev^d Mr Thos Morrit for $500£$ for Serveing the Cure of this from March 25th 1734 to March 25th 1735

Item One other payble to Anthony Atkinson for 40 pounds for defraying the Parochial Charges for yᵉ year 1734

The Same Day being Easter Munday the Parishioners Quallified to Chuse Vestry men and Church Wardens for the ensuing year proceeded to an Election and Chose

	Meredith Hughes Esq	⎫
	Anthony Atkinson	
Memᵈ	Mr Jnᵒ Lane	
all Quallify'd	Mr Jnᵒ White	⎬ Vestry
at yᵉ Same Time	Mr Anthʸ White	
	Mr Jnᵒ Avant	
	Mr Franˢ Avant	⎭

Mr Daniel Shaw	⎫
Mr Jnᵒ Barton	⎬ Chʰ Wardens

(19)

At a Meeting of the Vestry at yᵉ Parish Church on Munday April yᵉ 26th 1736

Present	Meredith Hughes Esq	⎫
	Mr Jnᵒ White	
	Mr Anthʸ White	
	Anthʸ Atkinson	⎬ Vestry
	Mr Jnᵒ Avant	
	Mr Franˢ Avant	⎭

Mr Danˡ Shaw	⎫
Mr Jnᵒ Barton	⎬ Chʰ Wardens

An order Drawn on Gabriel Manigault Esq Treasurer payble to the Revᵈ Mr Thoˢ Morritt for 250 pounds for Serveing the Cure of this Parish from the 29th of September to the 25th of March last past

Item One other order payble to Anthʸ Atkinson for Forty pounds for defraying the Parochial Charge for the Year 1735

Item The Same Day being Easter Munday the Parishioners met to Chuse Vestry men and Church Wardens for the Ensueing Year and Elected

Meredith Hughes Esq
Captn Anth^y White
Anth^y Atkinson
Mr John Lane   } Vestry
Mr John Avant
Mr Fran^s Avant
Mr Jno Thomson Junr

Mr John White   } Ch^h Wardens
Mr John Brown

Memorand^m. The Rev^d Mr John Fordyce Arrived here Septr 1736 Missionary for this parish in room of the present Incumbant Mr Morritt

At a meeting of the Vestry September 1736

Agreed that Mr John White undertake to repair the Plastering &ca of the Parsonage House and to fence in, a Garden place with Posts & Pales

At a meeting of the Vestry at the Parish Church on Munday Ap^l 1737 11th

Present   The Rev^d Mr Fordyce
Captn Anth^y White
Mr John Thomson
Mr John Avant   } Vestry & Ch^h Wardens
Mr Fran^s Avant
Anth^y Atkinson
Mr Jno White

An order was drawn on the Treasurer Gabriel Manigault Esq payble to the Rev^d Mr Thos Morritt for 250£ for Serveing the Cure of this Parish from the 25th March to ye 29th Septem^r last

Item   One other order on D^o payble to the Rev^d Mr John Fordyce for Serveing the Cure of this Parish from the 29th September to the 25th March last past

Item   Another order was drawn on Gabriel Manigault Esq Treas^r payble to Anthony Atkinson for forty pounds to defray the Parochial Charges for ye year 1736

The Same day Being Easter Monday the Parishioners Met at the Parish Church to Choose Vestry Men and Church Wardens for the Ensueing year and Elected

Captⁿ Meredith Hughes
Captⁿ Anth^y White
Mr John Thomson
Mr John White } Vestry
Mr Fran^s Avant
Anth^y Atkinson
Mr John Lane

Mr John Avant
Mr John Brown } Church Wardens

(21)

An order was drawn on Gabriel Manigault Esq Treasurer payble
1737 October } to the Rev^d Mr Jno Fordyce for his half-year Salary due for Serveing the Cure of this Parish from March 25th to September ye 29th last past

At a meeting of the Vestry at the parish Church on Munday April 3d 1738

present
Meredith Hughes Esq
Captⁿ Anth^y White
Anthy Atkinson } Vestry & Ch^h Wardens
Mr Fran^s Avant
Mr Jno Thomson
Mr Jno Avant

An order was drawn on the Treasurer payble to the Rev^d Mr John Fordyce for Salary due to him for Serveing the Cure of this parish from ye 29th Septemb^r to ye 25th of March last

Item   Drew an order on ye Treasu^r for forty pounds Parochial Charges for ye year 1737 payble to Anth^y Atkinson

The Same day being Easter Munday Several of the Parishioners met to choose Vestry Men and Church Wardens for ensueing year and Elected

Meredith Hughes Esq ⎫
Mr Jn° Lane |
Mr Jn° White |
Captⁿ Anth^y White   ⎬ Vestry
Mr Jn° Thomson |
Mr Fran^s Avant |
Anthy Atkinson   ⎭

Mr Jn° Avant   ⎫
Mr Abrah^m Staples ⎬ Church Wardens

An order was drawn on the Treasurer Gabriel Manigault Esq Pay-
1738   ⎱ ble to the Revd Mr Jn° Fordyce for Serveing the Cure
Nov 25th ⎰ of this Parish from y° 25th March to 29th Sept^r
(22)
At a meeting of the Vestry at the Parish Church on Munday April
y° 23d 1739
present   The Rev^d Mr Fordyce
              Mr Jn° White   ⎫
              Anth^y Atkinson |
              Mr Fran^s Avant   ⎬   Vestry
              Mr Jn° Thompson | & Church Warden
              Mr Jn° Avant   ⎭

An order was Drawn on Gabriel Managault Esq Treasurer payble
to the Rev^d Mr Fordyce for y° Salary due to him for Serveing the
Cure of this Parish from y° 29th Septr to y° 25th March last

Item   One other order payble to Anth^y Atkinson for Forty pounds
to defray y° Parochial Charges of y° year 1738

Item Resolved that Anth^y Atkinson undertake to Build a Corn
house at y° Parsonage Allso a Shade or P A^h on the front of the
Parsonage House

Item   The Same day being Easter Munday Several of the Par-
ision^{rs} met at the Parish Church to Elect Parish Officers for y°
Ensueing Year and Chose

The Rev^d Mr Jno Fordyce
Meredith Hughes Esq
Mr John Lane
Mr John White
Captⁿ Anth^y White } Vestry
Mr John Avant
Mr Fran^s Avant
Anth^y Atkinson

Mr Abraham Staples
Mr John Thomson Junr } Ch^h Wardens

Mr John Keen   Sexton

(23)
1739

Septr 29th   An order was Deliver'd to the Rev^d Mr Fordyce for the Salary due to him for Serving the Cure of this Parish from ye 25th March to ye date hereof drawn on Gabriel Managault Esq Treas^r

At a meeting of the Parishioners at the Parish Church on Munday Novemb^r 26th pursuant to an Advertisement to Choose two Vestry men in the room of Mr John Lane and Meredith Hughes Esq Deceased Mr Peter Lane and Mr Peter Tamplet were Elected

1739

Decr 12th   A letter was Signed by all the Vestry & Church Wardens and Sent to the Hon^{rble} Society to return thanks for their Hon^{rs} Pious Care in Sending the Rev^d Mr John Fordyce Missionary to this Parish

At a meeting of the Vestry At the Parish Church April ye 7th 1740 present

The Rev^d Mr Fordyce ⎞
Anth^y Atkinson
Mr John White
Captn Anth^y White
Mr Peter Tamplet   ⎬ Vestry
Mr John Avant
Mr Fran^s Avant
Mr Peter Lane ⎠

Mr Abra: Staples   ⎫
Mr Jn° Thomson   ⎭ Church Wardens

An order was drawn on Gabriel Manigault Esq Treas^r payble to
The Rev^d Mr Jn° Fordyce for the Salary due to him for Serving
the Cure of this Parish from the 29th of September to the 25th of
March last past

Item   One other order was drawn on the s^d Treas^r payble to
Anth^y Atkinson for Forty pounds to defray the Parochial Charges
for the Year 1739

Item   Ordered that Anth^y Atkinson pay to Josias Dupre the Sum
of fourteen pounds being the Ballance due him for Officiating
Six years in the Clerkship of this Parish Over and above his
Subscription to the Church and price of his Pew

Item   Ordered that Anth^y Atkinson & Mr John Thomson Junr Pay
to Mr Jos^e Dupre the Sum of 20£ for work done to the Parsonage

Item   The Church Wardens past their Accounts and the Ball^e
of £7–14–6 Remains in Mr Thomson's hands

Item   The Same day being Easter Monday Several of the Par-
ision^rs met to Chuse Vestry and Church Wardens for the Ensuing
Year Elected or Chose

The Rev^d Mr Jn° Fordyce ⎞
Anth^y Atkinson
Mr Peter Lane
Mr John White
Mr Abra: Staples   ⎬ Vestry
Mr John Avant
Mr Fran^s Avant
Captn Anth^y White ⎠

Mr Jn° Thomson Junr ⎱
Mr Peter Tamplet   ⎰ Ch^h Wardens

1740

Septem^r 29th.   An Order was drawn on Gabriel Manigault Esq
Treas^r payble to the Rev^d Mr Jn° Fordyce for the Salary due to
him for Serving the Cure of this Parish from the 25th of March
last past unto this day.

At a meeting of the Vestry the 24th day of Novemb^r 1740 The
Rev^d Mr Fordyce and all the Vestry & Church Wardens present
to receive a Title for One Acre and half of Land for a Churchyard
or Burying place.   The Writings for the Same were then Signed
& delivered by Mr John Peter Somerhoof & William Forbes
Agreed with Mr Alex^r Davidson to make new Doors and Window
Shutters for the Church, to paint the Same inside & out to paint
the Outside of the Church & the Cornishes, Corner-facings, front
of the Gallary, the Pillars and the Rails about the Alter, to polish
the Pulpit, and Alter Table and to Number the Pews, to find all
Materials (Except Hinges) and Compleatly to finish the Same for
the Sum of One Hundred and Eighty pounds

(25)

At a Meeting of the Vestry at the Parish Church ye 30th March
1741

pres^t   The Rev^d Mr John Fordyce
            Mr Jn° White   ⎫
            Captn Anth^y White   ⎪
            Mr Peter Lane   ⎬ Vestry
            Mr Abrah^m Staples   ⎪
            Mr Jn° Avant   ⎭

            Mr Peter Tamplet   Ch. Warden

The Same day Mr Peter Tamplet Acc^t was Examined and find
the ballance remaining his hands the Sum of £14 11, 3.^d
Item   Resolved that the two front Seats in the Gallery be made
into two Pews, one whereof to be appointed for the use of the
Donor of the Lands for the Churches Use as above said

Item   An Order was drawn on the Treasurer payble to the Rev^d
Mr John Fordyce for Serving the Cure of this Parish from the
29th of September last to the 25th Instant
Item   One other Order was Drawn on the Treasurer payble to
Anthony Atkinson for Forty pounds to defray the Parochial
Charges for the year 1740
Item   The Same day being Easter Monday Several of the Parish^ns
met to Chuse Church Officers for the ensuing year and Elected or
Chose   The Rev^d Mr John Fordyce Minister

Mr John White ⎫
Captn Anth^y White ⎪
Mr John Thomson Junr ⎪
Mr John Avant   ⎬ Vestry
Mr Fran^s Avant ⎪
Mr Abrah^m Staples ⎪
Anth^y Atkinson ⎭

Mr Peter Tamplet ⎫ Ch^h Wardens
Mr Crafton Karwon ⎭

Mr Crafton Karwon   Sexton

At a meeting of the Vestry on Sunday May 3^d 1741
present   Mr John Avant ⎫
Mr Fran^s Avant ⎪
Mr Jno White ⎪
Mr Anth^y White ⎬ Vestry
Mr Jno Thomson ⎪
Mr Abra: Staples ⎪
Anth^y Atkinson ⎭

Mr Peter Tamplet Ch Ward^n

Perused a Letter Rec^d from Doct^r Bearcroft Secre^ry to the Hon^le
Society directed to the Vestry of this parish demanding an Ime-
diate Election if no objections to Mr Fordyce who had Com-
plaind in his Letter to their Hon^rs dated Jan^ry 1st 1739 that the
Vestry had refused to Elect him.
Resolved to meet on Thursday following and to write to Mr
Fordyce to desire a Coppy of the said Letter

At a meeting of the Vestry on Thursday May 7th **1741**
present   Mr Jn° White
                M^r Jn° Thomson
                Mr Jn° Avant
                Mr Fran^s Avant } Vestry
                Mr Abra: Staples
                Anth^y Atkinson

                Mr Peter Tamplet } Ch^h Ward^s
                Mr Crafton Karwon

A Letter was Signed and Sent to the Rev^d Mr Fordyce by Mes^{rs} Staples and Tamplet, to desire a Coppy of the above S^d Letter to ye Society and to request Mr Fordyce to meet the Vestry
Item The Rev^d Mr Fordyce brought with him and read to the Vestry that paragraph (and delivrd a Copy thereof) wherein the Complaint was contain'd, and insisted on his Election notwithstanding the Vestry aquainted with the Complaints of Sundry of the Parishioners

(27)
On Monday June 22^d 1741 The Vestry and Church Wardens met at the parish Church and were all quallified by William Romsey......Except Abraham Staples
Pursuant to the Direction of a Precept from the Honble Church Commissn^s an Election was held at the Parish Church on Wednesday the 24th day of June 1741 where the Rev^d Mr John Fordyce was rejected by a Majority of votes.

1741
August 7^h The Vestry rec^d a Letter from the Revrd Mr Comis^ry Garden Dated the 23d of July the purport whereof was to dismiss the Revrd Mr. Fordyce from any further Care or Charge of this Parish
Allso received one other Letter from the Revrd Mr Jn° Fordyce dated August 4th 1741 the Contents thereof, to Inform the Vestry that he would not Officiate any more in the Parish Church
August 16th The abovesaid Precept was inclosed & directed to Mr Willm Smith Clark to the Church Commissioners in Charles

Town and delivered to William Hughes to send from Geo: Town

August 29th   At a meeting of the Vestry at the Parish Church A Letter was Signed and Sent by Anthony Atkinson to the Revrd Mr Commis^ry Garden to intreat his Advice Direction and Assistance

Octob^r 10th   An Order was drawn on Gabriel Manigault Esq Treas^r payble to the Revd Mr Jn° Fordyce for Serving the Cure of this parish for 4 1/2 Months Viz^t from the 25th March to the 7th of August last

Novr 8th   The Vestry Received an Answer (to the Letter Sent by Anthony Atkinson as above) from Mr Commissary Garden with proposals for Mr Fordyces return to the Church

Item   November ye 8th 1741   The Rever^d Mr Fordyce returnd to the Church to Officiate as heretofore

Pursuant to the Direction of a Second precept from the Honble Church Commissioners, a Second Election was held at the Parish Church on Tuesday the 9th day of March 1741 where the Reverend Mr John Fordyce was duly Elected Rector or Minister of this Parish

(28)

At a Meeting of the Vestry at the Parish Church on Monday April 19th 1742

present   The Revrd Mr John Fordyce ⎫
               Mr John Avant   ⎪
               Mr Fran^s Avant   ⎪
               Mr John Thomson   ⎬ Vestry
               Anth^y Atkinson   ⎪
               Maj^r Anth^y White ⎭

               Mr Peter Tamplet   ⎫ Ch^h Ward^s
               Mr Crafton Karwon ⎭

The Same day the Vestry Signed and delivered a Title to the Pew No 3 to Mr Josias Garnier Dupre, also one other Title to the Pew No 14 to Mr Caleb Avant.

Item   Examined the Accounts of Anthony Atkinson for the Estate of Meredith Hughes Esq Dec^d and find the ballance thereof transfer'd to the Said Anthony Atkinsons Accompt

Item Examined the abovesaid Anthony Atkinson Acc^ts and find the ballance thereof due from him the sum of £37 3,5½^d to be paid to Mr Alex^r Davidson in part of £212 due from the Vestry to the s^d Davidson.

Item. An order was drawn on the Treasurer payble to Anthony Atkinson for the Sum of forty pounds to defray the Parochial Charges for the year 1741 as the Law directs.

Item. Ordered that Anthony Atkinson pay to Mr Josias Gar: Dupre the Sum of Ten pounds Curr^t money for Serving the Office of Clerk of the Parish for the year 1741 which was accordingly paid.

Item. Ordered that Anthony Atkinson pay to Mr Crafton Karwon the Sum of five pounds for Officiating as Sexton for the year 1741.

Item. Examined the Accounts of Mr Jno Thomson and Mr Peter Tamplet late Church Wardens and find the ballance remaining in Mr Peter Tamplets hands the sum of £3, 15,9^d

Item. Mr Peter Tamplet and Mr Crafton Karwon Church Wardens for the Year 1741 past their Accounts and the ballance remains in Mr Peter Tamplets hands

(29)

Item Examined the Accompts of Major Anthony White and find the ballance remaining in his hands the sum of £26, 18, 9^d

Item The Same day being Easter Monday the Parishioners met at the Parish Church to Choose Church Officers for the ensueing year and Elected

Captn John White
Messrs William Brown
John Barton
John Pyatt   } Vestry
John Thomson Junr
William Gardner
John Bonnell

Messrs Peter Tamplet
John Brown   } Church Ward^s

Memorand^m The abovesaid Vestry did not meet to Qualify
or do any manner of Business relateing to the Church Dureing
this year

At a Meeting of the Parishioners at the Parish Church on Easter
Monday ye 4th April 1743 the following persons were Elected
for Church Officers for the Ensuing year

      Viz^t Mr William Brown ⎫
      Mr Jasper King |
      Leonard Outerbridge |
      John Avant   ⎬ Vestry
      Jos^s Gar: Dupre |
      Edward Hendlin |
      Richard Walker   ⎭

      Mes^rs William Gardner ⎫ Ch^h Wardens
      Leonard White   ⎭

      Thoe^e Shicorn Sexton

(30)

At a meeting of the Vestry May 23d 1743

Present
    The Rev^d Mr John Fordyce
    Capt John White
    Mr Edward Hendlin
    Mr Josias Gar^r Dupré
    Mr William Brown
    Mr Jasper King
    Capt Leonard Oterbridge

Vestry Men
The said Vestry be-
ing e l e c t e d on
Easter M u n d a y
April the 4th were
Duly Qualified Ac-
cording to Law
this day by John
Bassnet Es^r

    Mr Leonard White
    Church Warden

(31)

Item The Same day, the Said john Bassnett Esqr was Elected
as Church Warden, for the Ensuing Year in the place of Mr
William Gardner, who chose rather to Demit than Serve.

Item The Said John Bassnett Esqr and Mr Leonard White
were Duly Qualified as the Law Directs.

Item The Said Mr Josias Gar^r Dupre was Elected Register of this parish, and Qualified the same time for Said Office according to Law.

Item The Same time Sign'd an Order for the parochial Charges on the Treasurer for the Sum of £40 payable to Mr Anthony Atkinson for the year 1742 out of which the said Mr Atkinson is to pay Mr Dupre £10 for Clerks Salary for said year.

At a Meeting of the Vestry Munday August 1: 1743

Present
    The Rev^d Mr John Fordyce ⎤
    Capt John White   ⎥
    Mr Edward Hendlin   ⎬ Vestry Men
    Mr Jasper King   ⎥
    Mr John Avant   ⎥
    Mr Leonard Outerbridge   ⎦

    John Bassnett Esqr ⎤
    Mr Leonard White   ⎦ Church Wardens

Item The Said Day Mr John Avant, who was Chose as one of the Vestry Last Easter Munday was Qualified According to Law by John Bassnett Esqr.

Then Resolv'd by the Said Vestry and Church Wardens, that Mr Alexander Davidson be allowed Interest from January 1st 1741/2 for his Account of Work then due by the Church

Item Then also Resolv'd, that Mr John Bonnel pay Interest on his Note of hand, also Due to the Church, and payable to Mr Anthony Atkinson

At a meeting of the Vestry at the Parish Church on Monday March 26th 1744.

Present
    The Reverend Mr John Fordyce ⎤
    Capt. John White   ⎥
    Mr John Avant   ⎬ Vestry
    Mr Josias Gar^r Dupre   ⎥
    Mr Edward Handlen   ⎦

    Mr Leonard White Ch. Warden

Item   The Same Day Drew an Order on the Treasurer payable to Leonard White for Forty pounds to defray the Parochial Charges for the year 1743.

Item   The Same Day being Easter Monday Several of the Parishioners met to Chuse Vestry and Church Wardens for the Ensuing Year

Elected or Chose   Col^n Anthony White
                   John Bassnet Esqr
                   Capt John White
                   Mr John Avant   } Vestry
                   Mr Edward Handlen
                   Mr Willm Brown
                   Mr Josias Gar^r Dupre

                   Mr Jasper King   } Church Wardens
                   Mr Leonard White

(32)

At a meeting of the Vestry May the 14th 1744

Present   The Reverend Mr John Fordyce
             Captn John White
             Mr John Avant   } Vestrymen
             Mr William Brown
             Mr Josias Garner Dupré

             Mr Jaspar King   } Church Wardens
             Mr Leonard White

At which time the said Vestry & Church Wardens were qualified according to Law by William Fleming Esqr

Item   Tuesday June the 26th 1744.   This day John Bassnett Esqr was qualified according to Law as a Vestry Man of this Parish by William Fleming Esqr

Item   At a meeting of the Parishioners on Monday August the 6th 1744.   James Boyd was chosen Vestry Man in the Place of Col^o Anthony White who declined & was qualified according to Law by William Fleming Esqr

At a meeting of the Vestry Thursday September the 13th 1744.

Present   The Reverend Mr John Fordyce ⎫
                Captⁿ John White   ⎪
                Mr William Brown   ⎬ Vestrymen
                Mr James Boyd   ⎪
                Mr Edward Hendlen   ⎪
                Mr Josias Garner Dupré ⎭

Mr Leonard White   Church Warden

Then Signed a Title for Mr Jaspar King's Pew No 15 which formerly went in the name of Mr John Wallis on Condition of his paying Mr John Hayes's Subscription which the said John Wallis had always refused to pay.

Item   Then the said Day Signed Advertizements for raising a Tax for Relief of the Poor.

(33)

		£ S. D.
1743/ Leon^d White Church Warden for		
Mony Rec^d at the Communion	Dr	
May 22^d Whitsunday to Cash rec^d		6 .2..
Decr 25 To Do / at Christmass		5 12..
1744 March 25 To Do/ at Easter		9 9.6
May 13th To Do/ at Whitsunday		7 18.6
Decr 25th To Do/ at Xtmass		4 3...
1745 April 14. To Do/ at Easter in Curr^y & Silver		10 7...
Then rec^d from Mr Fordyce, Cash in his Hands, Rec^d at Easter April 3^d 1743 £9 and at Williamsburg July 1st at Communion 40/ both which Sums accounted for on Easter Munday April 15th 1745		11

£   54:12..

1743	By Sundry Accounts ....Cr	£	s	d
May 22d	By Mr Shieron for Wine Whitsunday	1	....	
Decr 25th	By Do/ for Wine......................	1		
1744 March 25	By Do/ for Wine at Easter.........	1	....	
May 13th	By Do/ for Wine Whitsunday.........	1	....	

1745 Apr. 14.	By Mr Blyth for Wine at Easter.....	2	10	...
	By Philip Lake for puting in new pannel in the Church Door, Stoping a Leak in the Roof over the Gallery and puting on Lock on the Door	2	10	...
	By Mr Johnston for Do/Lock......	1	17	6
15.	By Cash pd Mr Fordyce on Mr Wooddrops acc^t in p^t pay^t of a Silver Cup for the Communion Table for which he hath produced Receipt	40		
	By Cash return'd out of Said Mony being bad Bills	19		6
	By Ballance remaining the Hands of Leonard White..........................	2	15	

Nota Bene Mr White pass'd the said Mony & has made himself Dr for 19/6^d by carrying it forward £54   12 ...

which makes to Ballance................... £3,14,6^d—0,19,6

Page (36)

                               2   15

                               £3.14.6

(34)

1744	Leonrd White Church Warden Dr	£	S	D
	To Cash Rec^d from the Publick Treasurer for Parochial Charges for the year 1743	40	......	
1745	To Do for Parochial Charges for the year 1744	40	......	
		£ 80		

1744   Contra................Cr^t
              By Mr Dupré for Reg^r & Clks Sal-⎫   17   7 ...
              ery and Tax as pr agreement   ⎭
              By Mr Shieron as Sexton for 2 years   10 ......
              By Wm Saunders for Mending ⎫
              Plaster in the Church Gallery, & ⎪
              Work done at the Parsonage as Pr ⎬   3   15
              account.......................⎭
              By Ballance remaining in the Hands
              of Leonard White................   48   18
              _____
                                                 £ 80
              _____

1745. April 15th. At a meeting of the Vestry Easter Munday
Present   The Rev^rd John Fordyce ⎫
             Mr John Avant   ⎪
             Mr James Boyd   ⎬ Vestry-Men
             Mr Edward Hendlen   ⎪
             Mr Wm Brown   ⎪
             Mr Josias Dupré   ⎭

             Mr Leon^rd White   Church Warden

The Same Day Signed an Order on the Treasurer payable to
Leonard White for the Parochial Charges for £40 for the year
1744
Item   Sign'd other Advertisements for Raising a Tax for the
Poor at 1/ 3^d per Head on the Slaves of this parish, for defray-
ing the Expences of John Onion and his Wifes Sickness to Doctor
Dick & Peter Tamplat & C° The Said Tax to be paid on or
before the 15th Day of August next.
Turn over   Item

(35)
1745   ⎫
April 15th⎭ Item The Same Day the Following Gentlemen
were Chosen by a majority of Voices for Vestry Men & Church
Wardens for the Ensuing year

Vizt Cap¹ John White ⎫
Mr John Avant ⎪
Mr Edwᵈ Hendlin ⎪
Mr Wᵐ Brown ⎬ Vestry Men
Mr Wᵐ Forbes ⎪
Mr Jasper King ⎪
Mr Josias Dupré ⎭

Mr Leonard White ⎫ Church Wardens
Mr John Naylor ⎭

The Said Vestry-Men were Quallified the Same Day by Wᵐ
Fleming Esqʳ according to Law, (Excepting Capt White & Jas-
per King who were both absent)
Item. The Church Wardens were Quallified the same Day as
the Law Directs.
At a Meeting of the Vestry on Thursday June 13th 1745
Present

The Revᵈ John Fordyce ⎫
Capᵗ John White ⎪
Mr Edᵂᵈ Hendlin ⎬ Vestry Men
Mr Wᵐ Brown ⎪
Mr Josias Dupré ⎭

Mr John Naylor ⎫ Church Wardens
Mr Leonʳᵈ White ⎭

Captain John White was then Quallified by Wᵐ Fleming Esqʳ as
the Law Directs
Item Then agreed with Mr Josias Duprè to Build a Kitchen
and Washhouse, 25, by 12. a Fram'd House and Floor'd above
throughout, boarded with Feather Edg'd Boards, and Stair-Case:
The Said Kitchin to be finish'd by the 1st Day of Octʳ 1745. And
the Said Vestry above mentioned have agreed to pay Mr Duprè
£75 for doing said Work &c.
(36)
1745
June 18th Brought Over
and finding all Wooden Materials.
Item Agreed also that he find all Manner of Iron work, vizᵗ

Hinges, Nails, & Locks, Exclusive of the Said £75 & charge the Same to the Vestry.

		£	S	D
	Leon'd White to Ballance of Money Rec^d at the Communion brought forward from Page 33 as per Account given in and settled April 15th..................	3	14	6
Septr 29.	To Cash rec^d at Communion this Day	5	....	
	To Do/Xtmas Day...............	6	10....	
1746 March 30	To Do/Easter Sunday..............	5	4....	
May 10th	To Do/ Whitsunday..............	6	9	6
		£ 26	18	

1745	Contra Cred^r			
	By 1 Bottle Wine Xtmas Day......	0	15....	
	By Cash to Mr Naylor for 2 Bottles	2	....	
	By Cash to John Andr^{ee} for Work } done at the Parsonage as pr Order. }	6		
	By Ballance Due to the Church in Mr Whites Hands.................	18	3	
		£ 26	18	

(37)

Leonrd White Church Warden

1745	For Parochial Mony Rec^d & in his Hands Dr........................	£	S	D
	As pr account given in April 15th.	48,	18,	
1745	To Cash from the Treasurer by the } the Hands of Mr Fordyce for the } Parochial Charges of 1745........ }	40		
		£88,	18	

1746   Contra   Creditor

By Mr Duprès Salery & Tax pd to
Mr Mckiver.................... } 16,2 . . . . . .

By Cash to the Rev^d Mr Fordyce
for the remaining part of the Com-
munion Cup the whole valued... } 20 . . . .
from England being charg'd £60,
Curry according to Receipt pro-
duced for the Second payment

By Cash pd Mr Duprè as Clk and
Reg^r........................... 15 . . . .

By Mr Shieron as Sexton.......... 5 . . . .

By order payable to Doctor Dick... 29,10 . . . . . .

By Ballance due to the Parish...... 3,6

                                     £88,18

Leonrd White Do Ballance Due to
the parish as pr account Page 36 } 18,3

To Do/ as above................. 3,6

                                     £21,9 . . . . . .

1747   By Cash p^d Mr Naylor, on Shieron's
acc^t as Sexton } 10 . . . .

Ballance Due to the Parish   £11,9 . . . . . .

1746. At a Meeting of the Vestry on Easter Munday March 31st 1746.

Present   The Rev^d Mr Fordyce
               Captⁿ John White
               M^r Wm Forbes
               Mr John Avant   } Vestry Men
               Mr Wm Brown
               Mr Josias Dupre

               Mr John Naylor   } Church Wardens
               Mr Leonard White

Item   The Same Day Sign'd an Order on the Treasurer payable
to Mr Leonard White for £40 Currency to defray the Parochial
Charges of this Parish for the Year 1745, as the Law Directs.
Item   The same Day Ordered that Mr Leonard White should pay
Dr Dick the Sum of £29–10/ for his attendance on John Onion
& Wife during their Sickness as pr his acc^t given in to the Vestry
Item   The Same Day agreed by the Vestry that a Double Chim-
ney Should be built at the West End or Side of the Parsonage
House
Item   The Same Day the following Gentlemen were duly Elected
for Vestry-Men and Church Wardens for the Ensuing Year

Viz   Capt Jno White
             Mr John Avant
             Mr Edwd Hendlen
             Mr Wm Brown   } Vestry Men
             Mr John Naylor
             Mr Leonrd White
             Mr Josias Dupree

             Mr Wm Forbes, & } Church Wardens
             Mr Alex Brown

                                              Turn Over

Tuesday May the 20th 1746.   The Following Persons were Qualified as Vestry Men, as the Law Directs, by Wm Fleming Esqr Viz

             Captain John White
             Mr John Avant
             Mr Wm Brown
             Mr John Naylor   } Vestry Men
             Mr Leonrd White
             Mr Josias Dupre

Item   The same Day Mr Alex^r Brown was Qualified as a Church
Warden, according to Law
At a meeting of the Vestry june 12th 1746

Present The Revd Mr Fordyce ⎫
Captain John White ⎪
Mr Wm Brown ⎪
Mr John Naylor ⎬ Vestry Men
Mr John Avant ⎪
Mr Josias Duprè ⎪
Mr Leon^rd White ⎭

Mr Wm Forbes ⎫
& Mr Alex^r Brown ⎭ Church Wardens

Agreed the same Day by the Vestry and Church Wardens, that Capt John White do agree with Mr Arthur Foster for 6000 Bricks for a Double Chimney to the Parsonage House, & Underpinning Kitchin and Wash House

Item   The same Day Mr Wm Forbes was Quallified as a Church Warden as the Law Directs

Item   Order'd, that Mr Leon^rd White do compare his present Acc^ts Given in this Day with his former given in on Easter Munday. Turn back⎫ April 15th 1745 and to bring the same to a true to Page 37⎭ Ballance and make them Ready against the next Meeting of the Vestry

Page 37 Accn^ts there Ballanced

(Page 40)

At a meeting of the Vestry Oct 22d 1746

Present

The Rev^d Mr Fordyce ⎫
Captain Jn° White ⎪
Mr Josias Duprè ⎪
Mr Wm Brown ⎬ Vestry Men
Mr John Naylor ⎪
Mr Leonard White ⎭

Mr Alex^r Brown   Church Warden

The Same Day Examined Mr Leonard Whites acco^ts as Church Warden for 2 years 1744 & 1745, and find that he is indebted to the Parish for mony in his Hands as pr acco^t Page 37 the Sum of £ 21 9/ Currency.

Item   The Same Day drew an Order on the Publicke Treasurer for Sundry Charges payable to Captain John White for Repairs of the Parsonage, as pr account annex'd with that Order the Sum of £201 : 2 : 9ᵈ

At a meeting of the Vestry, & Church Wardens on Easter Munday, April 20th 1747

Present   The Revᵈ John Fordyce ⎫
              Mr Wᵐ Brown   ⎪
              Mʳ Josias Garnier Duprè ⎬ Vestry Men
              Mr John Naylor   ⎪
              Mʳ Leonard White   ⎭

              Mr Alex Brown   Church Warden

The Same Day Sign'd an Order on the Publick Treasurer payable to Mr Fordyce for defraying the Parochial Charges for the Year 1746, for £40/ Currency

Turn over to Page 41

(Page 41)
April 20th 1747.   This Day it was agreed that Mr Josias Duprè Mʳ Alexander Brown Mr John Naylor should send each of them a Negro that could Squair Timber for Steps for the Three Doors of the Church, and Mr Fordyce one Negro that could Labour or Saw, and to be at Church on Saturday the 25th Current about 9 of the Morning A.M. Do. where Mr Brown was to receive, and Direct them to do the said Work, and which work is to be done without any Charge by consent of parties concerned
Item, The Same Day the Following Gentlemen were Duly Elected by a Majority of Voices for Vestry-Men & Church Wardens for the Ensuing Year, Vizᵗ

              Capᵗ John White   ⎫
              Mʳ Jno. Avant   ⎪
              Mr Wᵐ Brown   ⎪
              Mr Josias Garnier Duprè ⎬ Vestry Men
              Mr Jnᵒ Naylor   ⎪
              Mr Leonard White   ⎪
              Mr James Lane   ⎭

Mr Wm Forbes   ⎫
Mr Alex^dr Brown ⎬ Church Wardens

Item, The Same Day The following Gentlemen were sworn into their Several offices by Wm Fleming Esqr Viz^t

     Mr Wm Brown   ⎫
     Mr Josias Garnier Duprè ⎬ Vestry-Men
     M^r Jn° Naylor   ⎪
     Mr Leonard White   ⎭

     Mr Alex^r Brown   Church Warden

Item. The Same Day, Agreed by the Vestry & Church Warden then Present that Mr Fordyce take the Dimensions of the Brocken Windows in the Church, and that he may agree with a Glazier in Charles Town, for new Leaded Windows to supply what are wanting.

(Page 42)
1747) The Revd John Fordyce by virtue of an Order ⎫
drawn by the Vestry and Church Wardens on the ⎪
Publick Treasurer April 20th Easter Sunday as pr ⎬
page 40th for the Parochial Charges of this Parish ⎪
for the year 1746 Dr   ⎭ £   S   D
To Cash Rec'd from the Treasurer.............. 40

Contra........................Cred^r
May 30th   By Cash paid Wm Saunders, as pr his
        acco^t & Receipt....................... 26   10....
        By Do/ paid Mr Naylor for nails for the
          Parsonage......................... 5   10....
        By Do/ paid Capt Wm Wooddrop Nails
          Do/ 6^d & 4^d......................... 5   1   3
June 4th   By John Andrews, in full of his acc^t as p^r
          Rec^t........................... 3   10....

Ballance due to Jn° Fordyce 11^sh/3^d......£40   11 3

At a meeting of the Vestry and Church Wardens on Easter Munday April 11th 1748   Present

The Revd John Fordyce ⎫
Captn John White ⎪
Mr Wm Brown ⎬ Vestry Men
Mr Josias Garnier Duprè ⎪
Mr Leonard White ⎭

Mr Wm Forbes ⎫ Church Wardens
Mr Alex^r Brown ⎭

The Same Day Sign'd an Order on the Treasurer for £40 Currency,
payable to Mr Fordyce for Defraying the Parochial Charges of
this Parish for the year 1747.

Item, The same Day the following Gentlemen (as on the other
side) were Duly Elected by a Majority for Vestry-Men & Church-
Wardens to Serve for the Ensuing year

Turn Over

(page 43)
1748 April 11th Viz^t Captain John White ⎫
Mr Wm Brown ⎪
Mr Jaspar King ⎪
Mr Wm Forbes ⎬ Vestry-Men
Mr Leonard White ⎪
Mr Alex^r Brown ⎪
Mr Anth^y White Senr ⎭

Mr James Lane ⎫ Church Wardens
Mr Meredith Hughes ⎭

Item, The same Day the abovesaid Vestry Men were all Duly
Qualified by Wm Fleming Esq, as the Law directs

Item, The said Day the Rev^d Mr Fordyce was Chosen Reg^r &
was Qualified for said Office, at the same time.

Item, Then Examin'd the Church Wardens acco^{ts} &c and find
there is a Ballance Due to the Parish in the Hands of Mr Forbes

for the Sum of..................................... £5   5   6
In the Hands of Mr Alex^r Brown pr acc^{ts}........... 3   4   3
In the Hands of Mr Leonard White as pr Accts Re-⎫
corded Page 37...............................⎭ 11   9....
In the Hands of Mr Fordyce as part pay^t of Mr Jasper
Kings Pew.................................... 6........

£25   18   9

Dr

The Revd John Fordyce to the above mentioned
Order payable by the Publick Treasurer...........£40........

By Reg^r £ 5/, Mrs Karwon £5/.................. 10.......
By Cash paid Mr Duprè......................... 30.......

£40.......

Septr 6th Wm Hughes was unanimously Elected as Church Warden
in the Room of his Brother Meredith who Departed this Life the
23d of May Last; and the said Wm Hughes was Duly Qualified
for the said Office by Wm Fleming Esqr Monday Decr 12th 1748

(Page 44)
1749. At a Meeting of the Vestry and Church Wardens on Easter
Munday March 27th 1749 Present
>   The Revd John Fordyce ⎫
>   Captain John White   ⎬ Vestry Men
>   Mr Wm Brown   ⎭
>   Mr Jasper King
>
>   Mr William Hughes ⎫ Church Wardens
>   Mr James Lane   ⎭

The Same Day Sign'd an Order on the Treasurer payable to Mr
Fordyce for the Sum of £ 40 being the Parochial Charges for the
year 1748.
Item, Sign'd Another Order on the Treasurer Payable to Mr
Fordyce for the Sum of ....£76 2 9^d Granted by the General
Assembly for the Repairs of the Parsonage.

Item, Mr James Lane, Church Warden, produc'd his accounts, and were Examin'd, and find there is a Ballance in his Hands of Mony Rec^d at the Sacrament the Sum of £ 13 16/.

Item, The Following Gentlemen were Duly Elected as Church Officers for the Ensuing year Viz^t

Captn John White
Mr Wm Brown
Mr Jasper King
Mr Leonard White   } Vestry Men
Mr Anth^y White Senr
Mr Wm Barton
Mr John Pyatt

Mr Wm Hughes   } Church Wardens
Mr James Lane

continued

Page 45 } March 27th 1749, Easter Munday—
1749.

The same Day the following Gentlemen were duly Quallified according to law by Wm Fleming Esqr

vizt

Captain John White,
Mr Wm Brown,   } Vestry Men
Mr Jasper King,
Mr John Pyat,

Mr Wm Hughes,   } Church Wardens
Mr Jas Lane

June 10th. This day the following Gentlemen were Quallified as Vestry Men, Viz^t—

Mr Wm Barton
Mr Leonard White   } Vestry Men
Mr Anth^y White

1750. At a Meeting of the Vestry & Church Wardens on Easte1 Munday April 16th 1750.

Present   Rev^d Mr John Fordyce,
             Major John White,
             Mr Jasper King,
             Mr Wm Barton,   } Vestry Men
             Mr Anth^y White,
             Mr John Pyat,

             Mr James Lane   Church Warden

The Same Day the said Vestry Sign'd an Order on the Publick
Treasurer for £40/ Currency, payable to Mr Fordyce for defraying the Parochial Charges for this Parish for the year 1749.
Item, The Same Day Mr James Lane, Church Warden Produc'e'd
his acco^{ts} for two years past, which were Duly Examined and
passed, and find that there is a Ballance in his Hands due to the
Parish of mony rec^d at the Sacraments the Sum of £24, 17, 9^d
Item, The same Day the following Gentlemen were duly Elected
as Church Officers for the ensuing Year Viz^t

             Major John White,
             Mr Wm Barton,
             Mr Anth^y White Senr,
             Mr John Pyatt   } Vestry Men
             Mr James King
             Mr Wm Hughes
             Mr James Lane

             Mr John Walker   } Church Wardens
             & Mr Thomas Hendlin

Item   The same Day, the following Gentlemen were duly Quallified
according to the Law by Wm Fleming Esqr Viz^t Major John White
                                                   Turn Over

Page 47 }
1750   }   April 16th Easter Munday
                  Major John White
                  Mr Wm Barton
                  Mr Anth^y White Senr   } Vestry Men
                  Mr John Pyat
                  Mr James Lane

Item the same Day agreed with Mr Alex^r Davidson to make frames for the Semicircles & Ovals of the Church Windows at 7 shs /pr pane.

The Revrd Mr Fordyce to Cash rec^d from the Treasurer for Parochial Charges 1749...........................Dr £ 40....

C^r By Mr Duprès Tax............................	16	2
By Registers Salary............................	5....	
By Mr Wright as Sexton........................	5....	

Page 48th }
1751 }

At a Meeting of the Vestry on Easter Munday April y^r 8th 1751. Present The Rev^d Mr John Fordyce

the S^d Day the following Gentlemen Were Duly Elected to Serve as Vestry Men & Church Wardens for the present year Viz^t

Major John White
Mr Anthy. White
Capt Wm Hughes
Mr George Atkinson   } Vestry Men
Do^r Jno King
Mr Fran^s Avant
Mr Jas Lane

Mr Wm Barton }
Mr John Pyat   } Church Wardens

June ye 18th. this Day the following Gentlemen ware Duly Qualified according to Law by Paul Trapear Esqr Viz^t

Major John White
Capt Wm Hughes   } Vestry Men
Mr Fran^s Avant
Mr Ja^s Lane

Mr Wm Barton }
Mr John Pyat } Church Wardens

July ye 13th this Day Mr George Atkinson Ware Duly Qualified by John Man Esqr as Vestry Man.

(49)

At a Meeting of the Vestry on the 13th July 1751
Present

Major John White ⎫
Mess^r Fran^s Avant ⎪
Jam^s Lane ⎬ Vestry Men
George Atkinson ⎭

Mess^r Willm Barton ⎫
John Pyatt ⎬ Chur^h Wardens

Item For want of a full Vestry adjourned untill Wednesday the 23d Instant

At a Meeting of the Vestry & Church Wardens at the Parish Church on wednesday 24th July 1751
Present

Major John White ⎫
Mess^r Jos^s Gar^r Dupree ⎪
Anthy. White ⎬ Vestry Men
Jam^s Lane ⎪
Geo Atkinson ⎭

Mess^r Willm Barton ⎫
John Pyatt ⎬ Church Wardens

Item   This day Mr Anthony White, & Mr Jos^s Gar^r Dupree who was Chose in the Room of Doct^r Jas King who refused to quallifie were This Day quallified to Serve as vestry men for the Ensueing year

Item   Same Day George Atkinson was Chose as Register

Item   Same Day Major John White produced his acc^t Dated 1745 which was Examined and found a Ballance due to S^d White the Sum of £3, 13,^s which s^d Vestry agreed to allow.

(50)

The Same Day Drew an order on Jacob Motte Esqr Treasurer for forty Pounds in favour of Mess^r Willm Barton & John Pyatt

Item Drew an order in favour of Major John White on Mr Dougal Campbell as adm^t or to the Estate of Alex^der Brown for £ 3, 4, 3, being a Ballance due from s^d Brown as pr page 1743

Sam Day Examined the Acc^t of Mr Jam^s Lane late Church Warden and find the Ballance remaining in his hands the Sum of £24, 17, 9

At a Meeting of the Vestry and Church Wardens at the Parish Church on Wednesday October 23^d 1751

Present

Major John White	
Mess^r Anth^y White	
Fran^s Avant	Vestry Men
Jam^s Lane	
Geo. Atkinson	

Messrs Willm Barton	Church Wardens
John Pyatt	

Item   Same Day Sign'd a Letter to the Bishop of London and another to the Honorable Society for a Minister in the place of the Rev^d Mr Fordyce Dec^d and sent them to the Rev^d Mr Garden by Maj^r John White

At a Meeting of the Vestry at the Parish Church on Tuesday 7th Jany 1752.

Present

Major John White	
Capt Wm Hughes	
Messr Jo^s Gar Dupree	Vestry Men
Anth^y White	
Geo. Atkinson	

Mr Willm Barton	Chur warden

(51)

Item   Same Day Perused an account against the Rec^d Jno Fordyce Estate and found the Ballance to be £135, 9, 6 due to s^d deceased

Item   Same time sign'd an order for the same on Mess^r Paul Tra...... and Thos Hasell Ex'ors to s^d Estate Payable to John Pyatt and William Barton

Same Day appointed Mr William Barton to agree with a Workman to repair the Parish Church

At a Meeting of the Vestry at the Parish Church on Munday March ye 30th 1752

Present   Maj^r John White

Maj^r John White
Mr Jos Gar Dupree
Anth^y White   } Vestry Men
Fran^s Avant
Ja^s Lane

Mr John Pyatt } Church Wardens
Willm Barton

An order was Drawn on Jacob Motte Esqr Treasurer for the Sum
of £40. to defray the Parochial Charges for ye year 1751

Item Same Day being Easter Munday the Parishioners met to
Chuse Vestry Men and Chur. Wardens for the Ensuing year and
Elected as on the other Side

Item Same Day William Mitchell was taken on the Parish at £90
per year

Easter Munday March 30th 1752

Maj^r John White
Captⁿ Robt Stewart
Mr Anth^y White
John Pyatt   } Vestry Men
Geo. Atkinson
Jo^s Gar. Dupree
Fran^s Avant

Mr William Barton } Church Wardens
John Glen

At a Meeting of the Vestry and Church Wardens at the Parish
Church on Thursday Aprill 9th 1752

Present

Maj^r John White
Mr Jo^s Gar. Dupree
John Pyatt   } Vestry Men
Fran^s Avant
Geo. Atkinson

Mr Willm Barton   Church Warden

Item The above Gentlemen were this Day Duly Quallified as
the Law Directs.

Item Sign'd the order order drawn on Paul Trapier Esqr and Thos Hasell for the Sum of £135, 2, 9 being a Debt due from the Revd John Fordyce's Estate, the former assignment being laid aside.

Item Same Day Thomas Wallbrock was taken on the Parish at £90, pr y^r.

(53)
At a meeting of the Vestry and Church Wardens at the Parish Church on Thursday 11th June 1752
Present

Maj^r John White	
Mr Jo^s Ga^r Dupree	
John Pyatt	Vestry
Fran^s Avant	
Geo. Atkinson	

Willm Barton	Ch Wardens
John Glen	

Item This Day Mr John Glen was Qualified into the Office of a Church Warden for the ensuing year

Item Signed an order on Mr Jam^s Lane for the Sum of Twenty four pounds, Seventeen Shillings, and Nine pence, being the Ballance of his Acc^t as late Church Warden

Item Same Day Mr Peter Lane rendered an account for his Expen^s for Burring Mary Nannamone who died at his house the Sum of £10, 15

Item Ordered that Mr William Barton do pay the above acc^t to said Peter Lane.

Item This Day Captn William Hughes was Chosen to Serve as a vestry man in the room of Mr Robert Stewart who refused to Serve in Said office

On the Other Side

(54)
Item This Day Mr William Flinn mett said Vestry agreable to appointment to Examin the Parish Church and to undertake and agree for repairing the same, Agreed to undertake Said Work but would not agree for no sertain Sum untill further Examination

Item.   Same Day Agreed with Mr Jo⁵ Ga Dupree to furnish Said
Flinn with all wooding Materials for repairing the Said Parish
Church

At a Meeting of the Vestry and Church Wardens at the Parish
Church on Tuesday 26th October 1752

Present   Maj John White ⎫
              M Jo⁵ Gar. Dupree |
              John Pyatt   ⎬ Vestry Men
              Anth White |
              Fran⁵ Avant |
              Geo. Atkinson   ⎭

       Joh Glen   Church Warden

Mett and went and Viewed the Parsonage House and found it very
much out of repair.

Item   Ordered that Mr William Barton & Jnᵒ Glen do Emediatly
Get a Workman to repair said Parsonage House.

Item   this Day Mr John Pyatt Prodused his Receipt from Mr
Will Barton Present Church Warden in full for Ballance of his
Account when Church Warden

(55)

At a Meeting of the Vestry and Church Wardens at the Parish
Church on December 17th 1752

Present

              Maj Jnᵒ White   ⎫
              M Jo⁵ G. Dupree |
              M Jnᵒ Pyatt   ⎬ Vestry
              Mr Anthy White |
              Geo. Atkinson   ⎭

              M Will Barton ⎫
              Mr Jnᵒ Glen   ⎬ Ch War⁵

Item Met and Agre'd with Mr Jo⁵ Gar. Dupre to get Stuff Emediately for the repairs of the Parish Church and to make a Sufficient
quantity of good Sypress Shingles all to be made of sound Hart,

which s^d Shingles he is to Deliver at the Parish Church for £, 4 pr ^m with the rest of the Timber

Item   Resolved that William Barton do Emediately agree with Mrs Fleming for the Rent of her House Quarterly to accommodate Our Missionary when he Arives

Item Same Day went and Examined further into the Parson^s House and found it Past all repairs and Came to a......result to Petition for Assistance to Build a new House.

Item   Ordered that George Atkinson do Draw up a Petition to represent the bad state of our Parsonage House and Glebe Land and to Crave their Assistance to rebuild ye Same The s^d Petition to be made ready agaenst ye next meeting.

(56)
Memorand^m   The Rev^d Mr Michael Smith arriv^d here Decem^r 24th 1752 Missionary for this Parish in the room of the Rev^d Mr Fordyce Dec^d

At a Meeting of the Vestry at the Parish Church on Tuesday January 30th 1753.
Present

Maj^r Jno Wihite
Mr Jo^s Gar. Dupree
Mr Jno Pyatt
Mr Fran^s Avant   } Vestry
Mr Anth^y White
Geo. Atkinson

Mr Jno Glen
Mr Willm Barton   } Ch^h Ward^s

Item. Sign'd a Petition to the Assembly to Crave their assistance to Rebuild the Parsonage House.

Item   Agreed to Meet again on Thursday the 9th February

Agreable to appointment mett on Thursday the 9th February 1753 at the Parish Church where were Present.

Maj^r John White
Geo. Atkinson   } Vestry Men

William Barton   Wm Barton

For want of a full Vestry were obliged to adjourn untill the next Meeting.

(57)
At a Meeting of the Vestry and Ch^h Wardens at the Parish Church on Ester Munday Aprill 23^d 1753
Present

Maj^r John White ⎫
Mr Jo^s Gar. Dupree ⎪
Anth^y White ⎬ Vestry Men
Fran^s Avant ⎪
Geo Atkinson ⎭

Mr William Barton ⎫
John Glen ⎬ Ch^h Ward^s

Item Sign'd an Order on Jacob Motte Esqr for the Sum of £,40 to defray the Parochial Charges for 1752.
Item Same Day Examined Mr William Barton's Acc^t of the Poor, Alowed and gave him an Order on the Ch^h Wardans for the Ensueing year for the Sum of £115, 13, 3 ye am^t of his acc^t Same Day Examined his Acc^t as Churchwarden for 2 years and find a Ballance in his hands of ....£, 13,8,3

Item Same Day Sign'd an advertisement to Assesse the Parish for the Sum of £133, 13/3 to defray the Exspencies of Messrs William Mitchell and Tho Wallbruck the Poor & C^a

Item Sign an order on the Publick Treasurer for Six Months Salery due to the Rev^d Mr Smith.
for serving the Cure of this Parish.

Same Day found in his acc^t the Sum of £ 135, 9, 6 in favour of the Parish Being Moneys rec^d from Paul Trapier Esqr Due from the Estate of the Revd John Fordyce Est^s to the Glebe of this Parish Sup^r Willm Barton's acc^t for 1751 & 2

(58)
Item The Same Day being Ester Munday the Parishioners Mett to Chuse Church Officers for the Ensuing year and Elected—

Maj^r John White ⎫
Messrs Jo^s Gar Dupree ⎪
John Pyatt ⎪
Anthy White ⎬ Vestry Men
Fran^s Avant ⎪
John Handlen ⎭

Messrs George Atkinson ⎫ Ch^h Wardens
Willm Barton ⎭

Messrs Peter Lesesnee ⎫ Overssers of the Poor
Jam^s Thomson ⎭

Mr Thos Jewning   Sexton

At a Meeting of the Vestry and Wardens at the Parish Church
on Thursday 28th June 1753
Present

Maj^r John White ⎫
Mr Anth^y White ⎪
John Pyatt ⎬ Vestry Men
Fran^s Avant ⎪
John Glen ⎭

Mr William Barton ⎫ Ch^r Wd^s
George Atkinson ⎭

(59)
Mett and Sign'd Advertisements for the Inhabitants to give in a
List of theyr Slaves to the Collector of the Poor Tax
Item same day Chose Mr William Walker to act in Capasity of a
Vestry Man in the room of Mr Jno Handlin D^d

At A meeting of the Vestry and Church Wardens at ye Parish
Church on Thursday ye 6th of September 1753

Present   Maj^r John White ⎫
Mr John Pyatt ⎪
Anthy. White ⎬ Vestry Men
Fran^s Avant ⎪
Willm Walker ⎭

Mr William Barton ⎫ Ch^h Wardenes
George Atkinson ⎭

Sign'd an Order on Jacob Motte Esqr Publick Treasurer for one half years Salary due ye 25th Septem^r payable ye Revd Mr Michael Smith for Serveing the Cure of this Parish

Item Shaderick McCormack an orphan Child was this day taken on the Parish at £30 Expense pr year.

Item Same Day Rec^d a Letter from ye Rev^d Mr Smith wherein he acquainted ye Vestry that he had Purchased 22 H^d of Neet Cattle of Mrs Fleming and desire'd an order for the Money if the Vestry thought fitt.

Resolved and return'd for answer that we could not satisfie him at this time, as it was at Mr Trapiers upsion whether he return'd the Cattle Due for the Estate of ye Rev^d Mr Fordyce to the Glebe or pay the Cash for them, which by the next Meeting we should Endeavour to know and at that time he might depend on a Positive Answer.

(60)
At a Meeting of the Vestry and Wardens at the Parish Church on Tuesday 25th September 1755
Present

> Maj^r John White ⎫
> Mr John Pyatt   ⎬ Vestrymen
> Willm Walker   ⎭
> George Atkinson   C^h Wd^n

Item for want of a sofisient Number of Vestry Men were obliged to adjourn.

At a Meeting of the Vestry and Wardens at the Parish Church on Thursday 11th October 1753
Present

> Maj^r John White ⎫
> Mr John Pyatt   ⎪
> Anthy. White   ⎬ Vestry
> Fran^s Avant   ⎪
> Willm Walker   ⎪
> John Glen   ⎭
>
> Mr Willm Barton ⎫
> Geo Atkinson   ⎬ Ch^h Wd^{ns}

Item   Sign'd an order of Paul Trapier Esqr Payable to the Revd Mr Michael Smith for the sum of Twenty Eight Pounds Currency in part due from ye Rev^d Mr Fordyce Estate on acc^t of Cattle due to the Glebe land of Parish of Prince Frederick.

Item   This day the Rev^d Mr Smith agree'd to remove out of Mrs Fleming's into the Parsonage House, and that Mr William Barton was ordered to have said House Cleansed accordingly.

At a Meeting of the Vestry and Church Wardens at the Parish Church on Thursday the 10th of January 1754
Present

Maj^r John White ⎫
Mr Anth^y White ⎬ Vestry men
John Pyatt ⎪
William Walker ⎭

Geo. Atkinson   C^h W^n

Mett and Sign'd an order on Jacob Motte Esq for the sum of Six Hundred Pounds Currency Granted to the Glebe House of this Parish.

Item   Ordered that George Atkinson do draw up Petition to the Generall Assembly of this Province for further assistance for Building an House on the Glebe of this Parish and to have it ready by Saturday next.

To be Sign'd on Sunday following.

At a Meeting of the Vestry and Wardens at the Parish Church on Saturday ye 16th March 1754
Present

Maj^r John White ⎫
Mr John Pyatt ⎪
Anth^y White ⎬
Fran^s Avant ⎪
John Glen ⎪
Willm Walker ⎭

George Atkinson

Mett and Sign'd an order on Maj^r John White Payable to Mr Cornelias McCarty for the Sum of Six Hundred Pounds Currency for Work done to the Parsonage House.

Item   Agree'd to Rate the Parish Inhabitants at 1/6 pr head on Slaves only to defray the Expenses of ye Poor for ye year 1753

Item   Wrote and Sign'd a Letter to Mr William Williams and to Mr John Simson requesting them to Come and Make Oath to what they know concerning the Scandelous aspersion layd to Mr Smith's Charge.

At a Meeting of the Vestry and Wardens and other the Inhab^{ts} at the Parish Church on Easter Monday ye 15th Aprill 1754.

Viz^t

Maj^r John White	
Mr John Pyatt	
Anthy. White	Vestrymen
Willm Walker	

Mr Willm Barton	
Geo. Atkinson	Ch^h Wards

Mett and Proceeded to Election and Chose the following Persons to Serve as Church Officers for the Ensuing year

Viz

Maj^t John White	
Capt Willm Hughes	
Mr John Pyatt	Vestry Men
Anth^y White	
Geo. Atkinson	

Mr Jos. Gar. Dupree	
Fran^s Avant	Ch^h Ward^s

Mr John Williams	
Fran^s Lesesnee	Overseers

At a Meeting of the Vestry and Wardens at the Parish Church on Wednesday ye 19th June 1754.

Present   Maj^r John White ⎫
            Mr Willm Barton │
            John Pyatt   │
            Anth^y White   ⎬ Vestry men
            Willm Walker   │
            Geo. Atkinson   ⎭

            Fran^s Avant   Ch^h Ward^n

Mett and sign'd Advertisements for Collecting the Sum of £141 Currency to defray the Expenses of the Poor for ye Y^r 1753.

Item Mr James McPhersan was Elected as Ch^h Warden in the place of Mr Jos. Gar. Dupree who declin'd serving.
The said James McPhersan was this day quallified.

Item Allowed Mr William Barton's acc^t for last year and Sign'd an order on the Present Church Wardens Payable to s^d Barton for ye Sum of £113, 12, 6 Being ye Expen^{se} ye Poor 1753.

Item George Atkinson Renderd his acc^t for Last year, the Sum of £7, 7, 6 and allowed for Maintaing Sarah McCormack taken on the Parish. Sign'd him an order on Present C^h Ward^s for s^d Sum of £7, 7, 6

Item Sign'd an order on Jacob Motte Esqr Publick Treasurer Payable to ye Rev^d Mr Smith for one half years Salary due the 25th of March Last.

Same day sign'd an Order on Jacob Motte Esqr for the Sum of Two Hundred Pounds Currency Granted by the Generall Assembly to the Glebe of this Parish.

Same Day Axamined Mr William Barton's Acc^t as Chur^h Warden and find a Ballance Due to s^d Barton the Sum of £ 19, 13, 9

On Sunday the 7th of July 1754.
The Rev^d Mr Michael Smith Desire'd the Vestry to meet together after Service, which were

Present   Maj^r John White ⎫
               Mr Anth^y White ⎪
               John Pyatt   ⎬ Vestry Men
               Willm Barton   ⎪
               Willm Walker   ⎪
               Geo. Atkinson   ⎭

               Mr Fran^s Avant   Ch Ward^n

When mett   gether Mr Smith Declared that he Intended to
Leave this Parish and that that was our warning to Provide our-
selves with another Minister for he had Got a Parish on the Neck.
At a meeting of the Vestry at the Parish Church on Monday the
13th of January 1753
Present
               Maj^r John White ⎫
               Mr Anth^y White ⎪
               John Pyatt   ⎬ Vestry Men
               Willm Barton   ⎪
               Willm Walker   ⎪
               Geo. Atkinson   ⎭

Mett and Agree'd to Rate the Parish 1/6 p^r head on Slaves to defray the Exspences of the Poor for ye y^r 1754.

Item Sign'd an Order on Maj^r John White payable to Cornel^s
McCarty for the Sum of Two Hundred Pounds Currency for work
done at the Parsonage,

Same Day Sign'd an order on Mr William Barton Payable to Mr
Cornelias McCarty for the Sum of ....£, 137..
At a Meeting of the Vestry and Ch^h Wardens at ye Parish Church
on Easter Monday the 31st March 1755.
Present
               Maj^r John White ⎫
               Mr Willm Barton ⎬ Vestry Men
               Anth^y White   ⎪
               Geo Atkinson   ⎭

               Mr Jam^s McPhersan ⎫ Ch^h Ward^s
               Fran^t Avant   ⎭

Mett and Allowed Mr William Barton's acc^t for ye Poor for ye y^r 1754 the Sum of £134, 7, 6

Item Mr Fran^s Avant passed his acc^t as Ch^h Ward^n for the Board of John Wort for ye year 1754 for £90

Item   Agreed to allow Mr John Williams the Sum of £12 Currency for Burring of John Rogers, Dyed at his House.

Further Agree'd to allow Mr Anthony White the Sum of £50 Currency to main   Thomas Pew taken on the Parish this Day.

Same Day the Vestry Ward^s and other the Inhabitants there Present Proceeded to Elecation and Chose the following Gentl^m to Serve as Church Officers for ye Ensuing year.

Viz^t

The Revd Mich^l Smith	
Maj^r John White	
Mr Jos^h White Senr	
Willm Barton	Vestry Men
Jam^s McPharsan	
Willm Green	
Geo Atkinson	

Mr Willm Walker	Ch^h Ward^s
Willm Wilson	

Mr Mathew Nelson	Overseers
John Simson	

At a Meeting of the Vestry and Wardens at the Parish Church on July the 11th 1755.

Present

Coll^n John White	
Mr Willm Green	
Willm Barton	Vestry Men
Jam^s McPharson	
Geo. Atkinson	

Mr William Wilson	Ch^h Ward^s
William Walker	

Mett Chose and Elected Mr Jamˢ Mitchell to act as Vestry Man in the room of Mr Josʰ White Senʳ who declined Serving

Item Sign'd an order on Mr Jamˢ McPharsan Late Chʰ Wardⁿ Payable to yᵉ Present Chʰ Wardⁿˢ for the Sum of £32 Currency Parochial Money then in his Hands

Same Day Sign'd an order on Paul Trapier Esqʳ Payable to the Present Chʰ Wardens for the Sum of Thirty Eight Pounds Currency being the Ballᵉ Due from yᵉ Estate of yᵉ Rev Mr Fordyce Due to the Glebe of this Parish for Cattle.

Further Agree'd that yᵉ Present Wardens do agree with a Workⁿ to Pail in a Quarter of an Acre of Land for a Garden and to Clean out the Well Provi'd there is Parochial Money in thier hands suffitient.

At a Meeting of the Vestry and Chʰ Wardens at the Parish Chʰ on Monday the 12th January 1756.

Present   Collˡ John White ⎫
              Mʳ Willᵐ Barton ⎪
              Willᵐ Green   ⎬ Vestry
              Jamˢ McPhersan   ⎪
              Geo. Atkinson   ⎭

              Mʳ Willᵐ Wilson ⎫ Chʰ Wardˢ
              Willᵐ Walker   ⎬

Mett Assessed and Rated the Parish at the following rates Vizᵗ Lands at 1/pr hundred acres Slaves at 1/pr hᵈ Moneys at Interest at 6ᵈ pr 6£, Stock in Trade 3ᵈ pr 6£ to discharge the sum of £256, 7, 6 Being the Exspence of the Poor of the Parish for yᵉ Year 1754.

further ordered that the Present Chʰ Wardⁿˢ do Lock up the Church Doors and not admit the Revᵈ Mr Smith into the Church at his return untill the Vestry be called to gether to hear his Reasons why he was so long absent from his Parish.

At a Meeting of the Vestry and Chʰ Wardˢ at the Parish Church on Wednesday the 4th February 1756.

Present

> Col¹ John White
> Mr Jamˢ McPhersan
> Willᵐ Barton   } Vestry Men
> Willᵐ Green
> Geo. Atkinson

> Mr William Walker } Chʰ Wardˢ
> William Wilson

Mett the Revᵈ Mr Smith at his Return from the Northward and heard his Reasons for absenting himself from his Parish for three Months Last Past/Which were that he had been sick in his absence—and further told the Vestry that he had Provided himself with Another Parish in the North Province and that they might Provide themselves with another Minister, as soon as they could, but would Constantly attend in his function untill another Minister arived.

Resolved that yᵉ sᵈ Mr Smith should be no more admitted to Preach in this Church.

Further ordered that Geo. Atkinson do prepare Letters to the Honourable Society for another Minister to supply the Vacancy of this Parish and to have them ready by Sunday Next.

At a Meeting of the Vestry and Chʰ Wardens at the Parish Chʰ on Thursday the 12th March 1756.

Present

> Coll¹ John White
> Mr Willᵐ Barton
> Jamˢ McPharsan   } Vestry Men
> Willᵐ Green
> Geo. Atkinson

> Mr Willᵐ Walker } Chʰ Wardˢ
> Willᵐ Wilson

Mett and Sign'd an Order on Jacob Mott Esqʳ payable to the Rev Mr Michaˡ Smith for Six Months Salary Due to him the 25th of March.

Item   Rec^d an order from the Rev^d Mr Smith on Jacob Mott Esqr Payable to the Present Ch^h Ward^s from the Sum of Sixty Six Pounds Currency Being due to the Glebe of this Parish for 22 Head of Cattle Belong^g to s^d Glebe.

Item   Sign'd and gave the Revd Mr Smith a Discharge and Likewise Mr Smith gave the Vestry and Ch^h Ward^s a Discharge.

Same Day ye Rev^d Mr Mich^l Smith and the Vestry and Ward^s Sign'd and Passed Receipts to Each other in full of all of all acc^{ts} as to Parish Business Related.

At a Meeting of the Vestry and Wardens and other the Inhabitants at the Parish Church on Easter Monday the 19th of Aprill 1756.
Present   Coll^l John White ⎫
               Mr Willm Green   ⎬ Vestry Men
               Jam^s McPherson   ⎪
               Geo. Atkinson   ⎭

               Mr Willm Walker ⎫ Ch^h Ward^s
               Willm Wilson   ⎭

Mett and Proceeded to Election and Chose the following Gentl^m to Serve as Church Officers for ye Ensuing y^r Viz^t

               Coll^l John White ⎫
               Mr Anth^y White   ⎪
               Willm Green   ⎪
               Willm Walker   ⎬ Vestry Men
               Willm Wilson   ⎪
               Jam^s McPhersan   ⎪
               Geo. Atkinson   ⎭

               Mr Jam^s Crockett ⎫ Ch^h Ward^s
               Char^s Woodmason   ⎭

               Captⁿ John McDonald ⎫ Overseers
               Mr Saml Butler   ⎭

At a Meeting of the Vestry and Ch^h Ward^s at y^e Parish Church on Tuesday the 4th of May 1756.

$$\left.\begin{array}{l} \text{Coll}^1 \text{ John White} \\ \text{M}^r \text{ Jam}^s \text{ M}^c\text{Pherson} \\ \text{Anth}^y \text{ White} \\ \text{Will}^m \text{ Green} \\ \text{Will}^m \text{ Walker} \\ \text{Will}^m \text{ Wilson} \end{array}\right\} \text{Vestry Men}$$

$$\left.\begin{array}{l} \text{Mr Jam}^s \text{ Crockett} \\ \text{Char}^s \text{ Woodmason} \end{array}\right\} \text{Ch}^h \text{ Ward}^s$$

Mett and Sign'd an order on the Present Ch^h Wardens Payable to Mr Anth^y White for the Sum of Forty Pounds $^{2/3}$ Currency for Support of Thomas Pew.

Item   Doct^r Jam^s Crockett Rendered an acc^t of £20 Currency for Nesessarys found Willm Mitchell and gave him an order on present Ch^h Ward^s for y^e Same.

Item   Mr William Wilson Render'd his acc^t for las year for nesesarys and maintainance found Mich^1 Cary the Sum of £30, an order given for s^d sum

Item   Sign'd an order payable to Math^1 McCormack for the sum of £10 for the funerall Exspences of a Poor that Died at his House.

Item   This Day Mr Willm Barton Renderd his acc^t of the Poor for ye y^r 1755 for £100. an ord was sign'd on the Present Ch^h Ward^s for amount......of ye same.

Item   Mr Willm Wilson Render'd his acc^t of Boarding John Wort with Mrs Ann Pike for £90 Sign'd an order payable to Mrs Pike on Present Ch^h Ward^s for s^d £90....

Same Day Mr William Walker Produced his acc^t for ye y^r 1755 and Past wherein he is Indebted to the Parish the Sum of £1.9.3

Same Day paid it into the Hands of Mr Charles Woodmason Present Church Warden

This Day Rec^d an acc^t from the Rev^d Mr Mich^1 Smith wherein he says that Mr McCarty has charged him for the Sashes and

Glass of the Glebe House the sum of £106. and an aditional charge of £19.1—for Garden and Stable   Upon which the Vestry Waited on Mr Smith in a body who at Last Confest that it was a fraudulent thing in McCarty.

Item   This Day Asesed and Rated the Parish at the following Rates Viz^t Lands at 1/6 pr Hun^d acres Slaves at 1/6 pr h^d Moneys at Interest pr hund^d Pounds 1/ Stock in Trade 3^d To Discharge the Sum of £290,2,3 for the Exspences of the Poor for ye y^r 1755 and the aditional Sum of £20 as a Fund.

Same Day Mr James McPharson Render'd his acc^t for the year 1754 as Church Warden the sum of £40 Paroch^l Moneys £40.

To Cash Paid William Wilson as ye C^h w^d £32
To Ditto p^d Geo Atkinson as Regis^r   5
Towards ye Pulpit Cloth................   3

£40.......40

Same Day drew an order on Mr Willm Walker payable to ye Present Chur^h Wardens for the sum of £40 Currency Parish Money when in his hands.

[End of first part Parish Records
in the Register Book 1713–1756]

At a Meeting of the Vestry in Black River Church on Easter Monday April 19 1756 the following persons were duly elected Officers for the present year, viz

Col John White ⎫
Anthony White ⎪
William Wilson ⎪
Geo Atkinson ⎬ Vestry-Men
Ja⁸ McPherson ⎪
William Walker ⎪
William Green ⎭

Doct^r Ja⁸ Crockat ⎫ Church-Wardens
Cha⁸ Woodmason ⎭

Capt Ja⁸ McDonald ⎫ Overseers
Capt Sam¹ Butler ⎭

The Vestry then took into Consideration the State of the Parish which requiring much time to discuss, they adjourn'd to Thursday sennight next

The Parish being without an officiating Minister thro" dismission of the Revd Mich¹ Smith from this Cure, the Vestry requested Mr Cha⁸ Woodmason that He would read Prayers and a Sermon every Sunday, with which proposal he complied.

At a Meeting of the Vestry & Church Wardens of the Parish of Prince Frederic, at the Parish Church, on Tuesday April 27th 1756 Present

Col. John White
William Green

. . . .

William Wilson
Ja⁸ McPherson
Cha⁸ Woodmason
Geo Atkinson

The State of the Parish was examin'd; and but one of the Church Wardens being present, the Public accounts could not be audited.

On a Motion made, That this Parish is now without an Incumbent, and no Minister resident near at hand, to perform Ecclesiastical Offices, it was moved,

1ˢᵗ That Letters be wrote to the Lord Bishop of London, requesting a Minister for this Parish

2dly That Letters shᵈ be wrote to the Society for propagating the Gospel, to thank them for past favours, to excuse our long Silence, and to assign the Reasons that induced the late Vestry, to expel Mr Smith from this Cure.

3dly That an ansʳ be sent the Revᵈ Mr Alexʳ Garden, to his kind Letter to the late Vestry of March 4th last, and of thanks for his judicious Remarks and advices.

To which Motions the Vestry agreed, & ordered the said Letters to be prepared, and to be read, considered off, and signed on next Sunday, the Heads of which Letters being drawn.

Prince Frederick Parish   Sunday May 2ᵈ 1756

Divine Service ended, the Vestry Men & Church Wardens assembled to hear the Letters read, that they had order'd to be drawn, & laid before them, which they approved, and sign'd: The following is Copy of those wrote to the Rᵗ Revᵈ Thoˢ Ld. Bpp. of London.

Black River So Carolina
May 1st 1756

My Lord,

We the Vestry-Men & Chh Wardens of the Parish of Prince Frederic in Sᵒ Carolina, beg leave to address Your Lordship, as our Diocesan & spiritual Father in Christ, to acquaint Your Lordship, That this our Parish is now vacant, & destitute of a Minister, thro the Resignation and dismission of The Revᵈ Mr Michel Smith from this Cure. A Gentleman who has not been long resident with Us, but who in that short Space has rendered himself quite infamous, & obnoxious to ev'ry Individual almost of this Country thro' his flagrant Manners, and bad Conduct: for in 3 Years (the Time he was here) he has done more Injury to the cause of Virtue, Religion, and the Church, than his Successors can repair in many; We therefore put our Selves under

Your Lordship's paternal Care & Protection, desiring and hoping, that Your Lordship would be pleas'd to appoint some worthy good Clergyman to be our Pastor, whom We should be glad to see and receive as soon as possible. We hope that Your Lordship will not take it amiss in Us to observe, That this Parish is the largest, and most populous in this Province; Yet tho' numerous in Inhabitants We of the Church are widely scatter'd, and but few in number; The Parishoners being for the most part of the Communion of the Church of Scotland, and Settlers from thence and the North of Ireland; who have two Meetings, and large Congregations: so that this Parish above all other in this Province, merits Your Lordship's Care and thought; and requires a diligent, grave, & pious Minister to take Care of the Interests of the Church, which are hourly suffering, & will wholly sink if not timely and properly supported; for Mr Smith's bad & irreligious Manners, has caus'd Numbers to join themselves to other Congregations or to turn their Backs on the Church, and Divine Service; chusing rather to stay away, than sit under the hearing of a profligate Teacher. Our Back Country is fill'd with Numbers who ne'er heard the Word of God preach'd, or saw a Minister among them. Indeed Mr Smith did make a Tour into these remote Parts of the Parish, But He had better stay'd at home, for the Consequence has been, that thro' his indiscreet Carriage, (We sh^d rather say immoral Conduct) among them, instead of bringing them over, and joining of them to the Communion of our Church, he has unhappily driven them to send for Anabaptist Teachers from Philadelphia, who dip many, and form them into Congregations; so that the regaining of them, and making them Members of the Established Chh will (we judge) be attended with great Pains, if not an impossibility.

A Gentleman of Gravity, Virtue, & Prudence, will not fail of reaping a plentiful Harvest here both in Spirituals and Temporals—We have a neat Parish Church, genteel Parsonage, Glebe, Cattle, and other Emoluments, for accomodation of what judicious Minister Your Lordship may send over; whose Salary will be One Hundred Pounds Sterling & upwards paid half yearly by the Public Treasurer, besides Perquisites, wc^h may am^t to as much, or more or less, according to his Conduct; A Minister's Income here, depending much on his Carriage and Manners.

We shall only add, That the adjoining Parishes around Us, are
also destitute of Ministers, so that there is not a Clergyman
from Santee River to Cape Fear, to perform any Ecclesiastical
Office, or administer the Sacraments on any Emergency: so that
We hope Your Lordship will take the Premises into Y^r religious
Consideration, & grant our Request, who are with ye utmost
Duty and Respect

> May it please Y^r Lordship
> Your Lordship's most dutiful
> and obed^t Sons & hble Serv^{ts}
> John White
> Geo Atkinson

Ja^s Crockat   William Green
Ch^s Woodmason Anthony White
> Ja^s McPherson
> William Walker

The following is Copy of the Vestry's Letter to the Secretary
of the Society for propogation of the Gospel in Foreign Parts.

> Black-River S^o Carolina
> May 1st 1756

Revd Sir!

The Augmentation lately made by the present Assembly of
this Province, to the Salaries of our Parochial Clergy by increas-
ing their Stipends from 70£ to 100£ Stg & upwards, p^r Ann;
and thereby freeing the Society from a Burden they have long
born in maintaining Missionaries among Us, will, We doubt not
meet with the Societys Approbation On this Occasion Sir, We
take the Liberty to return the Society our humble thanks for
their Care of our Spiritual Concerns so many Years past; And
this both on behalf of our Selves, as well as all other Inhabitants
of this Parish Members of the Church of England, who wth grate-
ful Hearts will ever retain a Due Sense of the The Societys many
singular & repeated favours shown Us. The last Missionary
they sent Us over, was The Revd Michael Smith—for whom We
built a genteel House, and did ev'rything within our small Power
to render his situation agreeable, and Residence easy among Us.
He was rec'd here with great Alacrity—shown uncommon Marks
of Respect; and rec^d many singular Tokens of favour and Regard,

And as there are (nor have been for some Years) no resident Minister in two or three Parishes adjoining Us, He might have commanded a very plentiful income, nay, affluent Fortune, (beyond any Country Clergyman in this Province) had his Will been equal to his Power, and Virtue as shining as his Abilities, But unhappily for Him and for Us 'tis with great Concern We are obliged to say that this Gent^{ms} Manners have been so flagitious his Conduct so unhappy and imprudent, both in Spirituals and Temporals, as to subject Him to the Public Censure and Odium of this Whole Province, and thereby reducing Himself to the Necessity of resigning this Mission, and leaving this Province, and thereby forcing Us on the disagreeable Measure of dismissing of Him from this Cure, to which He never was, or could hope to be elected, from having shewn himself more fit to pull down and destroy, then to build up the Church of Christ.

Our long Silence may be interpreted remissness, or judg'd Ingratitude by the Society; but it has been owing to this Cause vizt. We were willing to pass over Mr Smith's Irregularities, and even (for a long while) winked at His Errors, and cover'd his failings, in hope, that Time, Experience, and Admonition might reclaim Him, and all His Miscarriages be obliterated and forgot—being inclined from Charity and regard to his function to impute his faults, rather to Levity, Indiscretion, and Human Infirmity, than to a bad, or a corrupt Heart: We delayed therefore laying Our Spiritual Concerns before the Society, till We saw the Effect of our friendly Counsels and forbearance, and what We could consistent wth Justice, Truth, & Our Duty, pronounce of this Gent^m —Sorry are We to say, that so far from reforming of His Conduct, and suiting it to the Dignity of His Profession, and the Maxims of Right Reason (We might add, of Common Sense) That He seemed to run counter to both, trampling on all Rules, and despising all Advice; He has oft left his flock without Notice, Necessity, or Our Consent; so that our Church has been frequently shut up, even for 3 Months together, without his taking of the least thought or Care, ab^t getting of it supply'd in his Absence, And in one of His late Rambles into the North Province, He bro^t home with Him a Woman, whom he lives with and calls his Wife; tho' in our strictest Examination of Him on this head, he could produce no Witness or Vouchers of ye Celebration of his Marriage with Her; so that We have cause to apprehend that if he is contracted, it must be agreeable to some assertions He has made in Public Company, vizt "That it was in his Power as a Priest, to marry himself to any Woman whatever, without the Intervention of a Third Person." Nor has He as yet realiz'd his Marriage, or given the Public any satisfaction in Relation to it, further, than by publishing the Bans of Marriage between Him, and this Woman one Sunday in the Church But as We are inform'd That Mr Smith has said, "That the Society shew so little Regard to what may be urged by the Laity ag^st any of their Missionaries, as to credit the Assertion of any single one of them, prior to the joint Testimony of any Body of People in America, We beg leave Sir further to declare, That we are Mr Smith's Friends, and Well-Wishers; and what We here say, arises not from Party Prejudice, or ill Will, but from a strict Regard to Truth, the Dictates of our Consciences, the Obligations of our Oaths and Office, and what is incumbent on Us as Men & Christians, and in Honour bound to the Society to declare, lest we suffer in our own Characters,— The Society in their annual Memorial, desire that they may be inform'd of whatever is remiss and scandalous in their Missionaries; And therefore We will make no Apology for these Declarations, or for what We apprehend to be just and right, further, than by for enclosing a few Papers to corroborate our Assertions, and to shew that the bad Character Mr Smith Sustains is founded on facts, and not wholly built on the Base of Common Fame, We are   Revd Sir

The Societys most obliged and
Your very hble Serv^ts
The late & present Vestry Men &
Chh Wardens of the Parish of
P. Fred^k S^o Carolina
Jno White
Geo Atkinson
Ja^s Crockat   William Green
Chas Woodmason   Anthony White
Ja^s M^cpherson
Willm Walker

The papers above alluded too, & sent with the above Lett^r were 1st An Affidavit of Margaret Simpson, & 2dly An Affidavit of Wm Williams, relative to Mr Smith's bad Carriage in his Travels into the interior Parts of the Parish, 3dly A Scandalous & Libertine Paper Mr Smith affix'd up at Blk River Church, in Justification of Fornication, from Scripture. 4^{thly} Memoirs of Mr Ab^{rm} Jordan, to shew that no Marriage Ceremony according to the Laws of the Land, ever passed between Mr Smith & Margaret Jordan with whom He now cohabits & calls his Wife.

The Vestry wrote also to the Rev^d Mr Alex^r Garden to this Effect

Revd Sir

The late Vestry recd Your kind & obliging Letter of March 4th, and after reading the Contents, could no longer hesitate to execute what had been so long wished for by all Good Men, vizt the dismission of Mr Smith from this Cure; but the latter part of Y^r judicious Letter being of a tender & serious Concern, required longer Deliberation, to which (& the busy Season) it has been owing, that the other Matters You pressed devolved on Us to execute; and we have accordingly wrote the Society, and his Lordship of London, the Reasons of our silencing of Mr Smith, which We hope they'l approve, one Copy of each We have left open for Your Perusal, hoping that You will be so kind as to second our Petitions with Your Interest, for procuration of another Minister, as soon as possible: We return our joint thanks both for Your late as well as former favours shewn this Parish, which we shall ever retain a just sense off; and with our best Wishes for Your health and long Life, remain with all Esteem and Respect

Revd Sir &c

Signed as before

The Vestry having rec^d a Letter from the Rev^d Mr Smith, signifying, That Mr Mac Carty, the Carpenter who built the Parsonage House, had arrested, and made him pay for the Sashes of the said House:

Resolved. That the Vestry meet as next Tuesday, to take under consideration the Contents of ye sd Letter.

Ordered That Mr Anth^o White wait on Mr McCarty, to enquire into the Validity of these Allegations,

Ordered That the Church Wardens wait on Mr Smith, to examine further into this strange affair.

Tuesday May 4th 1756

At a Vestry held in the Parish Church of Prince Frederic
Present

> Col John White
> Anth° White
> Wm Wilson
> Ja^s M^cpherson
> Wm Walker
> Ja^s Crockat
> Wm Green
> Chas Woodmason
> Geo. Atkinson

Mr Anth° White reported, that He had seen and spoken with Mr McCarty, who declared that Mr Smith had never paid Him for any Sashes, nor had he e'er received a farthing from Him on such acc^t The Ch^h Wardens reported That they had waited on Mr Smith, and on sifting of Him, ab^t Matters, had great Ground to conclude that there was some Collusion, or deception, for some iniquitous Scheme concerted between Mr Smith and Mr McCarty,
A Letter from the Rev^d Mr Smith was presented to the Vestry, relating in loose & general Terms, ye heads of accompts, between Him and Mr McCarty, wch giving no satisfaction, the Vestry waited on Mr Smith in a Body to enquire further Particulars,

   After a strict Scrutiny, they found the Chh Wardens surmises to be well founded, and that those accompts & rec^ts of Mr McCarty wch Mr Smith produced, and asserted he had paid, were false, and fallacious; formed only to counterbalance other like fictitious acc^ts bro^t by Mr Smith ag^st McCarty in consequence of a Quarrel between them. Mr Smith hav^g also bro^t a Bill of 19£ for Work done to the Stable &c. The same was deny'd Paym^t He hav^g had 30£ given Him by ye former Vestry (arising from Sale of the Materials of y^r Old Parsonage House) to discharge the said Bill.

The Vestry being informed That Mr Smith intended to send Mr Mac Cartys Bill & Rec^t home to the Society and thereby to impose on their kindness, directed Mr Charles Woodmason to add a Postscript to their former Letters, to this Effect, which was done accordingly,

Black River Ch^h May 4th 1756

Revd Sir! Postscript.

The Vestry having recd Letters from ye Rev^d Mr Smith affirming, "That he had been arrested by ye Carpenter who Built "ye Parsonage House, for the Sashes of the said House, and de-"siring reimbursement" they could not but be surpris'd at the Contents, as the s^d Carpenter had been paid One Thousand Pounds of this Curc^y for building of ye said House, Sashes, Closets, Beaufets, and all Conveniences included, They therefore sent to the said Carpenter, whose answer was, "That he had never "rec^d a penny from Mr Smith on any such acc^t"......They therefore waited in a Body on Mr Smith to examine into ye grounds of his Allegations; That he shewed a Bill and Rec^t of this Maccarty's, the Carpenter, for these Sashes; But on Scrutinizing into ye Validity of such Bill and Rec^t, They found it a contrived Affair of this McCartys to counterbalance a like fictitious acc^t bro^t by the s^d Mr Smith ag^st ye s^d MacCarty, neither of wch acc^ts had any foundation (as we could find) but only in Anger & Resentment; and to occasion quarrels and Contention. After expostulating with Mr Smith on his daring to endeavour to saddle ye Parish wth such an open & barefaced fraudulent Acc^t, his reply was, "That He made himself very easy ab^t the Matter, for if "We did not allow it Him, ye Society would, and that He should "send it home to them." To prevent therefore Sir, the Good-nature & Kindness of the Society's being imposed on in this Manner, (sh^d Mr Smith attempt) We here declare, that he never paid such Money, That ye s^d McCarty had been before paid for these Sashes, and why this McCarty arrested Him We find on inquiring to be owing to this "that Mr Smith being impatient "to get into the New House, broke it open, before finished, and also "broke open a Room in wch this McCarty had locked up these "Sashes." That after this act of Indiscretion, Mr Smith em-"ployed another Workman to put up these Sashes, and finish

"the House, unknown to this McCarty, & the Vestry. "That this
"McCarty, & Mr Smith falling out on this Head, they reciprocally
"arrested each other by Way of Insult, Mr Smith bringing a fal-
"lacious acc^t of Diet, lodging &c., agst McCarty, and ye other
"opposing this trumped up acc^t by another acc^t of like nature,
"in wch a Charge was made of these Sashes." But had Mr Smith
really paid the Man for these Sashes, We should immediately
have made Him repaid Mr Smith with Costs, and this We told
Him. But Mr Smith not offering to make this appear (indeed
it could not be) We judged it necessary to give the Society this
information, to be on their guard agst any indirect Steps Mr Smith
may take to impose on them.
After which they directed the Church Wardens to write to Mr
MacCarty, in these or like words,

Sir
   The Vestry having this Day recd Lett^r from Mr. Smith, with
an acc^t of Yours agst Him for the Sashes of the Parsonage House,
they waited in a Body on Mr Smith to enquire into ye Grounds
of such an extraordinary Charge: and on Examination find it
to be only the Issue of a Quarrel between You, and that You had
trumpted up a Charge of this Nature agst Him to oppose a like
fallacious acc^t bro^t by him agst You, in order to pay Him in his
own Coin. However ye Vestry could not but be amazed That You
could take so extraordinary a Step as this; and while they were at the
Parsonage House, took Notice, that there still remains sev^l Matters
unfinished, wch by your Contract You are bound to do; And therefore They have enjoined Us to address You hereon, to desire You
to repair to the Parsonage, and finish off whats remaining to
do there, within one Month from this date, otherwise they will
be forced to fall on Measures to oblige You, as will not be agreeable. The Vestry waits Your Speedy Answer for whom we are
                    Sir
                    Yr hble Serv^{ts}
                    Ja^s Crockat
                    Chas Woodmason

Ordered by the Vestry, That Mr Woodmason affix Mr Smiths
two Letters to the Postscript to ye Societys Letter & to acquaint

ye Society y^t ye Charge of £19,1,0 bro^t by Mr Smith ag^st the Parish, had been paid by the late Vestry, out of Monies arising from Sale of the Ruins of the old Parsonage House.

The Vestry then proceeded on other Public business and after rec^d the Parish acc^ts and auditing of them

Order'd

That   be p^d Ann Pike for One Years Board &c of Wort

That   D^o Wm Barton for Board of Mitchell

That   D^o Doct Crockat for Necessaries for Mitchell

That   D^o Antho. White for sickness and Burial of a Traveller

That   D^o Wm Wilson for D^o

That   D^o Wm Barton for Board of

That £10,0,0 D^o Nathl Mc Cormac for Board & Burial of a Traveller

To raise which Sum the Vestry assessed the Parish as under Viz^t

Negroes p^r Head	1/6
Lands per 100^d acres	1/6
Money at Interest per cent	1/
Stock in Trade per cent	6^d

The Vestry then drew an Order on the Public Treasurer for forty Pounds in His Hands, Parochial Money,

Out of which they ordered That £3,17,6 be p^d Wm Wilson for Repairs, fencing, &c at the Parsonage

At a Vestry duly Summoned to meet in the Parish Church of Black River on Monday the 2d Day of Aug^st 1756

Present

        Col John White
        Anth^o White
        Willm Green   Ja^s Crockat
        Ja^s M^cpherson Ch^s Woodmason
        William Walker
        Geo. Atkinson

The Vestry signed an Order to Wm Wilson & Wm Walker to pay the present Ch^h Wardens Forty Pounds Curr^y

Order'd the present Chh Wardens to pay Mr Geo Atkinson Five Pounds Curr^y for his Salary as Register to Easter Last.

Order'd That Mr George Atkinson the late Register deliver up to the Vestry at their next Meeting, all the Parish Books, Papers, Acct^s, and Registers in his hands, and complete the Parish acc^ts and render them fair & properly digested according to Law.

The Vestry then drew an Order on Mr Wm Wilson for £...... Curr^y Parochial Money, in his hands, ordering the Same to be rec^d by and paid to the present Wardens

Resolv'd, That Mr Josias Dupree be elected Parish Clerk of this Parish, and that the Chh W^dns do acquaint Him thereof and request Him to accept of the Same: And that if Objections sh^d be made by Him to the smallness of the Salary, The same to be augmented out of the Parochial Money

The Chh W^dns then acquainted the Vestry, That 32 Acadians were on their Passage for this Parish, here to be lodg'd, maintain'd, & accomodated, till otherwise provided for,

The Vestry came to a Conclusion, That the Chh Wardens lodge the said Acadians in the Parsonage House: But wav'd entering on the principal Subject Matter, vizt providing Victuals & Necessarys for their Reception.

The Church Wardens insisted warmly to have this Point fully settled & determin'd—But the Vestry treated the Affair so slightly as to tell the Chh Wardens, *They might do the best they pleas'd in the Matter*, and refus'd taking the least Charge or Care of the said Acadians; and proceeded in taking a View of the present ruinous State of the Parish Church; and then broke up, after naming Monday Three Weeks to meet again, to consult further about repairing of the Church.

The under is the Letter wrote Mr Josias Dupree pr. the Chh Wardens, agreeable to the Vestrys Directions.

Sir   Blk River Chh 2^d Aug^st 1756

At a Meeting of the Vestry this day, it was unanimously agreed to elect You Parish Clerk of Prince Frederic Parish, & We are order'd to acquaint You of the same, & to request the taking of the s^d Office on You, which will be highly obliging off & a great Benefit to the Parish. Should the present Salary be judg'd too small by You, for the attendance and Trouble You necessarily must be at, We are further impowered to enlarge the same out of the Parochial Money, to induce Your acceptance of the Place, & are

Sir

Yr most hble Serv^{ts}

Ja^s Crockat

Chas Woodmason

To Mr Josias Dupree

To which a Verbal answer was ret^d *"That it did not suit Him"*

An Acc^t how the Acadians sent to Prince Frederic Parish were distributed Tuesday 10th Augst 1756.

Joseph Durong	Andrew Burnet
his Wife	
Ann Lambert	dead 27th Oct 1756
their Children	
Mary Durong	Marg^t Wells
Josette Durong	Saml Gregg
Ann Durong	Willm Thompson
Marg^t Durong	Hannah White
Mary Ann Durong	Dead 13th Oct^r
Rosalie Durong	Andrew Burnet
John Daigle	Doctor James Crockat
his Wife	
Rosalie Richard	D°
their Child	
John Baptist Daigle	D°
Peter Lambert	Chas Woodmason
and of his Children	
Peter Lambert	D°
John Lambert	D°
Francois Leblanc	DD Nov 6th... ...Dead
his Wife	
Magdalen Cormie	DD 28th Oct......Died
their Children Viz^t	
Josetta Leblanc	Anna King
Ozick Leblanc	Henry Futhy
Magadalene Leblanc	Alex^r Swinton
Teaslie Leblanc	Henry Futhy
Margaret Leblanc	Richard Horsley

⎰ Paul Olivier......................John Rose..........Dead
⎨ & his wife
⎱ Magdalene Bourk................D⁰................Dead

⎰   Marg* Daigle Widow............Rev*d John Baxter
⎪   & her three children viz*
⎨ ⎰ Paul Forrait...................D⁰
⎪ ⎨ Larion Forrait................D⁰
⎱ ⎱ John Baptist Forrait...........D⁰

John Baptist Porrier   Col John White
Michell Porrierre   Doct Ja⁵ Crockat   Dead
Pierre Caisee   Rev*d John Baxter
Michell Lapierre   Col John White   Dead
Renaie Drowhany   Cha⁵ Woodmason

At a Vestry held at Black River Church, on Monday Aug*st 23*d
1756
Present

        Col John White
        Anth⁰ White
        Ja⁵ M⁰pherson
        W*m Green   Cha⁵ Woodmason
        W*m Wilson

The present decay'd Condition of the Parish Church was taken
into Consideration
Resolv'd, That the Parish Church is in a very decay'd State &
must of necessity be repair'd immediately, to prevent its falling.
That the Parochial Money in Hands of the present Wardens
together with what may arise from the present Years surplus
be apply'd tow*d the Repair.
That the late Incumbent Mr Mich*l Smith hav*g defrauded the
Parish of Sixty six Pounds Currency, Parochial Money in his
Hands that Ways and Means be fallen on for Recovery thereof.
Order'd, That Col John White, and Mr Anth⁰ White be a Committe for employing some Workman to take a Survey of the Build-
ing, & to lay their Report before the next Vestry.
That y*e s*d Committe draw up an Estimate of y*e Charges & Cost
requir'd to put y*e Chh in tolerable Repair, & what materials will

be wanting as Sills, Shingles, Nails, Glass, Boards, Lime, Paint, &c. And that they contract with some reputable Workmen and proceed in the Business, as far as the Parish Money will allow, & what Contributions they can collect.

That information hav^g been rec^d of some Movables of the Revd Mich^l Smith's being in the hands of Mr Wm Green, the Chh Wardens do attach the same, according to Law provided the Expence be under the Value of the said Goods. And then the Vestry separated without doing further. . . . .

. . . .
up, occasion'd by the Absence & Negligence of their late . . . ., and want of the Parish Books & Papers.
At a Vestry held in the Parish Chh of Black River, on. . . . .

The Rev^d Mr Wm Peasely appear'd, and offered to serve this Cure till arrival of a Minister from England,

But the said Gentlemen's Character being tainted; and Vestry of St Helena havg dismiss'd Him from that Parish for Irregularities, a Debate arose concerning the Admission of the said Gentleman, who produc'd the following Letter, of Recommendation from Capt Richardson one of the Representatives of this Parish in the General Assembly, [letter does not appear in Minutes] And then Mr Peasely laid before the Vestry. . . . . .by the Revd Richard Clarke, of Charlestown, to a gentleman of the Vestry of St Helena, in answer to one which Mr Clarke had rec^d from Him, subsequent to a Lett^r of Mr Clarke's to know the Imputations alledged agst Mr Peasely, and their Reasons for dismissing of Him, for Satisfaction of the Provincial Clergy of which the following is a Copy. [this letter also does not appear] And Col John White being going for Charlestown, was desir'd to wait on Mr Clarke, and to obtain from Him a Copy of the Letter he had rec^d from the Vestry of Port Royal, in ans^r to that wrote them by Him, in Name of the Clergy, But Col White did not produce any such Copy, only a short Note from Mr Clarke address'd to Himself wherein He says, That he apprehends that the Parish may admit Mr Peasely, on Probation provided he abides by his repeated Promises and Assurances of being a better Person for the future, or to this Purpose.

The Vestry not being conven'd hereon (Easter being near) Mr Peasely Officiated at the Church by desire of two or three of the Vestry Men, against the Consent and Opinion of the Church Wardens, and some Members of the Vestry.

March 1.   The Church Wardens apprentic'd out Shadrack Mac-Cormack a Poor Boy abt 7 Years of Age, to John Simpson Cooper, on Jeffrey's Creek, till the s^d Boy came of Age.

On Easter Monday April 11th, 1757, the Vestry met, and proceeded to Election of Church Officers for the present Year.

The Church Wardens proceeded by Ballot, to take ye Suffrages of the Parishioners:

Four Persons that gave in Votes, vizt John Walker, Eben Duncan, Ja^s Hepburn, and Alex^r Davidson, being objected too, as not conforming to the Chh of England, & qualified according to Law:

It was put to the Vote of the Assembly then present, if the said Persons are legally qualify'd to Vote,

And the Public Laws being produc'd and read:

A Debate arose among the Parishioners, thereon.

And the said Persons, tendering their Votes, & insisting on their Qualifications, as Freeholders, and hav^g serv'd Parochial Offices, the Church Wardens (to silence the Clamour) accepted of their Votes.

But a Scrutiny being demanded, and an appeal to Higher Powers threatened, the Church Wardens would not reckon in the Votes of the Persons Objected too, but marked them off.

And on casting up the legal Votes, they stood thus.

For Church Wardens		For Vestry Men	
James Crockat 18 take out 4	14	William Green	12
John White	2	William Hughes 18 take out 4	14
Anthony White	2	James Crocket	2
Josias Dupree	10	John White	10
John McDowell	9	Anthony White	10
Chas Woodmason	1	William Barton 12, deduct Hepburn & Jno Walker	10

For Church Wardens
JohnMcDonald 18 take out 4 14
———————————————————————

For Vestry Men
Jos Gar Dupree........... 11
John Conyers 15 deduct 2
  excepted against   13
William Walker........... 29
George Atkinson.......... 17
William Wilson 13 deduct 4 9
Cha⁸ Woodmason 17 take

Overseers
Claudius Pegee........... 29
Sam¹ Canty............... 29
Joseph Canty............. 3
Dan¹ Mcdonald........... 1

  out 4................... 13
Ja⁸ Lane.................. 22
Ja⁸ Mcpherson........... 19
Alex^r Rose............... 1
Vestry Men
Danl Mcginny............ 2
Ab^m Mashu Junr.......... 1
Robt Sutton.............. 1
Alex^r McRee............. 1

On which the Persons following were declared duly elected for the Year ensuing

Ch^h Wardens	Vestry	Overseers
Ja⁸ Crockat	William Hughes	Claudius Pegee
John M^cdonald	John Connor	Sam¹ Canty
	William Walker	
	George Atkinson	
	Cha⁸ Woodmason	
	James Lane	
	James Mcpherson	

Complaint being made to His Excellency the Governor by Col John White that an undue Election of Parish Officers for ye Year 1757 was made at the Parish Church of Pr Fred^k on Easter Monday: by the Church Wardens, The Church Wardens (to obviate all Objections that could be alledg'd against the Illegality of the former Election) Advertiz'd a new Election to be on Monday ye 25th April 1757

And the Parishioners being assembled, gave in their votes as follows

Church Wardens		Vestry Men	
James Crockat............	19	William Walker...........	28
John Macdonald..........	32	Jas Mcpherson...........	19
Josias Dupree	12	Charles Woodmason........	18
		James Lane..............	29
		John Connor.............	18
		William Hughes...........	18
		George Atkinson..........	19
		Anthony White...........	13
Overseers		John White..............	13
Thos Bossard.............	16	William Barton...........	12
Claud Pegee.............	19	Josias Garnier Dupree......	12
William James...........	12	William Green............	12
Saml Canty.............	14	Wm Wilson..............	3
		Arch Baird..............	1
		Danl Mcginny............	1

On which the following Persons were declar'd duly Elected and publickly Advertiz'd accordingly vizt (and sworn in by Arch Baird Esqr

Chh Wardens	Overseers	Vestry Men	Register
James Crockat	Claud Pegee	William Walker	Chas Woodmason
Jno Mcdonald	Saml Canty	James Mcpherson	
		Chas Woodmason	
		James Lane	
		John Connor	
		William Hughes	
		Geo. Atkinson	

At Vestry held in the Parish Church of Pr^ee Frederic on Wednesday the 18th May 1757
Present

Ja^s Crockat ⎫ Chh W^dns
Jno Mcdonald ⎭

Wm Hughes ⎫
Ja^s M^cpherson ⎪
Jno Connor ⎬ Vestry Men
Ja^s Lane ⎪
Chas Woodmason ⎭

The present State of the Parish Chh was taken under Consideration and on a Survey of Repairs lately made and necessary to
be executed It was Resolv'd

That the Work lately done to the repairs of the Church being
very imperfect, and insufficient; An Absolute Necessity arises,
that the said Work be examined by some skilful Workmen, and
be more substantially ececuted.

That a Committe be appointed to Contract wth proper Workmen, for the finishing of the Church, and putting of it into good
Repair, as far as the Parochial Money will go. And the Persons so Constituted, were,

Mr Ja^s Mcpherson and

Mr James Lane

Ordered, That They Shingle, Sash, Weather board, & put the
Church into ye best Repair possible, as far as the Parochial Money
now in Hands of the Ch^h wdn^s/will admit; and to the best of their
judgment. Which Money amounts to 100

And Mr Robt Weaver having been apply'd too by the late Church
Wardens, to Survey the Work done to the Church by order of
the Committe appointed in Vestry ye 23^d Augst last

The following Ans^r was rec^d from Him—

To the Vestry and Church Wardens of Prince Frederic Parish,
At the desire of James Crockat one of the Church Wardens, I
have carefully examin'd the Repairs of Your Parish Church,
and find them so insufficient, both with regard to the Workman-
ship, and part of the Timber, that I think it will be a manifest
Imposition on the Public if either the Workman is paid or the
Church, cover'd up in its present Situation for I am clearly of
Opinion should the Church be cover'd as it is now, it is in dan-
ger of suffering by Hurricanes, or any violent Gusts of Winds
from

Gent^m

Your hble Servt

April 3d 1757   Robt Weaver.

At the Vestry held in the Parish Church of P. Frederick, on Wednesday the 18th of May 1757

Michael Cary was bro^t before ye Vestry, as an infirm and poor Person, an Object of Charity, and incapable of Labour hav^g lost his Eye Sight

When ye s^d Michael Cary was put under the Care of Mr Henry Yaw, to be boarded, and maintained by Him at ye Rate of £60, pr. ann from this Day: to find Him in suff^t Meat, Drink, Washing, Lodging, Linen, and Cloaths

At the same time Willm Mitchell, a Parish Pauper, was taken by William M^cdonald, to be boarded by Him for one Year, from this Easter Monday at ye rate of £80, per ann—Cloathing excepted. May 18, 1757

Mr George Atkinson late Register, deliver'd up the Parish Books, wch on Examination, found to have no Entries made in it of Marriages, Burials, and Baptisms, for 3 Years past,

I Geo. Atkinson Register of the Parish of Prince Frederick for the y^r 1756 am Register'd as above for not Registering Children Baptized, Mariges, Deaths, &c Do Declare that there was no Minister to give s^d acc^{ts} to George Atkinson for 3 years was........

At a Vestry held in the Parish Church of P. Frederic on Wednesday the 18 May 1757

The Want of a Worthy Minister for this Parish being very great, and no Ans^{rs} being rec^d either from the Bishop of London, or the Society, to the Letters wrote them, for a Successor to the Rev^d Mr Smith

And it being reported, that the Revd Mr Andrews had declin'd the Lectureship of St Philip's, and intended to embark for England by some safe Opportunity:

And it being further hinted to some of the Vestry, that Mr Andrews's departure would not immediately take place:

It was Resolved to address Mr Andrews to supply this vacant Parish during his Stay in Carolina, or to accept of the Cure of the Parish in Case his Inclinations should induce Him wholly to settle in the Province.

And the Register being order'd to draw up a Letter, He immediately withdrew, and presented the following, which being read, was approved off, and signed by the Gentlemen then present.

Black River Church 18 May 1757

Revd Sir.

The Occasion of this address, arises from a Rumour which reach'd Us, Viz^t That You are about resigning of the Lectureship of St Philip's and retiring from Charlestown, till some safe and favourable Opportunity presents to carry Your family to England. We should be pleased to find this Report verify'd shou'd its Issue terminate in *Winyaws* being made Your Residence.

The amiableness of Your Character As a Minister and Christian strict Morals and Integrity of Manners in private Life as a Gentleman would alone excite in Us (and all here who Love Religion and Learning) such pleasing and agreeable Desires: But when We reflect on our late and present unhappy fate as to Spirituals, and the reduced State of the Church in this Quarter, these Wishes are *higher* rais'd, and prompt Us to *perfect* their Attainment.

Permit Us then Sir to realize our Sentiments of You, by giving You this Call and Invitation, That should You quit Charlestown, and Y^r Affairs incline You to a Country Retreat, That You'd be pleas'd to favour Us with Your Company and to accept of this vacant Parish of Prince Frederic where We are ready to receive and establish You as our minister, whenever You please.

For We have not a Clergyman within fifty miles to perform any Ecclesiastical Offices in any Emergency, and how long We may rest thus unprovided, is uncertain (We having not yet had any answer from home to our Letters wrote 15 Months ago for a Minister) but would rather chuse to remain thus destitute and unhappy, than accept of obnoxious Persons, who disgrace the sacred Character and bring Religion and the Church into Contempt. Wherefore after looking up to Heaven for Divine Aid, We turn our Eyes Sir on You, to heal the Wounds, the Stabs that Vertue and Goodness has sustained here within few Years. We want a Person of exemplary Life, prudent Conduct, and uncorrupt Morals, to apply the Balms of *Example* and *Precept* to pierc'd and broken Souls: to be an Ornament to Religion, Support to our bleeding weaken'd Church and a Blessing to Civil Society: In this Light Sir We regard You from the Enconiums and Eccho's of the Public, and the testimonies of private friends.

And should You Approve of this Invitation and oblige Us with Your Presence, and Ministry, We shall be careful to confirm the reality of these Conceptions, by striving to support You genteely, and to make Your Residence among us, as easy and agreeable as Possible.

Our late incumbent acknowledg'd his Income to be near 1500£ pr Ann but We cannot Warrant his Assertions, nor enter into any *Particular* Engagements As this Parish is very extended, so also may be the Rectors Emoluments They partly depending on remote Persons and Accidents: For the Parish Church and Parsonage (which are both neat and pretty) being situated on the lower Verge of this Parish, will occasion require more Time and Travel for Minister and People to be thoroughly acquainted, than if built more Central.

These our tenders of Respect, are accompanied with our best Wishes for Your Health, and that You may long live among us to adorn Religion, and build up Living Temples to the Glory of H I M, whose peculiar Servant You are, and whose Service is Your Honour and Delight We are with due Esteem

Revd Sir

Your most obed^t and most hble Serv^{ts}

The Church Wardens and Vestry of the

Parish of Prince Frederic

James Crockat   Wm Hughes
John Macdonald   Ja^s Mcpherson
                                 Jno Connor
                                 Ja^s Lane
                                 Chas Woodmason

To which the following Answer was rec^d,

Charlestown June 14 1757

Gentlemen.

Your Letter dated the 18 May, I rec^d this day, and am greatly obliged to You for Your kind Way of thinking concerning Me. The partiality of my friends hath given me a Character much beyond my deserts,

There might be some Reason for the Report you Mention but that Reason is now superseded, since the Ships so long expected are arrived; on board one of which I have taken my Passage, and shall certainly sail for England in about three Weeks time. If when I am there, I can be of any Service to You either by representing Your Case to the Society at home, or in any other Method that You may think off, You may lay Your Commands upon Me, and they shall be faithfully executed by

Gentlemen

To the Church Wardens   Your most obliged humble Servant
and Vestry of the Parish   John Andrews
of Prince Frederic

And the underwritten (enclosing a Duplicate of ye former Vestrys

Letter to the Bishop) was sent to Mr Andrews by the Register.

Black River 28 June 1757

Revd Sir

The Distance at wch sev^l Members of our Vestry reside from the Church and each other, rendering it impossible for them to convene in Time to answer Your obliging fav^r of the 14th inst, I take upon Me in Name of the Body to write You.

"That they take extremely Kind Your offers of Assistance to procure them a Minister; which Xtian Task they entreat you to engage in immediately on Your Arrival in England: Whatever Gentleman may come over with only 3 Lines from You, will be accepted here, as next to Choice of Y^r Self, they would approve of Your Choice"

"That they need not trouble You with a Portrait of a Minister that would suit here, as Your better Judgment and Experience will paint the requisite Qualities, and their Sentiments may be gather'd from their late Letter to You.

But if that You sh^d rather chuse to persue the Old Tracts (which as to this Parish have been very crooked) they enclose a Letter to his Lordship of London, which they beg Your Care off, (and sh^d it suit, and be not too much Trouble) to deliver with y^r own hands.

"And that You would be pleased to quicken his Lordships Motions in our favour, by remonstrating,

"That our Parish Church, Parsonage & Glebe is daily falling to Ruin by being unoccupied.

"That there are now 4 Meeting Houses in this Parish, and two more talked of being built, (wch Increase would not have been thro' Weakness, Supineness, & Immorality of our Incumbents) Whereas, had we Godly Ministers, Chapels of Ease would probably be raised in their places, and less Room for the Sectaries to spread themselves.

"That the People of the Lower Part of our Parish, are a sober, sensible & literate People, those of the upper Part, far otherwise; whose Numbers daily increase by Refugees from ye other Provinces

"That if a Minister be not settled here soon, the defection from the Church will be so great, as hardly to leave enough Church Members to form a Congregation.

"That Itinerant Teachers from the N° ard, are Yearly making of Converts that illiterate Persons set up for Pastors That the Presbyterian Missionaries from the Northern Colleges, use unwearied pains & Diligence to extend their Influence & Interest, to the hazard of this whole Parish being soon entirely in their Hands.

"That this Prospect grieves every true Son & Well-wisher to the Church of England, while our Establish'd Clergy calmly look on, But that our Assembly, Alarm'd at our Situation, has lately divided this extensive Parish, taking a New one out of it, to be called by the Name of St Mark alloting also 100£ stg, pr ann for an Itinerant Minister to officiate at the Waterees, & ye Catawba Settlem^t So that we want 3 Ministers Sir at present, in this one Parish only.

I conclude in their Names, to wish You a quick safe and pleasant Passage that You may find & enjoy the establish'd Health You seek after, and be blessed with all temporal and Eternal Happiness. I am for the Vestry and Church Wardens of the Parish of Prince Frederic

Revd Sir

Y^r most obd^t hble Servt

Chas Woodmason Register

At a Meeting of the Inhabitants of the Parish of Prince Frederic at the parish Church on Easter Monday, 1758
There appeared Peter Lane, wth an acc^t for subsistance and Burial

of John Reed when Thirty pounds was allowed Him for the same. Also appear'd Thomas Cribb, & exibited an acc⟨t⟩ for Burial of a Traveller, who dy'd at his House when Ten pounds was allow'd Him. Ten Pounds was also allow'd Ann Pike for Burial of Henry Wort. Also appear'd Rich⟨d⟩ Cockburn w⟨th⟩ an acc⟨t⟩ for Burial of Edw⟨d⟩ Filley, a Soldier, when Ten Pounds was allowed Him.

The following Persons were chosen Vestry Men, Viz⟨t⟩

Col Jn° White
Josias Garnier Dupree
Capt Anth. White
William Barton
Jn° MacDowell
Dan¹ DuPree
Isaac Carr

And $\begin{cases} \text{John Godfrey} \\ \text{Josias Dupree} \end{cases}$ Chh Wardens

$\begin{cases} \text{John Connor} \\ \text{Hugh Thompson} \end{cases}$ Overseers

Peter Lane Register

The Church Wardens presented their acc⟨ts⟩ which were as follows

To Cash pd Mich¹ Gordon for Himself & a Negro for sawing of Boards, getting of Sills & Stuff for repair of the Chh by Order of the Vestry	45,0,0	By Cash recd of the Chh Wardens of y⟨e⟩ preceding Year	60,0,0
To Math¹ Clark, for Do	15,0,0	By Parochial Money of Mr Motte	40,0,0
			100,0,0
To Cash pd Ja⟨s⟩ Lane for Carting of Timber & Securing of the Parsonage House from Fire	14,0,0		
Ballance in hand	26.		
	£100.0.0		

Drew Orders on the New Vestry for the Monies due to Peter Lane
Thos Cribb & R'chd Cockburn & Ann Pike

Drew Order on the Old Chh W^{dns} for the Ballance in their Hands

Drew Order on Mr Motte for last Years Parochial Money

Drew an Order of £20 on D^o in fav^r of he Revd Samuel Fayerweather for two Sermons preach'd by Him in the Parish Church

And then the Regist r deliv'd all the Books & Papers off the
Par sh n His Hands, to the New Vestry & Chh Wardens.

On summing up the Monies due from the Parish of Prince Frederic
for subsisting & Burial of Poor Pe sons, it stands thus

To Henry Yaw for subsisting Mich^l Cary......... 51, 13, 4
To Wm Macdonald for subsisting & Burial of W^m
    Mitchell.................................. 38, 10, ..
To Ann Pike for subsisting & Burial of Jno Wort. 25, .0...
To Richd Cockburn Thos Cribb & Peter Lane........ 50......
                                        £165, 3, 4

At a Meeting of the Vestry Munday the 1st day of May 1758

Present
            Col John White
            Capt Anth^n White
            Mr Isaac Carr   } Vestry
            Mr John McDole
            Mr Jo^s Ga^r Doepree
            Mr Dan^ll Doepree

Pres^t
            Mr John Godfrey   } Chh Wardens
            Mr Josias Doepree

The Same Day agree'd with Isaac Bates for the makeing And the
Del:vering of Twelve Thousand Good March^tble Hart Cypress
Shingles at Five pounds Curr^y pr Thousand, at the Parrish Church
of Prince Frederick to be Delivered Above High Water Mark to
Peter Lane at the Said Ferry Landing &c

The Same Day Above Written Assess'd the Parrish

        Slaves pr head........................ 1/6
        Lands pr 100.......................... 1/6
        Mony at In^ts pr L^b..................... 9^d
        Stock n Trade........................ 9^d

At a Meeting of the Vestry & Church Wardens at the at the Church of Prince Frederick Parish on Tuesday the 12ᵗʰ September 1758

Present

> Colᶦ John White
> Mr Josiah Grnʳ Doepree
> Mr Franˢ Lessne
> Mr John McDole
> Mr Isaac Carr
> Mr Danᶦᶦ Doepree

Vestry

Mr John Godfrey   Church Warden

Its agreed that Colᵒ John White and Capᵗ Anthony White is to take upon them to Repair the Church And Make itt all Sufficient Good and Substantiall, By the Judgments By the Vestery, to be Vewe'd the first Tuesday in February 1758—the Vestery is then Agreed to Meet again to Settle the Same and Order Payment.

An Ordʳ given in Favour of Colᵒ John White on Jacob Motte Esqʳ Publick Treasurer for the Money allowed By Act of Assembly For the Repair of the Parsonage House, &c.

N B, The Above Ordʳ in Favour of John White By the Vestry and Church Wardns of the Parish of Prince Frederick Return'd not Accept'd &c.

Revernᵈ Sir

Wee the Vestry Men And Church Wardns of Prince Frederick Parrish beg Leave to Acquaint You, that on Our Application to yᵉ Revᵈ Mʳ Andrews to Send us a Ministʳ the Revᵈ Mʳ Cooper Came out for Our Parrish, & that Influencᵈ as Wee Suppose by Sum who Represented Us to Him in a disagreeable Light, He acceptᵈ of Prince William Parish which Wee Imagin'd Might possibly be yᵉ Case should Wee send for A Nother, Wee therefore in Consideration of yᵉ Melancholy Condition of our Parish For want of a Ministʳ to Officiate to Us in Holy things and hearing that Mʳ Peasly, who has Lived on Peede for Twelve Months last past, has behaved there to yᵉ Satisfaction of yᵉ Peop!e Who in a Verry Precarious Situation, as that Parish not as yet Settled, have Invited Him to Supply yᵉ vacant Cure of our Parish which he has Accepted of and is Expected, with His Famaly in A Short time to Reside among Use

Now Sir as Wee are Apprehensive that two Persons only Who Wee
have had Reason to think Doe not Seek yᵉ pease of yᵉ Parish may
endeavor at Easter next to Set aside this our Caull of Mʳ Peasely,
and throw Us into the Same Confution & Distraction they Did
Sum time Since.   Wee beg Leave to ask You Wheather a Succeed-
ing Vestry Can Repeal any Lawfull Act of Yᵉ preceeding and if
they Can what Steps may be Propʳ for Us to take, to prevent their
Makeing Void this Our Act, in Mr Peasely Favouʳ Who Wee hope
by His Good Behaviour, May Remove ye Preajudices that Sum
Persons, have against him and Reconcile yᵉ Contending Parties
of our Miserably Divided Parish.   Some of Us seem to think that
an Application to His Excellency as Ordinary of ye Province, and
to the Church Commissnʳˢ may be necessary But Wee Shall Defer
taking this or any other Step' till Wee Are Favoured with Yʳ
Advice which Will be Earnestly Expected, By Revernᵈ Sir

30 Decʳ 1758. Yʳ Most Obedint and, Humᵇˡᵉ Servᵗˢ

      John White ⎤
      Anthᵒ White ⎬ Vestry Men
      Danˡˡ Doepre ⎦
      Josiah Doepree   Ch Warden

At a Meeting of the Vestry and Church Wardens of Prince Fredrick Parrish, on Easter Munday the 16 of April 1759
The Church Wardens presented their accounts, which is as follows

By account Rendered by Col John & Anthᵒⁿʸ White..............£186, 17, 6	By Cash Received of the Church Wardens of the pre-seeding Year	£26
By Cash paid....... 56.....	By Parrochoall Money	40
Ballance Due.......£130, 17, 6		£66
to Coll John & Anthᵒⁿʸ White.........................£66		

Vestry ⎰ Colᵒ John White
        Capᵗ Anthᵒ White
        Isaac Carr
        John McDole
        Francˢ Lessesne

By Cash pᵈ Peter Lane
for Register & Sexton 10
John Godfrey ⎱ Church
Josiah Doepree ⎰ Wardens

Drew Orders on the New Vestry for the Moneys Due to
Peter Lane for Mical Carey........................... £ 75
To Joseph Wood for a Child   paid A. W................ 5
Mary Brown for Daneil Smith   paid A W............ 30
To Edward plowden for Mrs Nolings & Children pd J. C.... 50
To Jn° Godfrey for John Smith two Months paid A W.... 6

     ─────
     £166
     ─────

The Same day Gave an Order to Capt Anth° White and Mr John
Connor, on Jacob Mott Esqr Publick Treshu^r for the Parochal
Charge Forty Pounds
The above We Rec^d and Payd the same to Coll Jn° White out of
£130, 17, 6 as above due to Jn° & Antho White.

         Jn° Connor   } C W
         Anthony White   }

Elected in this day 16 April 1759 Easter Munday Vestry Men
and Church Wardens for ye Ensuing Year

         Col° John White
         Mr Josiah Doepree
         John McDole
         Franc^s Lessesne   } Vestry Men
         Jno Godfrey
         Isaac Carr
         William Wilson

         Antho^n White   } Church Wardens
         John Connor

         Abraham Micheau Jn^r } Overseers
         Hugh Thompson
         Peter Lane   Register

At a Meeting of the Vestry 17th April 1759 Assessed the Parish
for the poor Tax

         Lands at............................... 1/6
         Slaves................................. 1/6
         Moneys at Interest..................... 9^d
         Stock in Trade........................ 9^d

To Jacob Mott Esq Publik Treash^r
    Prince Frederik Parrish 6 May 1759
S^r

    Be pleased to pay to ye Revrn^d Mr Sam^{ll} Fenner Warren ye sum of Twenty pounds Curn^y for Officiating in the Parrish Church of Prince Frederick, on Sunday ye 25 Day of March Last, the Sixth of this Ins^t

    We are Sr Y^r Hum^{bl} Serv^{ts}

Anthony White	Ch Wardⁿ	John White	
		John McDole	Vestry Men
		Isaac Carr	
		Wm Wilson	

SOUTH CAROLINA

    Parish of Prince Frederick &c &c.

    May it please Your Lordship
    For the Spring of 1757 Wee Laid before y^r Lord Ship the State of Religion & of the Church of England inn this Quarter, Together With our Want of a Minister. And Y^r Lord Ship from y^r paternal Care of this Distant Unknown Part of y^r Diocess, was pleased to Note our Representation's and Releive our Spiritual Necessities by Recommending this Cure to the Revern^d Mr Cooper: whome My Lord Wee have not the Happiness to Enjoy For on his Arival in this Province, Finding that the State of things in this Parish were now Greatly Different From What We Reported to y^r Lord-Ship. He therefore declin'd this Parish, And Accepted that of Prince William, Vacant by the Death of Mr Lewis, We Must own My Lord, that the temporal State of this Parish is now on a deffor'nt foot. And Greatly Reduced within these Three Years, and on these acc^{ts} 1st Our Assembly Wisely Considring the Great Extent of the Parish and the heavy w^{gt} on the Shoulders of the Incumbent; have Erected the Upper Part into a Seperate Parish, Now known by the Name of St Mark, who as yet are Unprovided with a Minist^r.
2d^{ly} to Lessen the Duety of the Ministers of this and of Prince George Parish, the Assembly have appointed two Itiner'nt Ministr^s to Visit the Back Country. 3dly The Adjacent Parishe's of Prince

George & St James'^{s}, have Since that thime Been Filled, Whereby
the large Harvess of Fees be Report^d by our Late Incumbent, Mr
Smith is Curtailed So that at Present the Utmost Any Gen^t Can
hope to Raise here will not Amo^t to More than one hundred &
Eighty pounds pr annum.   Our Chh & Parson'^{g} is in Good Order,
But the Parochial Cattle & Other Effects are Dispersed, and Lost
through Want of a Resident Minister to Look to them.   From
this Contraction of our Parish, which is Reduced to name Limits
and from the Removal & Death's of Many of our Church Mem-
ber's, Our Congregation Now Consists but of Very Few & Those
Widely Scatter'd or Distant from the Church, 9 prctm of our
Inhabitants being of of the Chh of Scotland.   Yet, hope Wee That if
a Worthy Good Man Such another as Mr Cooper, who had the
Good of Souls and the Chh at heart, Was Settld Among Us that
our Congregation Would Annually Increase, and the Church of
England recover from ye Languishing State it is Now Fallen into
among Us.   The Want of Such a Sensable Exemplary Paster here
is possible by ye Decay of Relig'on and Morals, and the Daily
Poversion of Numbers of the Ignorant Commonalety from the
Church by the Subtle Deceptions of Many itinerant Anabpt^s
and other Teachers Sent in annually Progresses this way from
Pennsylwaina, the Den of the American Hydra of Schism, and
Enthusiasm Wee......Supply our Selves with an Ejected Offici-
ating Minist^r whose Caract^r has unhappily Sufferd throe the
Noxious Blast of Calumny, but are fearful of giveing Offence to
ye r gid Presbyterians Around Us As they might make this a
Plea for Continuance of a Seperation & to open wide ye Rents of
Religion the Shed'y of Every Good Man, to Close therefore we
Chuse, to wave, our Private Concernes for the Greate Good of the
Church, & to Remain Sum time Longer Destitute of Spiritual
Food, till Y^r Lord Ship be pleased be pleased to Appoint Som
Pious Clergy Man to the perticular Charge of this parrish and to
Limit him to this Cure only, that We be not Rejcted a Second
Time for aA Richer parrish.

   Who Ever May be Appointed our paster may be Certain of an
Easey Quiete and be pleased, an happy and Pleasent Situation, A
Sedate & Contemplative Mind will meet with nothing to impair

or Riffle his Studies if devoted to the promoting of Knowlidge, and the Salvation of . . . .

We are

(In Name of & by Ord^r of the Vestry)

May it please Y^r LordShips

Y^r L^dShip's Most Dutiful ande

Most Obed^t Sons & Servants

To Jacob Mott Esqr Publik Treashu^r

S^r/   Prince Fredrck Parrish 16 July 1759.
   Be Pleased to pay to the Revern^d Mr Samuel Fayrweather The Sum of Forty Pounds Curn^y for Officiating in the Parrish Church of Prince Fredrick Four Sundays.

£40 . .   Wee are Sr Y^r Hum^{ble} Serv^{ts}

John Connor's ⎱ Chh   John White ⎱
Anth^o White ⎰ Wards   John McDole ⎱ Vestry Mne
                           Wm Wilson ⎰

Prince Fredrick parish 27 May 1759—

Rev^d S^r
   Having Wait^d a Long Time in hopes to Find You as good as Y^r Word, and that you would have sent for y^r Child—According to y^r promise and the time being Elapsd Wee, the Church Wardens of his Parrish take this Oppertunity of Conveying the Child to you by the Barer Thomas Cribb Nothing Doubting but Yl^d be kind Enought to Pay the Charges, For as Wee hear y^o are in good cercumstances, You Know Wee Can't answer, to the Parrish, for the Maintenance for Your's, But, ho'ever for what is past, we put up With, but this Charge We hope yl^d not Refuse to pay Mr Cribb, Which is twenty pounds, Curr^y, Also wee hope You'dd Consid^r that Y^o are in Arrears to this Parrish, For Cattle you Sold Which Cattle were the property of the Parrish, which Money wee beg Youl Remitt by Some Safe hand as soon as possible this beeing q^t Needfull. From Y^r Hum^{ble} Serv^{ts}

Anth^o White

John Connor

Chh Wardens

North Carolina June ye 10th 1759.

Gent^n

Your Letter by Mr Cribb with the Child I Recived & was Much Surprised that you did not acknowlege the Receipt of a Letter I Sent you Some time ago. I therein Request^d that you would inform me what Expence the Parrish was at for the Children Because Ime inform^d they were both thrown upon the Parrish and Mr Green and Mr Wilson Both make a Demand upon me of Sixty pounds for the Borde of y^r Children. Ime obliged to y^r offer of not chargeing for what they have had but shall take it a particular Favour if you will Send me a Line informing me how Long they had been upon the Parrish & what Charge you had been at, and if Can Contrive to make a Remittanee I will; Coin is not to be got here, and our Curn^y will be of no value, therefore if a Good horse, will Serve to make Remtn^e I will send one in Value Equal to ye Charge you have been att, I know Mr Anth^o White used to Delight in a good horse, and as Ime Frequently Riding in the Country I Can Provide him one of any value from £50 this Money Down to £15 which I will Engage Shall com as Cheep to him as if he had Bought him in Your Said Province, I have paid Mr Cribb for Bringing the first Boy But was not provided with Cash to pay for the Last. And he Could not Stay till I Could be Supply'd but you May Depend Upon it I will pay him, Wishing you & the whole Parrish thro. you happiness I am

Gent^m

Yr Most Obedn^t Servt

Mich^l Smith

To
Messrs Anth^o White &
John Connor; Chh. Wardns
of Prince Fredrick Parrish
    S^o Carolina—

Gent^n Church Wardens &c

The Barer Michael Carry Who has had Y^r Indulgence to Reside in GeorgeTown for twelve days under My Care, I have Don for him what appear'd to Promise his Speady Relief, but as he was Limited to a time and that is Now Expired, he Now Returns

on y^r Bounty again, as the Space has been Soe Short Since the
Operation I cannot yet Give Judgement of the Ishue, but still beg
y^r furthur Indulgence If he has not profited by this Operation, my
only View, is the poor Man's Relief, and Soe far as in me Lys, to
Effect a Cure, I will act it with Chearfulness, and without Expec-
tation of Reward, May you Prosper in all Such Laudable Inten-
tions, this poore Man's Case Comes under that Charateristick
I am Gent^n

Geo:Town 8 June 1759   Y^r Most Hum^{ble} Servant
Robert Gibb
Regestred 17 July 1759.

S^r/ Mar^h 2. 1760—
   Please to pay the Revd Mr Saml Fareweather the Sum of Thirty
pounds for offitiating three Times in the parrish Church of prince
Frederick, & Oblige y^r Hum S^{ts}

To Jacob Mott Esqr Publick Treasurer	William Wilson John White John Godfrey, John McDowell	} Vestry
	Anthony White	Warden

Easter Monday Ap^l the 7th 1760—
Anthoney Martin White an acc^t for Taking Care of
Jno Rose 15 Days................................... 3, 10
An Connor an acc^t for Taking Care of an Infant 46
Days... 8, 16, 4
Joseph Wood an acc^t for Taking Care of an If^t Child . 56, 3, 8
An acc^t of Mary Brown for Sundrys for Danl Smith a
Child 9, 9
Cash p^d for Caring the s^d Child to Cape fare payd by
Antho White, & Jno Connor C. W................. 20, 0, 0
To 1 years of Michal Cary to Mr Bartholomew Spencer
Paid by Capt White, & Jno Connor................ 70, 0, 0
To 1 Years Board of Elizabeth Rawlings to Edward
Plowden.. 50, 0, 0

———————
£217, 19, 0

Ap¹ the 7ᵗʰ 1760   These orders were given to the above persons for their several sums only £20 which was pᵈ to Anthony White out of Surpluss money the sᵈ 20 being for Carying a Child to Cape fare, to the Revᵈ Michael Smith his Father

Recᵈ by Jnₒ Connor and Anthoney White from the 16ᵗʰ of Ap¹ 1759 to the 7ᵗʰ of Ap¹ 1760

Cash.. 175, 14, 9
Cash for Fines...................................... 12, 0, 0
Cash for the Communion........................... 4, 5,
                                                   £191, 19,9

This Day the following Persons were Chosen for Parish officers for the year 17607 &c

Vestry Men {
Jnº White
Antho Martin White   C W {
Danˡ McGinney
Isaac Carr
Jaˢ Lane
Joseph White Junʳ
William Walker   Declined Serving
Wᵐ Green
}

C W {
Jnº McDowel
Moses Miller
}

Joseph Wood
Hugh Thompson } Overseers

This day gave an order to Jnº McDowel & Moses Miller on Jacob Mott Esqʳ for 40 pound parochal Money

Antho White
Jnº Connor } C. W.

Jno White
Wᵐ Wilson
Isaac Carr } Vestry

The Above Order I endorsed to Anthº White

Register Wᵐ Finletter   Jnº McDowel

for the use of the Repairs of the Church done by the said Anthy White

At a Meeting of Vestry of the Inhabitants of the Parish of Prince Frederick on Monday June the 2ᵈ 1760

Present {
Coll. John White
Jos: White
Danˡ McGinney } Vestry
Anthy M. White
John McDowell } Wardene
}

Gave an Order to the Revd. Sam[l] Fairweather for the Sum of Twenty Pound Currency for Officiating Twice.

(Copy of the Order)   Prince Frederick Parish June y[r] 2[d] 1760

S[r]/   Be Pleased to pay to the Rever[d] Samuel Fairweather, the Sum Twenty Pounds Curr[y] for Officiating Twice in the Parish Ch[h] of Prince Frederick

We are Sir Y[r] Humb[le] Serva[ts]

	John White	⎫
	Joseph White Jn[r]	⎬ Vestry
	Anth[y] M. White	⎪
John M[c]Dowell Warden	Dan[e] M[c]Ginney	⎭

Coppy of the Certifycate Given to the Rev[d] Sam[l] Fayerweather

South Carolina

These are to Certify that the Rev[d] Samuel Fayerweather has Officiated in Our Parish of Prince Frederick Winyaw for the Space of three Years Last Pass'd at Sundry times, and in all that time he behaved in every respect Becoming a Gentleman of his Sacred Function.

Blk mingo Jun: y[r] 14, 1760   As Witness Our hands

John White	⎫
Joseph White Junr	⎪
Anth[o] M. White	⎬ Vestry
Dan[l] McGinney	⎪
Jam[s] Lane	⎭

Warden John M[c]Dowell

Enterd June 26th 1760

At a Meeting of the Vestry of The Inhabitents of the Parish of Prince Frederick Tuesday July 8th 1760.

In Order to Assess the Parish,

Presant

Vestry	⎧ Collo[l] John White		
	⎪ Jos. White Jun[r]		
	⎨ Dan[l] M[c]Ginney	Warden	John M[c]Dowell
	⎪ Jam[s] Lane		
	⎩ Will[m] Green		

Who Assess^d the Parish at the following Rates—

Viz^t	Lands at pr hundred acres..............	1/6
	Slaves pr head........................	1/6
	Mony at Interest aprct................	/9
	Stock in Trade D^o	/9

Item   The Same Day Willm Green was Chose in the room of Wm Walker who Declined Serving as a Vestry Man

1760 September 30.   The Vestry mett in Order to Consult on affairs relating to the Parish, and sending a Letter to the Bishop of London, and another to the Reverend Mr Clark.   When the following Officers were Presant Viz^t

Vestry
$\begin{cases} \text{W}^\text{m}\text{ Green} \\ \text{Jos}^\text{h}\text{ White Jun}^\text{r} \\ \text{Jam}^\text{s}\text{ Lane} \qquad \text{John M}^\text{c}\text{Dowell} \\ \text{Anth}^\text{y}\text{ M White} \quad \text{Chh Warden} \\ \text{Isaac Carr} \end{cases}$

The Vestry had a Rough Draught of the Above Letters drawn up by the Register, and Orderd that Coppies of the Same should be drawn by the Saturday following when they Appointed to meet in Order to sign the said Letters in Request of a Minister.

1760 Octo^r 4th   The Vestry Mett According to Appointment, in order to Peruse & Sign a Letter to the Bishop of London, and another to the Revd Richd Clark when the following Vestry were Presant Viz^t

Vestry
$\begin{cases} \text{Jos. White Jn}^\text{r} \\ \text{Anth}^\text{y}\text{ M. White} \\ \text{James Lane} \\ \text{Isaac Carr} \\ \text{Daniel M}^\text{c}\text{Ginney} \\ \text{W}^\text{m}\text{ Green} \end{cases}$

Wardens $\begin{cases} \text{Jn}^\text{o}\text{ M}^\text{c}\text{Dowell} \\ \text{Moses Miller} \end{cases}$

The following is a Copy of the said letters

[Note—Apparently a page or pages of Record Book here missing] As we shall waite with the Utmost impat onts till You shall be

Pleased to send us an Answer, We all join in our best wishes for
Your health. . .   Long Life,
and shall Remain   Revd Sr Your Most Obligd
with all Esteem & Respect   and most humble
                                Servants Anth^y M. White

Vestry $\left\{\begin{array}{l}\text{Jos. White Jun}^r \\ \text{Jam}^s \text{ Lane} \\ \text{Isaac Carr} \\ \text{Dan}^l \text{ M}^c\text{Ginney} \\ \text{W}^m \text{ Green}\end{array}\right.$

Ch. Wardens $\left\{\begin{array}{l}\text{Jn}^o \text{ M}^c\text{Dowell} \\ \text{Moses Miller}\end{array}\right.$

N B This is the Third Letter sent Home

Easter Monday March 23^d 1761
   When the following Members were Present
Viz^t $\left.\begin{array}{l}\text{James Lane} \\ \text{Dan}^l \text{ M}^c\text{Ginney} \\ \text{Isaac Carr} \\ \text{Anty}^y. \text{ Mart White} \\ \text{Jos. White Jun}^r \\ \text{W}^m \text{ Green}\end{array}\right\}$ Vestry

       John McDow'l   C. Warden

Mr Joseph Woods Presented his acc^t as follows—
To boarding John Brian 7 Months, at £70 pr an^m...   40, 16, 8
To Boarding an Orphan Child 5 Months at 50£ pr.an^m £20, 16, 8
To Burring & Charge for Orphan Child &c.........   5.....
The Same Day Mr John McDowell Renderd his acc^e for
Boarding Mich^l Cary 12 Month & Clothing £70, 0, 0 ....
Item the Same Day Gave Orders for the Charges of the Year 1760
Viz^t, To Jno McDowe'l an Order on the New Vestry for £70,
Paid by Francis Lesesne.........................   70, 0, 0
To an Order To Joseph Woods for Sixty Six Pounds
13/8, Francis Lesesne paid......................   66, 13, 8
The same put up an Adver^t for the Money Assess'd, being
One hundred fifty Six pound 13/4
The Same Day drew a Parochial Order on Jacob Mott Esqr

Publ^k Treasurer, payable to Daniel McGinney & Francis Lesses   y & endor:ed to Capt Antho^y White to discharge part of a Debt for the Repair of the Parish Church, & Registers Sallary.

Vestry

- Wm Green
- Jos: White Ju^r
- Isaac Carr   Jno McDowell   Ch. War^d
- Anth^y M White
- James Lane

The Same Day proceeded to Election when the following were Chose as Church Officers, Viz^t

Jno Godfrey
Wm Barton
Wm Green
Isaac Carr   } Vestry
Jam^s Lane
Jos. White Jn^r
Anth^y. White

Danl McGinney } Ch.
Francis Lessney } Wardens

Francis Goddard }
Jos^h Woods   } Overseers
Wm Findlater   Register

At a Meeting of the Vestry & Wardens of the Parish of Pr nce Frederick—Wedn:sday May y^r 27th 1761.

Present

Willm Green
Isaac Carr   } Vestry
James Lane

Danl McGinney } Wardens
Francis Lessesne

Who Orderd that a Letter should be Wrote to the Reverend Mr Keith to Give the Parish a Sermon which was Accordingly do :e, Item the same Day Proceeded to assess the Parish at the Following Rates Viz^t

Slaves pr head........................ 1/8
Land pr hd........................... 1/8
Money at Intst pr ct................... /7$\frac{1}{2}$
Stock in Trade....................... /7$\frac{1}{2}$

In Order to Raise the Sum of £158, 13, 8, for the Relief of the poor of Said Parish, &c

At a Meeting of the Vestry & Wardens &c, June 10th 1761

Present   Wm Green
               Jn° Godfrey
               Anth^y White
               Jam^s Lane   } Vestry
               Isaac Carr
               Jos. White Junr

               Danl McGinney   Chu. Warden

Item   The Same Day Appointed James Minness as Sexton,

Item   The Same Day Perused the Reverend James Dormers Credentials Who arived & preach'd a Sermon the 7th Insta^t N B the said Credentials where Sign'd by the Lord Bish. of Chichester & Rochester, & were Dated July 15th 1759 & Septr 25, 1757 & produced no further Letters of Recommendation but the Letter sent to his Lord Ship of London, Dated Octr 4 1760, Sent from the Vestry for 1760.

Item   Same Day, Advertiz'd the Several Rates the Parish was Assess'd at.

At a Meeting of the Vestry June 18th 1761

               Capt Anth^y White
               Jam^s Lane
Presant   Isaac Carr   } Vestry
               Jn° Godfrey
               Wm Green

               Danl McGinney   Warden

Drew an Order on the Public Treasurer for £75, to Repair the Glebe which was delivered to Mr Jn° Godfrey. N. B. The above Order was Lost by the Person Deliv'd to. Also appointed Mr Minness to Clean out the Church, &c for which the Vestry was to pay him £5.

Item The Same Day it was proposed to the Revd Mr Dormer weither he Chused to enter upon the Glebe Immediately, or be Boarded who agreed to the Latter for Six Months.
September the 2^d, 1761
The Vestry Mett in Order to Adjust some small differences between

the Revd Mr Dormer & the Vestry Relating to some Reports—
when the following were Present

Viz^t Capt Anth^y White ⎫
           Jos^h White Junr ⎪
           Wm Barton   ⎬ Vestry
           James Lane   ⎪
           Wm Green   ⎪
           Isaac Carr   ⎭

        Daniel McGinney   Warden

When the Revd Mr Dormer had spoken to the Vestry relating the
Occurrences in hand which were answered in the following manner
that what was represented to his disadvantage his was very sorry
for, that some might be True and Some false. What was true he
hoped to amend & what was not he lightly regarded and then
Deliver'd the Under written Letter, Viz^t.

September the 2^d, 1761   Registered the 3^d of Septr 1761
James Dormer probationary Minister of Prince Fredericks Parish,
Do give solemn Notice that in the Space of Nine Months from the
Date hereof I shall infallibly leave this Province & Consequently
this Parish. I therefore beg of them to write Immediately for
my Successor in order to procure one in Time, And I Further
declare that I will assist The Parish (if wanting) in Dictating of a
Letter to the Bishop & if I return safe to England I Further
declare that I will report them well—

Item it was agreed that when the Letter was prepared that the
Vestry should peruse it & if approved of, Sign it the first Opportunity

The Reverend Mr Dormer produc'd a Letter accordingly which
was approved of, and returned, & Mr Dormers former Declaration
retracted By agreement of the Vestry then Present, on Mr Dormer's giving the Parish   Warning
           [here occurs a blank of several lines]

Item   The Same Day delivered to Mr Danl McGinney a liste of the Poor Tax to the Ammount of £210, 13, 8 which he is to Collect for the releife of the poor of the said Parish

Item it was Likewise proposed to the Reverend Mr Dormer weither he was disposed to enter the Glebe for the time he intended to reside in the Parish, To which the Revd Mr Dormer replyed that he intended to enter upon the Glebe in A Month or five weeks if the Room was Sceiled, to which it was agreed too by the Vestry.

It was agreed by the Vestry that Mr Jenkins should Officiate as Clarke, to give Constant Attendance, (Sickness or accidents Excepted) and Salary to commence from the   June 1761 being the time Mr Dormer first Preached in the Parish of P. F.

Mr George Atkins Delivered the Tittles of the Church 1761 Septr 20 Land to the Vestry which was not recorded, but prov'd before Jno Basnet Esquire, the Witnesses were

The Land was convey'd by Wm Forbes to Sommerhuff & Tamplat then Ch. Wardens for the Year   and their Successors [The top of Page is broken off]
Novr 23, 1761

	Wm Barton	
	Wm Green	
	Capt Anth^y White	Vestry
Presant	Joseph White Junr	
	Jno Godfrey	
	Francis Lessesne	Wardens
	Danl McGinney	

Receiv'd a Letter from the Revd Mr Dormer, on several Requests Viz^t to have the Parsonage Repaired & to Draw an Order on the Publick Treasurer for Six Months Sallary some time due.

Item.   The Same day Deliverd A list Ammounting to £24[?] to Mr Danl McGinney

Item the same day Drew an Order upon the Publick Treasurer for Six Months Sallary as follows.

S^r: Please to pay to the Revd Jam^s Dormer Six Months Sallary due the 25th of Sepr last past &c

Item   The Same Drew an Order on the Publick Treasurer for £75 to repair to the Glebe.   Delivered to be drawn for Present Church Wardens

N B   The Above Order was return'd by Francis Lessesne accepted

Jany 19 1762   At a Meeting of the Wardens and Vestry for the Parish of Prince Fredericks

Presant   Capt Anth^y White
            Jos^h White Junr
            Wm Green
            James Lane   } Vestry
            Jno Godfrey
            Wm Barton
            Isaac Carr

            Danl McGinney   Warden

It was Determined on Mr Dormer's Promises of Amendment as to some Accusations laid against him that the Vestry would Continue him on those Conditions, & if not performed should be obliged to act as Cases might serve

Feby 20th

Drew an Order on the Publick Treasurer for Six Months Salery due the 25th of March next—

The Coppy of a Letter wrote to the Right Rev^d the Lord Bishop of London for a Minister to Supply the Parish in the Room of the Revd James Dormer which is as follows,

P Frederick South Carolina Feby 25th 1762

May it please Your Lordship

We the Wardens and Vestry of the Parish Prince Frederick, in His Majestie's Province of S^o Carolina, beg leave to Address Y^r Lordship, upon an Occasion, the Natural importance of which, we Cordially hope, will be deemed our sufficient Appollogy.

We have (it is true My Lord) Addressed Your very worthy

Predecessor twice on the like Occasion, and can Boast the Singular Satisfaction to have found that our requests have not been unnoticed, from the Demission of two Gentlemen t⟩ th⸱s Parish, Viz, The Revd Mr Cooper, and the Rev^d Mr Dormer, (Our Present Resident Minister) We are extremely sorry to be thus importunate, but as the Revd Mr Dormer has publickly Signified his intention of returning Home in June, July, or August next the farthest, our Church and Parish must of Course remain unsupplied for a time, (those advantages only excepted which we may Occasionally reap from the Charitable dispositions of Neighbouring Clergy) who reside generally speaking at too wide a distance to Assist us often and as we are by no meanes Lukewarm Advocates for Xtianity and her perpetuity we therefore entertain the most sanguine hope that y^r Lordship will excuse us, when we address you thus Ardently Besides (My Lord) the remotest distance that we of this Province live at from y^r Protection and Care the Numbers of Different Sectaries that abound here; the Immediate ill Consequences resulting therefrom to the advantages of us, add to all which, The general prevalency of Presbyterianism in particular, These Circumstances Strongly call for our Assiduity our Importunity and our most serious thoughts.

But we further beg leave to subjoin, viz, that least your Ld Ship Should Suspect, much less surmise, that any Difference whatever can subsist between the Revd Mr Dormer & Ourselves, previously to his intended Departure, we can assure y^r Lordship of the Contrary and as a proof have desired Mr Dormer to write in connexion with us, to which he has Readily assented, and enclose his Letter, with ours, unsealed. We have now My Lord, only to recapitulate in sanguine Terms (what has been already generally implied), that you will take our distressed situation under Cognizance, and as speedily as possible advert to our Sollicitations, by the Remission of a Minister to the future Cure of this Parish and that for our Sakes; for Mans Sake but Principally and Chiefly for his sake—who we are far from being Ignorant or insensibly of it, both lived & Dy'd for the Sake of Man. We beg leave to Subscribe ourselves,

May it please your Lordship,

Your very devoted Sons & Serv^{ts} in X^t

Signed by the Wardens & Vestry

P. S. Your Lordship will be pleased to Notice Viz^t that the
Province of S° Carolina is (generally speaking) a Good Plentiful
Province, the Standing Sallary of Prince Frederick is £107, Sterling
Pr Ann, Certain and paid out of the Publick Treasury by 2 half
yearly payments, The Ministers perquisites by no means incon-
siderable. There is also a Glebe, a Parsonage capable of Repair, and situated continguously to the Parish Church.

Given at our Parish Church this 25th Feby 1762

March 1st 1762

Drury Lane an Orphan Child about 10 years of age bound an
apprentice to Jacob Burton Shoemaker till he arrives at the Age
of 21 years, by Danl McGinny Church Warden Sign'd by James
Lane Vestry Man.

Easter Monday

At a Meeting of the Vestry & Wardens of the Parish of Pr F—
April 12 1762.

Present Jos. White Junr ⎫
     Isaac Carr   ⎪
     James Lane   ⎬ Vestry
     Wm Green   ⎪
     Wm Barton   ⎭

     Fran^s Lessnee ⎫ W^d
     Danl McGinney ⎬

To Thos Cribbs Senr Acc^t Burrying &c Eliz Rawlins.. 10, 5, 0
To James Minyis Acc^t pr Mich^l Cary Board.......... 59,

Item Same Day Mr John McDowell Rendered his Acc^t
and Cleard all the Orders off & Stands Twenty Pounds
indebted in excluding the list of Defauters List

Same Day drew Orders on the New Vestry for the Above

Sums Vix^t: £10, 5/ & £59

Items Paid following sums to Jo^s. Woods............. 66, 13, 8
&c... 70, 0

Then Proceeded to Ellection, when the Following Persons Were Chosen Viz^t: Anth^y M White $\Big\}$ Wardens
Jam^s Norvell

John Greg $\Big\}$ Over^{rs} William Barton
Francis Goddard   Jam^s Lane
William Findlater . . Regist^r Danl McGinny
                                      Bartly Clarke
                                      Wm Wilson
                                      Joseph White Junr
                                      ✕Anth^y White—Refused Serving

At a Meeting of the Vestry and Wardens May 13 1762.

Present $\left\{\begin{array}{l} W^m \text{ Barton} \\ Dan^l \text{ M}^c\text{Ginny} \\ \text{Bartly Clarke} \\ \text{Jam}^s \text{ Lane} \\ \text{Jos: White} \end{array}\right\}$ Vestry

James Norvell   Warden

When the following Rates the Parish was assessed for—

Viz^t Land pr C.   6^d $\Big\}$
              Slaves pr h^d 6
              Mon^y at int^r 3   To Raise £89, 5
              Stock in Trade 3

Item   The same Day the New Vestry Chose Wm Walker in the Room of Capt Anth^y White, who refused Serving.

N B, The Parochial Order Was to be putt to the following Uses—
Viz^t To Mr Jenkins as Clarke. £20, 0
To James Minzes as Sexton &c Paid.   7
To Wm Findlater as Register £5 $\Big\}$
To Do For Extraordinary Services 3 $\Big)$ Paid.   8–
To James Lane for Lime Paid. 1,2, 6
To Danl McGinney   Paid.   3
                                                          ————————
N. B. The Above is for 1761. . . . . £39, 2, 6
                                                          ————————

1762

June 13   The Revd George Skeine Preach at the Parish Church it being his 1st Serm^n

Item the Same Day the Vestry agreed after a Months Tryal to Write Home to his Ld Ship of London, to Countermand our letters which was sent for A Minister

20th The Vestry & Wardens agre'd to Write home Directly to Counterm^d The Letters and gave Orders for a Coppy to be Drawn In Order to be Perused on the Wednesday folling.

Coppy of a Letter to his L^{d}ship of London

Prince Fredericks Parish June 23^d 1762

May it please Your Lordship we the Wardens & Vestry of the Abovesaid Parish, having wrote a letter to y^r L^{d}Ship bearing Date the 25th Day of Feby 1762 requesting y^r Lordship to remitt us a Minister in the Room of Mr James Dormer who Declines this Cure, whose reasons Should our former Letter come to y^r L^{d}ships Perusal, be more Satisfactory,

We beg leave to acquaint y^r Lordship that Since our last Letter We have (unexpectedly) an Offer made us by the Revd Mr Geo. Skene, who has an Open Mission, & Comes well recommended both for Ability Life and Conversation and Considering the Great distance of this part of y^r lordships Diocese, the uncertainty of our letters Comeing to y^r hands, or of a Minister's comeing out these troublesome Times, Thought proper to embrace this Present Opportunity, rather than Run the Risque of Labouring under the Many Inconveniencies We have for several years Past.

We beg leave Further to inform your L^{d}ship, That should this Not come to y^r hand, before a Minister Should be remitted to for this Cure, The Gentleman would be at no loss, as there are several Vacancies in this Province, who would Willingly embrace the Opportunity of Providing Themselves with A Minister,

We beg leave to Subscribe
Ourselves May it Please Your Lordship
Your Lordship's Most Devoted sons &
humble Servants in X^t

October 13th, 1762. Item This Day Drew an Order on the Publick Treaserrer, for the Revd George Skine for his half year Sallary,
Due which order was Deliver'd to Capt Anthoney White.

February 10: 1763 at a meeting of the Vestry, and Church
Wardens of the Parish of Prince Frederick,

Present   Joseph White   ⎫
             William Barton   ⎪
             Bartly Clarke   ⎬ Vestry Men
             Danl McGinney   ⎪
             William Walker   ⎭

             Anthony M White   Church Warden

James Rupert [?[Entered as Poor on the Parish of Prince Fredricks
By Richard Smith of Brittons neck, who is to Bord him at the
rate of
      £50 p^r year from the 11 March 1762 untill Easter Monday.
                              Turn over

February 10: 1763 brought over
    The Vestry and Church Wardens agreed to have the Parsonage
House Repaired by Easter monday next if Possible at which Time
The Reverend Mr George Skene intends to Remove into itt,
Itt is also agreed that A M White Church Warden Doe inquire for
A Proper Person or Persons to Repair the Same as Soon as Possible
he is also Desired to Inquire how the money is to be Recovered
March 1st 1763 Att a Meeting of the Vestry and Warden of
Prince Fredericks Parish,

Present   Daniel McGinney   ⎫
             Wm Walker   ⎪
                                  ⎬ Vestry
             Bartly Clarke   ⎪
             Joseph White   ⎭

             Antho^y M White   Chh Warden

Item, the Same Day went and View'd the Parsonage and With a
Workman and Valued the Repairs to be worth One hundred and
Twenty Five Pounds, for which an order was drawn on the Public
Treasurer, which if excepted a Couple of Workmen was to be
employed in order to do the same repairs.

Easter Monday April 4 1763
        At a Meeting of the Vestry &c
Then proceeded to Settle fines &c.........................
Present   James Lane
              Wm Barton
              Joseph White
              Bartly Clarke
              Wm Walker
              Daniel McGinney
              Wm Wilson

            Wardens { James Norvell
                      { Antho^y M. White

Received an acc^t of fines Sacramental Money &c

Decr 25..	£ 3, 0, 6
April 3^d..	3, 13
Do	1
	7, 13, 6
Parochial Order Last Ea Mond^y.....................	40
Paid Capt Anthony.................................	£47, 13, 6
deduct for Lime....................................	2, 8, 0
Wm Hunstable for Merchdze [?]....................	20
Glebe...	22, 8, 0
To Cash paid......................................	25, 5, 6

Item Drew an Order on the Public Treasurer for £40 Parochial
Money payable to Willm Walker

Item Same Day the following Acc^{ts} were Rendered in

Viz^t Mr Abraham Prior for Board of Mich^l Cary....	£22, 3, 4
Mr Thos Cribb Do........................	£36, 16, 8
& Drew Orders for the Same on the New Vestry......	£59, 0, 0

Then proceeded to Ellection, for Parish Officers the following Persons Viz^t

Thomas Gm Scott ⎫
Joseph White Junr ⎬ Wardens

William Barton ⎫
William Walker ⎪
Bartly Clarke ⎪ Vestry
Jehu Walker ⎬ Men
Moses Miller ⎪
Willm Wilson ⎪
Willm Green ⎭

Joseph Britton Esqr ⎫
John Gregg ⎬ Overseers
Theadore Gourdine ⎭

Willm Barton   Sexton

Richd King   Regist^r

April y^r 4th 1763: The Parish of Prince Fredericks to pd

Andrew Burnett for Medecins & Attendance ⎫
for Michal Cary.......................... ⎬ £11, 10, 0

An Order this Drew for five Months Board of ⎫
Jam^s Rupert [?], Payab^e to Richd Smith by ⎬
Mr Scott   Paid........................... ⎭ £20, 13, 8

D^o An Order Payab^e to Thos Cribb for Board ⎫
of Michal Cary by Joseph White Paid....... ⎬ £36, 16, 8

D^o An Order Payab^e to Abrah^m Prior for ⎫
Board of Michal Cary Paid by Joseph White ⎬ £22, 3, 4

This day Agreed upon by the Church Wardens
& Vestry that Mr Thos Jenkins is to Act No
longer as Clerk of the Church.

May 9th 1763   Dischargd an order to Willm Findlater for Register in year 1762 £8

Likewise an Order Paid Doct^r Andrew Burnett for Attendance to Michael Carey, Poor of the Above Parish.

By a Surplis Money Deliv^d by Frances Lesene

The Following Answer to a Letter wrote ye 25 of Febuay 1762.

Gentlemen,   London 25th May 1762

My Lord Bishop of London hath just Receiv^d your Letter of the 25th of February last and orders me to tell in Answer to it that he shall be Ready to pay a due Regard to the Request which you have therein Made to him, hence you may Depend on it that no Endeavours will be wanting on the Part of his Lordship to Procure for you as speedily as Possible a Clergyman of an un-exquestionable moral Character which affords the best Foundation for hoping that he will not Only be diligent in the Performance of his Ministeral Duty but will Also watch with Tenderness and care the flock Over which he Presides......

His Lordship feels a Peculiar Pleasure from the Zeal that you have Expresed for our most holy Religion, and therefore he doubts not but you and your Parts will give all Ready Attention to the Doctrines Propounded to you, and will moreover every One of you willingly and Chearfully pay that Reverence and becoming Deportment towards your Pastor and Teacher which your Duty Enjoins you to pay and the Office that he Bears among you requires.

You have his Lordships Prayers for your advancement, In True Religion and his Blessings attend you.

I am Gentlemen

Your Obedient humble Servant

Willm Dickes

At a Meeting of the Wardens and Vestry May 9th 1763,

Present   William Barton ⎫
            William Green ⎪
            Daniel McGinney ⎪
            William Willson ⎬ Vestrey Men
            William Walker ⎪
            Bertley Clerke ⎪
            Jehu Walker ⎭

Thomas G^m Scott and Joseph White Junr   Wardens

When the Following Rates the Parish was ases'd,

For

        Lands p^r 100,   1/
        Slaves p^r h^d   1/
        Money at intst 0/6^d   To raise £99, 13, 8
        Stock and Trade 0/6^d   For old Arrears unpaid   £74

Margeret Spencer Enter'd as Poor of the Parish of Prince Fredericks By Jno McDowel

Parchal Order By Order of the Vestry & Wardens Paid by Willm Walker

    To Capt Anthony White for Clerks fees for Too Year £3, 5

    To Willm Findlater as Regest^r £5, 0

Moneys Received of Jn° M°Dowel and Paid to Willm Barton in Part of Arrears Due him.................. £6, 19, 0

agreed to pay Richd Smith for the board of James⎫
Lepunt..⎭ 50 ....

This 25th Sepr Gave The Revd Mr George Scheen an Order on Mr Jacob Mott for Half years Sallery due him

    Easter Monday 23^d of Aprill 1764 This 23^d of Aprill 1764 Gave an Order to the Revd Mr George Schene On Jacob Mott Esqr for Six Months Sallary due him.

Item, Drew an Order on the Publick Treasurer for forty Pounds Parochal Money Payable to T G^m Scott and Joseph White

Present

Willm Barton	
Willm Walker	
Danl M°Ginney	
Jehu Walker	} Vestry Men
Willm Willson	
Willm Green	
Bartley Clarke	

Thos G^m Scott	} Wardens
Joseph White	

Agreed upon by the Pres^t Vestry & Wardens that Moses Britton Shall be Paid forty Pounds for Supporting John M°Dowell and family one year this to be paid Next Easter.

Likewise fourteen Pounds Payable to Thos G^m Scott for Nursing Rachel Downing and Child

Likewise Six Pounds Ten Shillings Payable to Doct^r Andrew Burnett for attendance to Rachel Downing.

Parochal Order Paid twenty Pounds for Clerks fees

Sexton Paid five Pounds

Register Paid five Pounds

Paid Capt White for Old Arrears five Pounds

Paid Thos G Scott in part for a book £5

Paid Willm Barton in Part of Old Arrears Twenty Pounds......

Joseph White paid Mr Barton for Old Arrears £12,16,9

Receiv^d of A^y Martin White Thirty Eight Pounds 13, 71/2 Likewise twenty five pounds, 10, 71/2

Agreed upon that Jno Macdowell shall be Paid four pounds 2/ for board of Margarett Spencer

    Then Proceeded to Election for Parish officers the following Persons

Francis Goddard	} Overseers	The Rev^d Mr George Schene
John Ervin		Willm Green
		Daniel McGuiney
		Jehu Walker
Daniel McGuiney Sexton		Willm Walker
Richd King Register		Richd Green
		John Wagenfeild

Willm Green, Daniel McGuiney, Jehu Walker, Willm Walker, Richd Green, John Wagenfeild } Vestry Men

Thos Gm Scott and Bartley Clarke   Church Wardens

Due to Abraham Prior fifty five Pounds for board of Michal Carey Due Likewise to Abraham Prior for Board of Margeret Spencer forty four Pounds Eighteen Shillings

Due to Richd Smith for Board, of James Repunt fifty Pounds

At a Meeting of the Vestry & Church Wardens of Prince Frederks Parish this 14 May 1764

Present

T. G. Scott	} Church	Revd George Skeene
Bartly Clark	} Wardens	Danl McGinney
		Wm Walker
		Jehu Walker
		Richd Green
		Wm Green
		John Wagenfeld

Revd George Skeene, Danl McGinney, Wm Walker, Jehu Walker, Richd Green, Wm Green, John Wagenfeld } Vestry Men

They assest the said Parish at

1/6 p^r 100 for Land

1/6 p^r h^d for Slaves   To Raise the Sum of 204.2

9^d p^r cent for Money at Interest

9^d p^r cent Stock in Trade

and Likewise agreed to have the Glebe House repaired agreeable to Mr Skeene's mind

At a meeting of the Vestry & Church Wardens the 15 August 1764 it was Resolved to send a Letter to John Murray Esqr to acquaint us whether the Assembly had provided for the Repairing of the Glebe house and Likewise appointed John Wagenfield Register in the Room of Richd King being gone out of this Parish

To pay Pryer	£110	
To pay Smith.........................	50	
To pay Britton.......................	40	£200
To pay John McDowell.................		4–2
Paid McDowell by Henry Bossard Junr....		£204,2

The Parish of Prince Fredricks
   Easter Monday 8th April 1765
At a Meeting of the Church Wardens & Vestry,
Recvd of Joseph White Poore Tax Money............ 8,13,2
By T G Scott
Recvd of Capt A White and Antho Martin
White List and paid to Wm Green 6,14,9
to impartmenes [?] Order
Recvd of Thos Gwillim Scott .... 22,19,10$\frac{1}{4}$
for Poore Tax for the year 1762
This day paid Mr Barton for Old Arrears .... 31,13,0$\frac{1}{4}$
By T. G. Scott & Clark
Easter Monday 8 April 1765
At a Meeting of the Church Wardens & Vestry
Recvd of Mr Fran^s Godard, Poore mony............ £25,9
for the yeare 1763
Recvd of Thos G. Scott, for Poore 74,2,5
Tax for the yeare 1763
By T. G. Scott and discounted in his severall Orders as Below
Recv'd of Bartly Clarke............................ 15–17

Paid Mrs Pryer in part,...........................	41–6–0
Paid Thoˢ Gwillim Scott in part ⎫ for Orders ⎭	74,2,5
21 June Received of Mr Bartly Clarke ⎫ and paid to Mrs Pryer, by Thoˢ G. Scott⎭	32,2,9
The balance of ye Communion Money in Mr Bartle⎫ Clarks hands applied to a Charitable source, by con-⎬ cent of yᵉ parcon, ⎭ Recᵈ by The Widow McIver	9,10,0

Easter Monday: 8ᵗʰ April 1765
Agreed to pay Thoˢ G. Scott Mary William
Order for the board of Michell Cary and Margᵗ Spencer   70..
[Interpolated]
Paid Elizabeth Scott as administˣ to T. G. Scott Est.
By Henry Bossard, Next Easter Munday, the bal-
lance due on the three demands of £70, £13,5, 71/2, & £3
Out of the Poor Tax he recd

Agreed to pay Thos G Scott for ⎫ Sundries to Rachell Downing & ⎬ .... her Child ⎭	13, 5,7½
& to be paid to T G Scott out of Next Yʳˢ P Order for⎫ Sundries for the Church........................ ⎭	£3,

Agreed to pay Richᵈ Smith   Paid by Mr Bossard
for boarding Lepunt   the Request   30
                                          of Richard Smith
To pay Moses Britton for board
John McDowell & Famely, Paid by Henry Bossard Junr   40

This day drawed the Parochall Order payable To Revᵈ Mʳ Skeen
and disbursed as under

To Thoˢ Jenkins Clarke...........................	20
Dan McGeney Sexton.............................	5
Thoˢ Gwillim Scott...............................	1,10
To Capᵗ A White for old arrers...................	13,10

                                                          ————
                                                            40
                                                          ————

Easter Monday 8 April 1765
this day Drawed an order on Jacob Mott Esqr for the Rev^d M^r
Skeens Sallary for half a Yeare

Agreed to pay William Bruce	} Brought forward	
For the Pairs of the Church, and making	} £153, 5,71/2	
a Coffin for Thompson who was drowned	} .... £ 3,10..	

Paid by Henry Bossard Jun to Bruce 7/

Agreed to pay Dr Burnets accot	} 6,10	
for sundries for Rach Downing		

£163, 5,71/2

Elected this day the following persons as Parish Officers

Revd George Skene ⎫
William Wilson ⎪
Henry Bossard ⎪
William Green ⎬ Vestry
Bartly Clarke ⎪
Jehu Walker ⎪
John Wagenfield ⎭

Thos G^m Scott ⎫ Chh Wardens
Henry Bossard ⎭

T. G. Scott Register

John Ervan ⎫
Thos Goddard ⎬ Overseers
Fran^s Britton Junr [?] ⎭

Coppy of a Petition sent to Governor William Bull & Counsell
To the Honourable Will: Bull Esqr Lieutenant Governor and
Commander in Chief in and over His Majesty's Province, of
South Carolina and,
To the members of his Majestys Honourable Council,
To the Honourable Rawlins Lowndes Esqr Speaker and the Rest
of the members of the Honourable the Common house of Assem-
bly of the said Province
The Petitions of the Church Wardens and Vestry: Men of the
parish of Prince Fredricks in Craven County, in the said Province

Most Humbly Sheweth

That the Church and Glebe buildings of the Parish are mutch
decayed, and out of repair, which requires Immediate amendment to make them Comfortable Habitable, and That your

petitioners are unable of themselves to do this Necessary woork
and being Informed that Provision is made by your Honours
annualy for these good purposes

Most Humbly pray your honours that sutch Provision may be
put into their hands for the above mentioned uses in sutch a
manner as to your honours in your Wisdom shall seem meet
And your Petitioners as in duty bound shall Ever Pray &c⁰

Vestry⎨⎧ George Skene Minstʳ
        │ William Wilson
        │ Bartly Clark   T. G. Scott   ⎫
        │ Henry Bossard Senᵒʳ   H Bossard Junr ⎬
        ⎩ William Green

Sent 2ᵈ July 1765 pᵗ Mʳ Cape
[The following half page of original is nearly illegible]
The Parish being assessed at the following Rates
1/pʳ head for Slaves   To Pay the acct of   16
1/pr C. Land
1/ pr ct. For Money at ints   Present Parish Officers
Henry Bossard Ch Warden   William Wilson
                                      William Green

This day James Lane was Ellected Church Warden and Register
in Room of the (dec) Thos Gᵐ Scott
[Much of what precedes is illegible in original]
1766 february yᵉ 11ᵗʰ the Vestry and Wardens being mett at the
Parsonige present   Wᵐ Willson   ⎫
   Henry Bossard Junʳ ⎫   Wᵐ Green   ⎬ Vestry
   Jaˢ Lane   ⎬ Wardens   Bartly Clark ⎭ Men

They aggreed to apply to the Assembly for two hundred and fifty
pounds ten shillings, as it appeard probable that it wold require
that Sum to Defray yᵉ several Chargis of the nessary repairs
thereof and at yᵉ same time proceeded to Vew the Works thereon
towards yᵉ sᵈ repairs, and Aggreed that the Underpining of yᵉ
House & yᵉ Oven be taken Down and yᵉ Lime paid for and further that yᵉ Workmen be had to vew & Value the Whole as many
other things seamd to be Dun in a Scandelous Mannʳ

Easter Munday March y^et 31 ᵗ1766   Present

Wm Willson }   HenryBossard }
John Wagenfield } Vestry   James Lane } Wardins
Wm Green }
Bartly Clark }

This Day sind an order payable to Capt Anthony Whight for Y^e Parochal Money Viz^t forty pounds for ye year 1765 and agreed to Distribute it as folloes—

Paid By Capt White into the hands Henry Bossard .. £20

To Mr Wm Barten for Sexton }
Paid By Henry Bossard } £5,0,0

To Ja^s Lane for Register }
Paid by Henry Bossard } 5,0,0

Omited To Mr Wagenfield for Register for Last Year }
Paid By Henry Bossard } 5,0,0

To Capt Anthony Whight for olde arrears

Aggreed to Pay Mary Williams for ye Bord of }
Michal Cary & Margaret Spencer, for one year. } £110,0,0

Agreed to pay Moses Britton for ye Bord of }
Andrew McDowel one year } 40,0,0

Aggreed to pay Richard Smith for ye Bord of James Lepunt one year.................................. 30,0,0

To Cash Paid Capt White By Henry Bossard, Junr..... £180,0,0

Easter Munday March ye 31st
This day
Asses^d the Parish at ye following Rates for Defraying ye Sum of One Hundred & Eightey Pounds for ye year 1765
Viz^t Slaves at 1/6^d pr hd
Lands @ 1/6^d pr hund^d, acres,
Money at interest @ 9^d, pr Ct.

The Communion Money in Mr Bossard hands }
paid to ye New Wardens } 5,2,8
Rec^d By William Wilson }
This day Gave Mr Scheen an Order for Six Months Salleyrey

Eeaster Monday   The undermentioned Are the Parrish officers
this day Elected 31st March 1766

Anthony White } Ch Wardens   Bartley Clark
William Wilson   Anth^y Ma^n White
William Wilson Register }   John Wagenfield
Danl McGinney Sexton   John Mcdowell } Vestry
                                                        Charles Baxter
Moses Britton }   William Green Junr
Alex^r Swinton } Overseers   . . . .
Abra^m Misheau   Dan^{ll} McGinney

At a Meeting of the Vestry on Monday July 17th 1766 The Un-
dermentiond was agreed to in Presence of

Bartley Clark }
John McDowell
Dan^{ll} McGinney
Anth^y M. White } Vestry
John Wagenfield   Anthony White } Ch/
Ch^s Baxter   William Wilson } Wardens
William Green Junr

To Take Mary Bonnell On the Parrish to Be Supported as An
Object of Charity, and the Wardens to Apply to a Doc^r to Prescribe
Toward the Retreavend. her Sencess
And that William Wilson is to Be Paid for Six weeks Board of
her and Necessary Cloathing Found her as will appear By his
acc^t Prior to this date
The Wardens to Imploy Some person to Clear and Clean the
Church Yard

Octr 1st 1766   This Day Gave Mr Skeen an Order for Six Months
Salleyrey, Allso Gave Capt White An Order On Mr Mott for
the Moneys Granted this Parrish for the Repair of the Gleeb
& signd By

William Wilson } Wardens   Dan^{ll} McGinney
Anth^y White   Bartley Clark } Vestry
                            William Green Junr

The Order Above Mentioned Paid to Capt White £215,10..
for the Repair of the Gleeb

By the Vestry and Wardens Present this 27th Novr 1766

Agreed to pay Chas Gea for work done at the Parsonage, in Making Chimneys Plastering and Glazing   £41,15
Paid by Anth^y White

To Pay William Bruce for Carpenters work in
Repairing the Parsonage and Building a Stable ......   £93,..
And Barn, Nails, Locks, and hinges Included

To pay William Wilson for Lime..................   £33, 5

To Pay the Revd Geo Skeen for Glass Brick s, Shingles,   £47,10
Boards & Board of Workmen

Paid out of the Aforementiond Order Recd £215,10
By Capt White from Mr Mott

Rec^d of Capt White £33,5, in full for the Above Lime

William Wilson

Agreed that Capt White is to Get an Estamate of the Expenses
for Painting and Repairing the Church, and allso for Pailing in
the Church Yard and, agreed that the Sum To be Petition the
Assembly for

William Wilson		Cha. Baxter	
Antho^y White	Wardens	Danl MGinney	Vestry
		Bartly Clarke	
		Anthony M White	

This day was an Order Drawn in favour of Mr Skeen's Ex'tor
To Mr Mott, for the Remains of his Salleyrey Being 1 Mo Sent
Mr Mott a second Order for the 1 M^o Salleyrey, the first being
Lost.

Drew an Order in favour The Revd Paul Turquan for officiating
one Sunday in the Parrish Church

To Jacob Mott Esqr

Easter Monday 20th Ap^{ll} 1767

Agreed to Pay Mary Williams for Board Michael
Cary and Margaret Spencer a Year   £120. . . . .
     Paid Mary Williams by WW

John Godfrey for Board Mary Bonnell 9 M^o............ £ 75,.....
     Paid By W Wilson

To Doc^t William Fyffe for Medicins for ditto..........   2,15

To William Wilson for Board ditto 1/2 M° ⎫
and 4 Yards Linnen   ⎬   16,10
                                          ⎭
                                          _____

                                          £214,5,–
Surplus Money.................................   20,

                                          _____

                                          £234,5,

The Parish this day asses᙭ at the following Rates to Raise the
Above Sum

                     Slaves 1/3 pʳ head
                     Lands 1/3 pʳ C

Money at Intˢᵗ 7 1/2
Money Recᵈ this day of Bartley Clark as Surpelus ⎫
Being in full of his Collection for the Year 1763 ⎬ £ 21,1,3
Paid to Anthony White Warden for 1766   ⎭
Cash in the hand Capᵗ White for Fines............. £ 7,
Gave an Order On Jacob Mott Esqʳ for £40 to Capᵗ
White Parochal Money
Ballance on the Last Parochal Order In Capᵗ Whites
hands after Paying Mʳ Wagenfield, Mʳ Lane Register,
& Mʳ Barton Sexton the whole £15, and Clearing and
Cleaning the Church Yard and the Gleeb Fences £7,
whole amᵗ £22, Ballᶜᵉ due £10
The other Parochal Order is to Pay the Undermen-
tioned Thoˢ Jenkins for Being Clark Paid By A White £ 20,
William Wilson for Being Register Paid by Capᵗ White   5,....
Danˡ McGinney For Being Sexton, Paid by Capᵗ White   5,

                                          _____

                                          £30

William Wilson ⎫   Cha. Baxter   ⎫
Antho White   ⎬ Wardens   Bartly Clarke ⎪
Wee the Vestry and Wardens   Isaac Carr   ⎬ Vestry
agree to Pay Mʳ Chaˢ Baxter   John McDowell ⎪
£25 Pounds for a Pawl for the   John Wagenfeld ⎭
Good of the Parrish Gratious

Easter Monday 20ᵗʰ Apˡˡ 1767

The Undermentioned Persons was this day Ellected as Parrish officers

John Wagenfeld ⎱ Wardins
Ch⁸ Baxter   ⎰

Anthony White ⎫
Bartly Clark |
William Wilson |
Alex͏ʳ Tweed   ⎬ Vestry
William Pawling |
Isaac Carr |
John Augus Finke ⎭

William Wilson   Register
Dan¹¹ M͏ᶜGinney   Sexton

This 26ᵗʰ Apr¹ Gave the Rev͏ᵈ M͏ʳ Pierce An Order On the Publick Treasurer for £40, for 4 Times Preaching in this Parrish Church,

At Meeting of the Vestry and Wardens this 24ᵗʰ May 1767 The Rev͏ᵈ James Cosgrive was agreed With to Be Rector of This Parrish, Till It should Please the Bishop to Send One Out for the Parrish, agreeable to a Letter Wrote him By the Vestry and Wardens On that head, and upon Like⁸ on Both Sides the above Mentioned Letter to Be Countermanded Provided no Minister Come in The Interim.

The Same day Gave him an Order On Gordon and Mills for £250 To Purchase Nesessaries for house Keeping which was to Be Reemburst as his Salleyrey Becomes Dew, Also Tho⁸ Jenkins Ellected Clarke of the Church the Same day

Present

John Wagenfield ⎱ Wardens   Bartley Clarke ⎫
Ch⁸ Baxter   ⎰   Anth͏ʸ White |
                                      Anth͏ʸ M͏ᵐ White ⎬ Vestry
Paul Michau ⎱ Overseers   Alex͏ʳ Tweed |
John James ⎰   John August Finke [?] ⎭

At The Meeting of the Wardens and Vestry this 13th October 1767
Present

Ch^s Baxter			Anth^y White	
Dan^{ll} McGinney	} Warden		Alex^r Tweed	
This day Chose in the Room			William Pawling	} Vestry
of John Wagenfield (decd)			Bartly Clark	
			William Wilson	

Drew An Order On the Publick Treasurer for Six Months Salleyrey
due the Rev^d Mr James Cosgrieve

At a Meeting of the Vestry & Wardens this 10th Novr 1767
Present

Alex^r Tweed		Ch^s Baxter	
William Pawling	} Vestry	Dan^{ll} McGinney	} Wardens
Bartley Clarke			
William Wilson			

Meet the Revd Mr George Spencer whoe Presented the Vestry
With the Lord Bishop's Letter To the Vestry & Wardens of this
Parrish, As also his Lordship's License Mr Spencer Being Ask'd
. . . . .Chose to go dyrectly to live at the Gleeb, whoe
Replyd he did not but Choose Rather to Board himself with
One of his Parishioners Till Spring.
This 15th Jany It was Agreed that the Wardins M^r McGinney
and Mr Baxter Was to Apply for Some Person to Board Mar-
garet Mathews to Be Cured of a Turrible disorder And it seems
she is Boarded with Doc^r Wood, at £10, p^r Month and To Cure
her for £50, and she is to Board five Months Being. . . . £100. . . . .

Recd of Margaret Matthewes in the hands of Mr Salling	}	4–13 9

£ 95–6–3

Easter Monday 4th Ap^l 1768 Vestry & Wardens Present

Dan^{ll} McGinney	} Ch Wardens	Alex^r Tweed	
Ch^s Baxter		Bartley Clark	
		John Augustus Finck	} Vestry
		Anth^y White	
		William Wilson	

The Wardens Rendered their Acc^t

To Paid Mary Williams for Board Michael Cary & Margaret Spencer	.... £111,5,0
To ditto John Godfrey for board Mary Bonnell.......	100,

To Ball^{co} due on Woods Acc^t for the Cure &	£211,5,...
Board Margaret Matthews,........................	£ 95,6,3

Parrish Charges for the Year 1767................. £306,11,3

Gave M^r McGinney and Mr Baxter An Order On Mr Mott For
The Parochal Money Being...................'........ £40
Gave the Rev^d Mr Spencer An Order On Mr Mott For Six Months,
Salleyrey due him
The Parochal order to Pay The Clerk Fees,
due at his deceas .... £ 11, 11,0
To Pay dan^{ll} McGinney as Sexton................ 5, 0,0
To Pay William Wilson as Register............... 5 ..
To Pay dan^{ll} McGinney For Cleaning Round the
Parsonage fence, to Prevent fire Burning them 10.
To Pay Ch^s Baxter for Work done in the Church
And Repairs at the Parsonage Pr Acc^t Rendered 4,10..

£26,11...

Then Proceeded to Ellection for Parrish officers when the Under
Mention'd was Ellected

John Augustus Frick Anthony White	Wardens	William Barton Dan^{ll} McGinney William Green Senr	
Peter Michau Alex^r Tweed Hugh Irvin	Overseers	William Wilson Isaac Carr Henry Bossard Junr James Lane	Vestry

Dan^{ll} McGinney   Sexton
William Wilson   Register

Mary Williams Agreed to Board Michael Cary, and Margaret
Spencer, Twelve Months from Easter Monday, For the Sum of
£110, and all Nesessaries, found them, By her the said M. Williams

Charles Wilson Agrees to Board Mary Bonnell & finde her all Convenient Nesesaries for the Sum of Sixty Nine Pound Commencing for.the 4ᵗʰ May, 1768.

This day the Parrish assest to Raise the Sum of £306,11,3 Slaves 1/6 Lands pr Cᵗ Acres 1/6 Money at Intˢ, 9 Pence Present

Anthoʸ White   ⎫ Wardins   William Wilson ⎫
John Augusᵗ Fincke ⎭   William Green   ⎪
                                     Jaˢ Lane   ⎬ Vestry
                                     Danˡ McGinney   ⎪
                                     H. Bossard Jr.   ⎭

The Same day the above Vestry & Wardens Present agree that Capᵗ White & Docʳ Fink is to agree with Some Person To do the Needful Repairs to the Windows and Dores of the Church, and the Money to Be Paid Out of Surpelus Parochal Money, Now in Hand.

Gave the Revᵈ Mʳ Spencer this 27ᵗʰ Sepʳ 1768 An Order On the Publick Treasurer, for Six Mᵒ Sallery.

Octʳ 5ᵗʰ 1768   This day the Vestry & Wardens Gave Mesʳˢ Theadore Gordine & William Michau An Order On The Publick Treasurer for £500 Being the Money allowed By the Publick for Building a Chapple of Ease On Santee in this Parrish The Above Mention'd Gentelmen Being Appointed Commissioners, for dyrecting the Building the Said Chapple.

The Meeting of the Vestry this 12ᵗʰ Janʸ 1769 Present

Anthony White ⎫ Wardens   Danˡˡ McGinney ⎫
Augustus Fink ⎭   Isaac Carr   ⎬ Vestry
                                William Wilson ⎭

The Intention of this days Meeting was to Know what Reasons the Revᵈ Mʳ Spencer Could assign for his Charge of Being Ill Used By the Parrish and that he was Determined to Leave it And On His Not Meeting the Vestry, Agreeable to Promise, William Wilson, As Register is Required to write him a few Lines Requesting him to Appoint a Day, shortly In Order that Matters

May Be Properly Adjusted, And On his Non Complyance therewith, it is the determination of the Vestry, that he Shall Leave
the Parrish, as they Are Contious what Ill Usage has Been is
from him, to the Parrish, Henry Bossard Sen[r] Is this day Ellected
a Vestry Man, in the Room of William Barton Sen[r]. (dec[d])
Coppy of the Letter wrote the Rev[d] M[r] Spencer
Rev[d] Sir

On Thursday Last Persuant to Appointment the Vestry, Mett,
& On Y[r] Not Meeting them Agreeable to Promise, I am Requested
To Trouble You with this scrole/desireing You'l Oppoint a day
Shortley for the Meeting of the Vestry, In Order to assign Y[r]
Reasons/for the Charge of Being Ill Used, By the Parrish, and
that You ware determined to Leave it, for the Vestry is of Op-
pinion what Ill Usage have been is Rather from You, to the Par-
rish, so would Be glad how soon Matters ware Properly Adjusted.
S[r] Y[r] Hbl Sev[t]

William Wilson Reg[t]

Jan[y] 13th 1769—

Easter Monday March 27th 1769

To Pay John Burns for Burying a Poor Woman and Nesesaries found By Name Marg[t] Stewart	£8, 0, 0
To pay Mary Williams for Board Michael Cary, and Margaret Spencer Twelve Months from Easter Monday Last	110, 0, 0
To Pay Ch[s] Wilson for Board Mary Bonel from the 4th May to 27th March Being Eleven Months at Sixty nine p[r] annum,	63, 5, 0
To Pay John Godfrey for Board Mary Bonnel one Month at £100, p[r] annum	8, 8, 9
	£189,13, 9
By cash in hand of Anth[y] White & William Wilson as will Appear By there Acc[t]	65,15,11
	£123,17,10
	20

Parrish is assest to Raise this Sum.................. £143,17,10

Slaves 1/ Lands p^r C^t 1/ Moneys at Int^s 6^{c}p.
By Anth^y White & Agustus Finke (Wardens)

> Peter McChau   ⎫
> Alex^r Tweed   ⎬ Overseers
> Hugh Irvin   ⎭

Gave the Revd Mr Spencer an Order the Publick Treasurer, for Six Months Salleyrey Allso Gave William Wilson An Order for the Parochal Money,

To Pay the Sexton   Paid.........£5
To ditto the Register   Paid   5,   10—

Ball^e Paid Anth^y White & John Finke ⎫
to Pay part Robt Davidson Bill for ⎬ 30
The Repair of the Church ⎭

                                                     40—

           Present   William Green   ⎫
                   Isaac Carr   ⎬ Vestry
Antho^y White ⎫   Dani^l McGinney ⎪
John Augt Fincke ⎬ Wardens   William Wilson   ⎭

Then Proceeded to Ellection When the following Persons was Ellected Parrish Members

> James M^{c}pherson ⎫
> Thos Wood   ⎬ C. Wardens

John Godfrey   ⎫   William Wilson Reg^r
Danl McGinney   ⎪   Danl McGinney Sex^n
WilliamGreen Senr ⎪
Anth^y White Junr ⎬ Vestry
James Lane   ⎪   William M^{l}Cortry ⎫ Over-
John Burns   ⎪   John Perrit   ⎬ seers
John Glen Senr ⎭

Omitted/ Before Ellecting of Parrish officers the Revd Mr Spencer was desired to Clear up the Charge of Being Ill Used By the parrish, for Which the Vestry Mett 12th Jany Last, But he utterly Denyed The Intention of Any Such Charge, But Being Ill Used By some In the Parrish he'd Let a Word drop in his heat that he was heartily Sorrey for and On Matters Being Canvis'd it appears that the Vestrys Charge against Mr Spencer's

Parrish hunting is Not Without foundation, and In Order To doe Justice to the Parrish, he's Promised to Joyn them in a Letter to the Bishop for Another Minister, that the Parrish May Be a Providing a Parson, while he's Precuring a Parrish.

Agreed with Cha⁸ Wilson for the Board Mary Bonnell, At £69 pʳ annum
Agreed with Daniel Williams this 11ᵗʰ May 1769 at £105 pʳ Annum to Board Michael Cary & Margaret

The Vestry Met this 27ᵗʰ June 1769
Present

Thos Wood	⎫ Church	John Burns	⎫
James McPherson	⎭ Wardens	Danˡˡ McGinney	⎬ Vestry
		William Greeen Senʳ	
		Anthʸ White Junʳ	
		John Godfrey	⎭

Proceeded to Business & Ellected William Wilson & William Green Junʳ Vestry Men In the room of John Glen Senʳ & James Lane whoe declined Acting, Agreed to Petition the assembly for Money To Repair the Church.
The Revᵈ Mʳ Spencer departed this Life 28ᵗʰ June 1769 The Vestry Mett, this 26ᵗʰ July, 1769 and It Was Agreed that William Wilson should Write, a Letter to the Lord Bishop Soliseting him to Send Us A Minister to Succeed the Revᵈ Mʳ Spencer
The first Monday in Aug⁸ᵗ Being the 6ᵗʰ Day of the Month Mʳ Peter Lane Was agreed With to Be Clark of the Church at £20 pʳ Annum

This 28ᵗʰ Febʸ 1770 A Petition Sent to the Members of this Parrish Requesting Money for the Repairs of the Church & Inclosing The Church Yard

Easter Monday Apˡˡ 16ᵗʰ 1770
To Pay Peter Lane As Clark, (Paid to Wᵐ Wilson 12 July 1770)..................................... £10,......
To Pay Danˡˡ McGinney As Sexton, (Paid By Tho⁸ Woodd, & Ja⁸ Mcpherson)........................   5

To Pay William Wilson As Reg^{sr}, (Paid 12th July 1770)
by J. M..   5
To Pay Dan^{ll} McGinney for having Round the Parsonage Pail...   10

Carried forward—

Gave Tho Wood & James M^cpherson An Order for the Parochall
Money (Received the 12 July by Wm Wilson £40—

Easter Monday 16th Aprill 1770
At the Meeting of the Vestry Present

	William Green	Thos Wood	} Ch. Wardens
	Dan^{ll} McGinney	James M^cpherson	
Vestry	Anth^y White Senr		
	William Wilson		
	John Godfrey		

To Pay Mary Williams for the Board Michael Cary and Mar-
garet Spencer from 27th March 1769 to 12th May at Which Time
they ware Boarded to Dan^{ll} Williams/Paid by an Order to R.
Green £13, 11,3 Mathew Orchad Aplyed this Day for the Ben-
nefit of the Parrish as Being Unable to Get his Liveing for some
time Past, and Look'd On By the Vestry and Wardens As an
Object of Charrity Taken On the Parrish to Be Supported By
the Moneys Arising from the Poor Tax

Proceeded to Ellect Parrish Members When the Undermention'd
Was Ellected

William Michau } Ch.   Thos Wood
Meredith Hughes } Wardens   William Green Senr
                            Dan^{ll} McGinney
                            William Snow   } Vestry
                            John Godfrey
                            James Mcpherson
                            Anth^y White Senr

James Mcpherson   Reg^r
Dan^{ll} McGinney   Sexton

Adam M^cdonald
Moses Brown Senr   } Overseers
Geo Burrows Senr

Geo Green Agrees to Take Mathew Orchad to Board with Him, for Twelve Months, to furnish him With Eavery Nesesary for £59.

Easter Monday 16th April 1770.
Charges to be Paid By Thomas Wood, & James McPherson, Chu^r. Ward^s.
Viz^t

To Pay Richard Green Mary Williams Order for Board Michal Cary & Marg^t Spencer 46 days		£13,11,3
To Pay William Wilson Danl Williams Order £80		
To Ditto William Green, Dan Williams ditto for Boarding M. Cary & M. Spencer 12 Months	25	105
To Pay Charles Wilson for Boarding Mary Bonnell 12 Months..		69
		£187,11,3

Settled & Paid   } To Pay Clerk Sexton Register
the 12 July 1770 } &ca (out of the P. Money) 20,10,—
Also Paid Capt Anthony White this Sum (£14,12,10,) (Augst 16)
Ditto Robt Davidson 30/

Moneys Received from, By Thomas Wood & James McPherson Church Ward. Viz^t

May 10 From Daniel McGinney, part of his Account, for Collect.....................................	£28,18,2
Augt 16 From Anthony White part of his acco^t for Coll^t....................................	51,15,4

It appears by Anth^y Whites List that he has to Coll^t } this Sum Which when Receiv'd shall be made Men- } tion of. £49,2,5 }

1771—

April 1st From Anthony White this day,............	12,14,7½
May 4th Rec^d From Anthony White, this day p^r Rec^t	10
	103 8,1

From Henry Bossard by Tho⁸ Henning.............. ....   46, 1,10
                                                   _____
                                                            149, 9,11
1773
April 13 From Cap⁴ White.......................   5,11, 9
                                                   _____
                                                          £155, 1, 8
    From Merideth Hughs,........................   31, 7, 4
    From Wᵐ Pauling & Anthʸ White................   1, 2, 3
                                                   _____
                                                          £187,11, 3

Thursday 10ᵗʰ May 1770
              William Wilson   ⎫
              Elias McPherson   ⎪
              James McPherson   ⎪
              Daniel McGinney   ⎬ Vestry Men
              William Green   ⎪ William Michau ⎫ Church
              Anthony White Senʳ   ⎪ Meredith Hughs ⎭ Warden
              William Snow   ⎭

Met In the Parish Church the above date, and agreed with Thomas
Nowland To Board Mical Cary & Mary Bonnel until this Day
Twelve Months for (Finding all Nesesarys for them)...... £94
To Board Margarett Spencer for (and find her)...........   55,
                                                   _____
                                                          £149,

Likewise Assest the Parish at Viz⁴
              Slaves 12ᵈ pr head   ⎫
              Lands 12ᵈ, pr hund. Acres ⎪
    Money at Inst. 6ᵈ pr hund. Pound   ⎬
              Faculties 6ᵈ pr Facultie ⎭
                        To Raise the Sum of £203,6,3

Met In the Parish Church the 16 August 1770, and Appointed
William Wilson & Elias McPherson Vestrymen in the Room
of Thomas Woodd and John Godfrey, who were Appoᵈ at Easter
Last, and Declined Serving
Moneys Paid by James McPherson, & Thomas Woodd to Sundry
Persons Viz⁴

1770, May 16 Paid Charles Wilson on account of Mary
Bonnell this day. £15, 10
    Paid Thomas Woodd for Sundrys he bought for
Mary Bonnell. 10
August 16 Paid Anthony White Senr Pr Chas Wilsons
desire On Acc^t of M^y Bonnell. 23, 10
    Paid William Green Jn^r part of Daniel Williams
Order. 15,
October 20   Paid Charles Wilson on Account. 3, 10

                                     67, 10
    William Wilson. 80
    Richard Green. 13, 11, 3

                                    161, 1, 3

1770 Dr James Lane with Prince Fredericks Parish C^r
Augt 27 To this Sum received—1770, By p^d Mary Will^s p^r of
Th Govr £20   Rec^t. £58,
To d^o from Sundrys By p^d Moses Britton as p^r List   14, 5

                                     £72, 5

To Ball, due Ja^s Lane 37, 4, 7.
         £15, 0, 5

         £72, 5
It appears by James Lanes List that he has to Collect for ⎱
1764 & 1765 Both Sums Added Amount to (E. N. In^d) ⎰ 190, 19, 7

Anthony White Se^r ⎫
William Green Se^r |
Elias McPherson   } Vestry Men
William Wilson |
James McPherson   ⎭

Meredith Hughes/Warden

Met this 5th day of December and signed a petition to the house of
Assembly, for to have the Church, and Yard, Repair'd, with An

Estimate, of the Expence; Likewise agreed to Remove the Poor people Viz^t Micheal Carey, and Margrett Spencer from Thomas Nowland. Also Agreed to have a Jury of Inquest Caulled to take up, and View the Body of Mary Bonn[1], that dyed 3^d November Last and was buried 4 Ins^t As we have some Reasons to think that she was Ill used by said Nowland and his wife; and to have said Thomas Nowland and his Wife Letishea taken Up before a Magistret & Jury, and Examined how, and in What manner she came by her death. A true Coppy of the Estimate sent with the Petition Viz^t

Glazing & Sashing	£75,
Painting & Meterels	130,
Plastering & Materels	30,
Posts Rails & Nails for Inclosing One Acre Land and Carpenters Work	150.

£385.

6 December 1770.

The depositions of Sundry Persons, Conserning the death of Mary Bonnell, before Samuel Nesmith Esqr and the Jury Viz.

Mary Williams deposition, Is that on Saturday Morning 3^d Novr Last, she heard a Person over at Thos Nowlands House before Sun Rise Crying, O lord, O lord, murder, murder, and at same time heard Mrs Lucretia Nowland Daming and Cursing, & further she sath not—

Michael Carys deposition Is that Saturday morning 3^d Novr Last Mary Bonnell Took out the table to Scouer, and Mrs Lucretia Nowland and she was disputing, and after that Mrs Nowland fell a Crying and beg'd him to help her in with Mary Bonnell, she beleaved she was dead. And Mary Bonnell beged him when she was down for god sake to Help her in, so he & Mrs Nowland help her into the bed, she dyed Emediatly and never said any more,—

Thomas Nowlands deposition, Is that on Saturday, 3^d Novr Last he got up Early in the morning and went for beef no person up in the house but his wife when he came back his wife met him as he Ret^d from market Crying and told him Mary Bonnell was dead within, That he ask'd her how it

happened she told him that Molly Bonnell fell down and
dyed before she & Michel got her to the Bed so he went
in & felt her and she was warm, at that time he thought
She was not dead—

Lucretia Nowlands, Examination, Is that 3ᵈ Novʳ last, before Sun
Rise Mary Bonnell cared out the table to be scoured, then
she Complain'd of her Stomack, and Everything looked
dark before her Eyes, and fell down, against a post in the
peach, then She and Michael help her to the bed and said
Lucretia put on a Clean shift Emediatly and let her lye
till her husband came home

Black Mingo 8. dec 1770.

Cornelus Nelsons deposition. Is that Saturday 3ᵈ Novʳ last about
3 oclock in the Afternoon Thoˢ Nowland came down to
him to get a Coffin made for Mary Bonnell, which surprised him much, being Thursday before at said Nowlands
house & saw Mary Bonnell well and hearty and she was
then very merry a singing, he asked said Nowland what
was her Alement the said Nowlands answer, he could
not Remember particularly, but that he left her in bed
when went to market for beef & When he Retᵈ she was
dead and he saith when they ware pitting Mary Bonnell
In the Coffin he saw Two Bruised different marks on Each
arm

Hannah Nelsons deposition, Is that on Saturday 3ᵈ Novʳ last in
the afternoon Thoˢ Nowland came down to Mʳ Nelson
and said he was going to get boards of Mʳ Shackᵈ for a
Coffin then she ask'd him who was dead Nowland said
Mary Bonnell and ask'd her to go and sett up that night
along with his wife Accordingly she went, but ask'd
said Nowland before she Came from home what Alded
Mary Bonnell he told her he noed of nothing more than
a pain in her stomack that she complained of but when
he went to market left her abed, when he Returned she
was dead, Likewise saith when she got to Nowlands house
the Sun was down the next morning Mʳˢ Nowland went to
take some cloaths off of Mary Bonnell, and she went
with her, and help to put on ahand, she saw two different

Bruses on Each arm Emediatly she askd Mrs Now^d how they came her answer was she fell down in the Peach and Clasped her hands Round a post and called for help and she and Michael help her to the bed then she put a Clean Shift on her, Likewise observed a small black spot on Mary Bonnell Breast, also Mrs Nowland told her that when Michael and she carried Mary Bonnell to the bed she laid her down on it couver her up thinking she had afainty fitt on her,

Black River 10 Decr 1770

Judith Pains, deposition, Is that on Saturday 3^d Novr Last In the morning before Sun Rise, she heard a woman Cursing and Swearing over at Thos Now^d house, and a person Cry out O lord, O lord, at Same time; with that she called Benj. Will^s to lissen to the same and he called to his Mother Mary Williams to lissen to the Same Noise, and She got out of her bed and heard the same.

South Carolina ⎱ ss An Inquisition Indented, taken, at Black River
Craven County ⎰ Church, in Prince Fredericks Parish, of said County the Sixth day of dec^r Inst. In the year of our Lord One thousand seven hundred and seventy before me Samuel Nesmith Esqr for our said lord the King for the County afors^d Upon the view of the Body of Mary Bonnell there lying dead upon the Oaths of James Lane foreman Bartley Clarke, Elias M^cpherson, Richard Green, Francis Green, William Green, William Green Se^r, Francis Futhy John Glen Se^r Daniel Williams, James McPherson & John McRee, good and Lawfull men of said county who being Charged and sworn to Inquire for our said lord the King, when, where, how, and in what manner the said Mary Bonnell came to her death, do say upon their Oaths, that it appears that Mary Bonnell did dy a hasty sudden death, but it does not appear to us to be Other ways than by the hand of God by the depositions of Mary Williams, Michael Carey Thos Nowland and Lucretia Now^d Information at blk River Church, where the Corps of said Mary Bonnell Was Raised, and viewed, by us, which being in such a dead state, by lying Thirty Six days under the Earth, that we could not fully Examine nor

gain other satisfaction, but having Intelegence of Evidences ad-
jorn'd to Blk Mingo the 8. Inst. and there heard the deposition of
Cornelius Nelson & his wife Hannah, and having Inteligence of More
Evidence adjourned to blk River Church 10ᵗʰ Inst. and there heard
the Deposition of Judith Pain, which is as will appear by the
Several Depositions & Information, Reference being thereunto
had, as well I Samuel Nesmith aforesaid as the Jurys aforesaid to
this Inquisition have Interchangeably put our hands and seals the
day and year within written.

Easter Monday Apˡˡ 1ˢᵗ 1771
Met at the Parish Church, William Michau, Meredith Hughes
C. W.

Anthony White, William Wilson, Wᵐ Green, Elias Mᶜpherson,
Vesʸ

Agreed to Pay John Hambleton, for Finding James Watts
in his Sickness at his house Ten days, & Burrying and
finding coffin Sheet and Other Nesesary Extras........£27, 7, 0

By Sundry Belonging to the said Watts & sold by John ⎫
Hambleton..⎭ 6, 9,

Ballᵉ..£20, 18

Agreed to Pay William Hughes for assisting to Bury ⎫
Robert Fordice & finding nesesaries, pᵈ By Wᵐ Michau ⎭ £4, 10,

Agreed to Pay Patrick Conner for assisting to Bury ⎫
Robert Fordice, & finding Coffin...........................⎭ £5, 10,

Agreed to allow Danˡˡ Mᶜkenet for Tending Joseph
Fulcher 5 Weeks in his Sickness & finding Extras for
him, Also a Coffin & Sundries for his Burial..........£40,

Agreed to Pay Charles Wilson for Board of Mary Bon- ⎫
nell 1½ Mᵒ after Easter Monday............................⎭ £8, 12, 6

To Pay Thomas Noland for Board Mary Bonnell.... ⎫
Margaret Spencer, & Michael Cary, Seven Month at ⎬ £87, 18, 4
£149 pr Annum...⎭

To Pay George Green for the Bord of Mathew Orchard ⎫
Twelve Months to this Day ....⎭ 59,

To Pay Mary Williams for Board Margᵗ Spencer &
Michael Cary Three Month to this Day............. 45,

£271, 0, 10

Am^t Brought Down...........................·.........£271, 0, 10
To Pay William Pawling for a Coffin for Mrs Price....   5,

                                                    —————
                                                    £276, 0, 10
                                                    —————

This Feby 9th 1772 After Sermon Was Over The Rev^d Mr Villette
Solicited a Majority of the Vestry, & Wardens of This Parish to
know if Agreeable to Them—He Might Board in Geo Town A Little
while Till he Can Reconcile himself to a Country Life, Which
They Agreed to, Provided he did not Neglect The duty of his
Parish, Which he made severall Promises Not to Be Neglectfull in
any Part of his Duty Whatsoever

Easter Monday Ap^{ll} 20th 1772 Mett At the Parish Church This Day

Anthony White Junr ⎫   Anthony White Senr ⎫
William Pawlings   ⎬ Wardens   Bartley Clarke   ⎬ Vestry
                     ⎭   Elias M^{c}pherson ⎭

Gave The Revd John Villette An Order On The Public Treasurer
for Six Months Sallery.
Also Gave Capt Anthony White An Order to The Treasurer for
Forty Pounds Being The Parochal Money Due To This Parish.
The Said White Paid Peter Lane As Clerk...............£20.
        Ditto William Wilson As Regest^r.............. 5
        Ditto William McGee, as Sexton................ 5
        Ditto The New Wardens, William Pawling, And
        Anth^y White.....................................£10.
                                                    —————
                                                    £40.
                                                    —————

The Said Burns & Grace Received of Meredith Hughes
The Sum of Ten Pounds Being Part of The Parochall
Money In his hands & William MeChau, when Wardens
Fines in William Pawlings hands, Got from Thos Handlin £10
Expended by Said Pawling for the Support of Sam^{ll} Price £15,
Fines Rec^d By Anthony White Junr.................. £7, 17, 6
Ditto, By William Pawling.........................   10
                                                    —————
                                                    £8, 7, 6
                                                    —————

The Said Eight Pounds 7/6 Paid into The Hands of⎫
The New Wardens...............................⎭

Carried Forward

Easter Monday Apr[ll] 20th 1772
Agreed to Pay Doc[t] Tho[s] Wood or Order The sum of fifty Pounds
for Margaret M[c]Gegor for Board & phisick............ £ 50,
To Mary Williams for Board of Margaret Spencer and⎫
Michael Carey—12 Months.   ⎭ 144,
To George Green, for Board Mathew Orchard 12 M°.... 59,
To William Pawling for Nesesaries found Sam[ll] Price.. 15,
_____
£268,
Also to William Paulin, for Burying, Mrs Price......... 5
_____
£273

The above acc[ts] Pay'd By the Wardens Being
Anth[y] White Jun[r] & William Pawling
Daniel Fitzpatrick applyed as an object of Charity and it was
Agreed he should Seek a Place to Board at & Acq[t] The Wardens
Therewith,
Then Proceeded to Ellection of Parish Officers, When The Fol-
lowing Ware Choose

John Burns ⎫ Wardens   Anthony White Sen[r] ⎫
William Grace ⎭   William Wilson |
                             William Pawling |
                             Bartley Clarke   ⎬ Vestry
Theodore Gordine ⎫ Over-   William Snow |
Moses Brown   ⎬ seers   AnthonyMar[n] White |
William Forrister ⎭   Anthony White Jun[r] ⎭

William Wilson Reg[y]
William M[c]Gee Sexton
Tho[s] Wood Clark

Rated the Parish in the Manner following To Raise the⎫ £273.
Sum of.......................................⎭

Slaves at 1/3 p[r] head
Lands 1/3 p[r] C[t].
Money at Interest ⎫ 7[d]1/2 p[r] C[t]
and Faculties   ⎭

Gave the Revd John Villette An Order for Six Month Sallery
Gave the Revd John Villette An Order for Seven Weeks Sallery
due him This 7th June 1772.
Wrote a Letter This 7th June To Mr John Mitchell To Know If
he's Acqt^d With The Revd William Miller's Character and The
Said Revd William Miller is to Act as Minister of The Parish
during the Pleasure of The Vestry.

At a Meeting of the Vestry The 15th July They discharged The
Rev^d Mr Miller On Acc^t of Some Infamous Behavior of his &
Gave him an Order on the Publick Treasurer for The time he
Preached And also Wrote Mr Cansor An Answer to his Letter
Concerning Mathew Orchard That if he The Said Cansor Would
pay The Wardens The fines in his hands That belonged to The
Parish & Be Orchard's Security That He Will Go To The North-
ward As he Purposes & Not Be any further Trouble to The Parish
They Would Agree to Give him Twenty Pounds As he desires
This 2^d Novr A Majority of Vestry & Wardens present Jacob
Otmer applyed for The Benefit of The Parish as an Object & Was
Received.

This 20th Feby 1773 Gave The Revd Mr James Stewart An Order
On The Publick Treasurere.

At a Meeting of the Vestry & Wardens This 12th Ap^{ll} 1773 Being
Easter Monday

Present　　Anthony White Senr
　　　　　Anthony Marⁿ White
　　　　　Anthony White Junr　⎬　Vestry
　　　　　·William Wilson　　　　　　William Grace　Warden
　　　　　William Pawling

Mary Williams Rendered her Acc^t for Board & Nesesaries found
Michael Cary, & Margaret Spencer 12 Month..£170
　　　Surpulos Money Rec^d of Meredith Hughes......... £31, 7, 4
and paid to James M^cpherson & Thos Wood, Also
By William Pawling & Anthony White Being the Ball^e
due them.. £ 1, 2, 3
　　　As Wardens for Parish Expece.................. £32, 9, 7

Still to Receive On Meredith Hughes List............ £31,
Still to Receive on W. Pawlings & A. White List...... 62, 9, 11
Money in the Hands of W. Pauling, & A. White for Fines   25, 15,
    Paid William Grace By A. White................. £15, 15,
Rec^d from Doc^r Cantzon By Benj^a Screven fines Paid⎱ 40,
    William Grace.................................⎰
Cash Paid By Anthony White Junr to William Westbury
Out of The Parochal Money in his hands for the Re-
pairs of the Church Steps,........................... £3. 5–
Paid William Grace The Ball^e in his hands............ £6, 15
William Grace to Pay Thos Johnston for the Board of ⎱ £71.
Sam^{ll} Price 2 Months, Which is added in his acc^t.......⎰
William Grace Rec^d Alms Money Amt^a to............ £5,
The Expence for The Sacrament.................... 3, 5

This Ball^e Grace is to Give to The Needy............ £2, 12, 6

William Grace Paid for hoeing^s Round The Gleeb.... 35/—

Aprill 22th 1773 Being Easter Monday—
William Grace and John Burns Paid Mary Williams acc^t £170
Paid Thos Johnston for Board Sam^{ll} Price, 2 M^o........   7,
Paid Mathew Orchard By The desire of the Vestry......   10.
Sundrys to Mrs Boshear............................   2–6–3

£189, 6, 3

By Cash Rec^d in Part By William Grace for fines.... £ 54, 10
Gave Capt White the Parochal Order............... £ 40,
Paid Thos Wood/Clark £20, ditto W. Wilson/Reg^r £5,⎱ 30,
and William McGee/Sexton £5.....................⎰
Application Being made By William Forester On The Behalf of
Mary McElroy A Poor Widow, Agreed to Make her Some Allow-
ance to Support her & 4 Children.
Application Being Made By Elezabeth Bosher for Some Relief
from The Parish in her Present situation, Tis agreed That She go
to M^{rs} McDowell in Order to Cure her & That Some Suitable
Cloath Be Bought By The Wardens for her Also her Mother to
be Assisted in her Present Indisposition.

Sam^{ll} Price Taken On The Parish
Proceeded to Ellection of Parish Officers When the following was Ellected

Anthony White Senr
Anthony White Junr
Anthony Marⁿ White
William Wilson
William Grace
Thos Wood
John McDowell
} Vestry

John Glen Junr
Wilson Wilson
} C. Wardens

William Wilson Reg^r &
Sexton
Thos Wood, Clerk

Apr^{ll} 23^d 1773
Agreed with William Craps to Board Sam^{ll} Price & finde all Nesessarys 12 M° for....................... £60,
William Craps agrees to Take Michael Carey Twelve Months and furnish him with all Nesesries for........ £70,
from this 8th of May—
Mary Williams agrees to take Margaret Spencer for } £75,
Twelve Month from Easter, finding all Necessaries for }
Mary Williams to Be Paid from Easter Monday, to The eight May For Michael Carey at the Rates she had Him Last Year............................. £3, 10

————————
£78, 10
————————

This 1th Sepr 1773 Jacob Otnevan Object of Charrity Taken on The Parish, & agreed with William Craps to Board & finde him With all Nesessaries Till Easter Monday at £50 p^r Year
Gave The Revd James Stuart An Order on the Publick Treasurer, for Officiateing Six Sundays in Our Parish Church Feby 28th 1774
The Parish debt to be Paid by Wm Grace & John Burns £189, 6, 3
For fines in Wm Grace Hands.................. £54, 10
Tax Rec^d By William Wilson & Paid W. Grace. £66– 2–9
Fines Rec^d By Doc^r Cantzon & Paid W. Grace.. 40
Tax Rec^d by Wm Pawling & Paid to Wm Grace
Being the Surplus of his Collection.......... 7–15–
ditto By Anth^y White Junr & Paid W. Grace... 20–18–6

————————
£189– 6–3
————————

At Meeting of the Vestry & Wardens this 4th Apr^{ll} 1774 Being Easter Monday—

Present   Anth^y White Senr
Anth^y White Junr   Wilson Wilson   Warden
Thos Wood
John McDowell   Vestry
William Wilson
William Grace

Cash Rec^d of Meredith Hughes The Ball^e of his Surpulis Money of Poor Tax, £4, 17, 6 Paid into the hands of Wilson Wilson, In part defray the Expense he was at As Warden........£4, 17, 6

To Pay Mary Williams for the Board of Margaret Spencer Twelve Months } Paid £75,

To Pay ditto for Board of Michael Cary from Easter to the 17th Ap^{ll} Being Two Weeks at £85 p^r Y^r } Paid 3, 15,

To William Craps for Board of Michael Carey from 17th Ap^{ll} 1773 to This day Being 11 M^o & 2 Weeks £70 p^r Year } ..64, 3, 9

To William Craps for Board of Sam^{ll} Price from the 23^d Ap^{ll} to this 4th Ap^{ll} Being 11 M^o 3 Weeks at £60 } ..57, 10,

To ditto for Board Jacob Otner from 1st Sept to the 4tth Ap^{ll} Being 7 M^o at £50 p^r Y^r .... } 29, 4, 6

To Pay M^{rs} McDowell for 2 M^o Board & Care made of Elizibeth Boshere } . 15,

To Pay Mary Williams for Burying one Weak and Some Troble of him in Sickness Paid } Paid 10,

To Pay William Wilson for 3 Yards Irish Linnen at 13/9 and 6 Yards Oznb^s at 5/ for Elezabeth Boshare } .. 3, 11, 3

To Pay Anthony White for 10 Yards Oznab^s at 5/ and Thread 3/9 for Elizibeth Boshare } Paid . 2, 13, 9

To Pay John Hambleton for Sundrys to Bury Thos Brown/a Coffin and Nursing him in Sickness he Agrees to Take p^d By W. W } Paid 5,

To Pay Thos Wood for Phisick for Thos Brown, p^d By W   5,

To Pay William Pawling for Sundreys found M^{rs}⎫
Boshere and Coffin & Burying her   ⎭ Paid   10.

£280, 18,3
Carried Over

Amount of Charges Br^t Over........................£280, 18, 3
Allowed the Widow McElroy, to Assist her, & 4 Chil-
dren twelve Month, Including Two Cows & Calves
Baught for her By Moses Brown and William Forester 100,

Last Years Expense........................£380, 18, 3
For Standing Fund........................ 20,

£400, 18, 3

The Ball^e of Parochal Money in the hands of William Grace
Rec^d of Anth^y White Junr Being Five Pounds Paid to Wilson
Wilson also the Ball^e of Last Years Parochal Order in the hands
of Anth^y White Senr Being £10 Paid to Wilson Wilson—
Gave Anthony White Senr An Order on the Publick Treasurer,
for the Parochal Money Being....................... £40,

To Pay Thos Wood as Cleark F By A W..............£20,
To Pay William Wilson as Reg^r & Sexton Paid by A. W. 10

30

The Ball^s of Fines in William Pawlings hands to be Paid to Wilson
Wilson Being £10
Also in the hands of William Wilson collected from the Defaulters
£1–11–9.
The above £10, in Wm Pawlings hands, discounted by Wilson Wilson
With Said Pawling, In Payment of his Demand, Against the Parish
and the Rest Paid, to those who have demands Against the Parish,
as Entered Above, and On the Other Side—
Then Proceeded to Election When the Under mentioned Persons
was Elected as Parish officers,

William Barton ⎫ C. Wardens   Thos Wood   Clark
William Snow ⎭   Wm Wilson Reg^r & Sexton

Anthony White Senr ⎫
Anthony White Junr |
William Grace |
John McDowell   ⎬ Vestry
William Wilson |
Wilson Wilson |
Thos Wood   ⎭

The Parish Asses'd at the Undermentioned Rates, to Raise the
Sum of £400, 18, 3,
          Lands & Slaves at 2/ p^r head & C^t
          Money at Int^s and Faculties 1/ p^r C^t.
Overseers Oppointed for the Parish, Wm Michau, Robert
McCawtrey William Gambell, & John Fitzjarrel—
Mary Williams agrees to Keep Margaret Spencer, Twelve
M^o, finding her all nesessaries, for £65,
John Goudge agrees to Keep Michael Cary at £65 pr Year
finding him all Nesessaries, Commencing from the 8th May
Charles Wilson Agrees to Keep Sam^ll Price at £50 finding
him all Nesessaries Commencing from 21st May—
William Craps, to be Paid for Board Michael Cary, from 4th Ap^ll
to the 8th May, Being One M^o 4 days at £70 p^r annum, £6, 18, 6
ditto, for Board Sam^ll Price, from 4th Ap^ll, to 21st May
Being 1 M^o 17 days at £60 p^r annum................. £7, 15, 6
                                                       ──────────
                                                       £14, 14, 0
Gave the Revd Mr Stewart an Order for Six Times Preaching in
Our Church 10th Feby 1775
Also Wrote the Bishop of London A Letter Relating to Sending
us a Minister

Easter Monday 17th Ap^ll 1775
                Present
     Anthony White Senr ⎫   William Barton ⎫ C. W.
     John M^cdowell | William Snow   ⎭
     William Wilson   ⎬ Vestry
     Wilson Wilson |
     William Grace   ⎭

Mary Williams Charge for Board Margaret Spencer
—Paid by W. B. } £65,

Charles Wilson's for Board Sam^{ll} Price, from 21st May
to this Day, at £50 p^r Year, Paid By W. B. } . .45,16, 8

John Goudge's Ditto, for Board Michael Carey, from the
8th May to this Day £65, p^r Year, Paid By W. B. 63, 15

William Craps for Board Michael Cary and Sam^{ll} Price
from Easter Last to the Time they went from him
to Wilson and Goudge at £130 p^r Year Paid William
Wilson By W. B. } . 14, 14,

Joseph Scotts Aco^t for Makeing 2 Coffins } £9, 14 The
to Bury two of M^{rs} McCleroy's 6 Chil- } Ball^e
dren, Paid to John Knox. } pd Craps   8,

                               £197, 5, 8

deduct Fines in the hands of Wm Snow and William
Barton. 4, 19, 3

                               £192, 6, 5
Add for a Standing Fund. 20, 0, 0

                               £212, 6, 5

The Ball^e Parochal Money in the hands Capt White. . . . £10,
Gave Capt White the Parochal Order. 40,

                               £50,

He pays Robert Davidson for makeing Two Window
Shutters & Bringing them to the Church and putting
them up. } . .£9,

he Pays William Wilson for Cutting down the Bushes
and Cleaning the Church Yard. } . . .2,

he Pays Doc^r Wood for Acting as Clark to Our Church
a Y^r. 20,
Ditto William Wilson as Reg^r & Sexton 10,

                               £41,
Ball^e Parochall Money in Cap^r White hands. 9,

                               £50,

The Parish Assest to Raise the Sum of £212, 6, 5
At the Undermentioned Rates
Slaves p^r head & Lands pr C. 1/3
Stock in Trade & Faculty p^r C^t pence 7½
Then Proceeded to Election When the Undermentioned Persons
was Elected

Thos North ⎱
Charles Fyffe ⎰ C. Wardens

Anthony White Senr ⎱
William Wilson
William Barton
John McDowell   ⎰ Vestry
William Pawling
William Snow
William Grace

William Wilson   Reg^r &
Sexton

W^m McCawtrey, Peter Lequex ⎱ Overseers
and Hugh Giles   ⎰

The second July 1775 Jacob Otner Taken on the Parish—
Gave the Revd Mr Stewart an Order on the Treasury for Preaching
Six Sundays in Our Parish Church dec^r 15th 1775—

Sam^{ll} Price Buried 1st January 1776—

This 8th Ap^{ll} 1776 Being Easter Monday
Present
Thos North C. W.

Anth^y White Senr
William Wilson
William Barton
John McDowell
William Snow

William Barton Pays this Day out of his Collection, Besides Pay-
ing John Goudge and Mary Williams and Chas Wilson & W^m
Craps & Joseph Scott £26, 2—William Snow pay £25, 16, 3 &
Great Part of his List to Collect
Chas Wilson Acc^t for Board of Sam^{ll} Price from Easter
Last to 1 January & Burying him Paid By T. North.. £ 43, 9, 2
Mary Williams Acc^t for Board Margaret Spencer 12
M^o Paid By T N.............................. 65,
John. Goudge Acc^t for Board Michael Carey 12 M^o
Paid T. N.. 65,

Richard Green Acc* for Board Jacob Otner from 27th
July to this day at £40 p* Year, Paid by Th* N 31, 17, 6
William Gambell for Board of Benjamin Gilbart 12
M° Paid T. North..................................   45,

                                       £250, 6, 8
For Standing Fund   20,

Carried Over................................... £270, 6, 8

Ap¹¹ 8th 1776

The Charge of the Parish Braugh Over............ £270, 6, 8
Deduct Cash in Tho* Norths hands Part of Fine from
John Hambleton.................................   2, 10

                                       £267, 16, 8
To Pay Tho* North for a Coffin to Bury Peter Hughes   5,

                                       £272, 16, 8
Deduct Cash Paid by Peter Lequex A fine for not ⎫
Acting as Overseer When Legally Oppointed Paid ⎬   10, ...
into the hands of Tho* North.................... ⎭

                                       £262, 16, 8
Cash Pa:d Out of the Surpules Renderd by Wᵐ Barton
& Wᵐ Snow to Mary M°Cleroy to assist in the Minte-
nance of her Poor Children £39, 2.
     Deduct the Other Part Surpelus Paid Tho* North   12,

                                       £250, 16, 8

Agreed to allow William Jones a poore Man up Pedee
the Sum of Twenty Pounds Provided he is in this
Parish
William Newman Oppointed Overseer in the Room
Peter Lequex He Paying his fine
     Gave William Wilson the Parochal Order..... ⎫ £ 40,
The Ballˢ Parochal Money in Capᵗ White hands... ⎰   9

To Pay W[.]lliam Wilson as Reg^r.....................   5,

To Ditto as Sexton.............................   5,

To Ditto for Cleaning the Church Yard, and hoeing
& Securing them from Fire.......................}   3,

$$£ \ 13,$$

Deduct th's Sum out of the Parochal Order
Given W. Wilson and the Ball^s £27 In his Hands
The Parish Asses^t at the Undermentioned Rates to Raise the
Sum of £250, 16, 8
  Lands p^r C^t and Slaves p^r head 1/3
  Stock in Trade & Faculty 7½ p^r C^t

Easter Monday Ap^{ll} 8th 1776
Then Proceeded to Ellection When the undermentioned Persons
was Choose

   Anthony White Senr]   William Shepherd }
   Anthony White Junr]   John Futhy   } Wardens
   John McDowell
   William Barton   } Vestry
   Will am Pawling
   William Wilson
   Thos North

Overseers/ John Hambleton, Hugh Giles, Paul Michau
William Wilson   Register & Sexton
Gave The Revd James Stewart an Order On the Publick for
Offitiating five Sundays in this Parish, Church this Y^r

Easter Monday Being 31st March 1777 Present,
 William Shepherd } Ch.   John McDowell,   }
 John Futhy   } Wardens Anthony White   }
          Anthony White Junr   }
          William Barton   } Vestry
          William Wilson   }
          Thos North   }
          William Pawling   }

Tho⁵ North Accᵗ for 2 Coffins To Bury Peter Hughes Children £5	£5
Mary Williams for Board of Margaret Spencer Paid by W Shepherd................................	65,
Richard Green for Board Jacob Otner Paid By W. Shepherd, £40................................	50,
Mʳˢ Coles ditto for Board Michael Carey Paid By J. Futhy..	67, 10
George White, for Board Benjamin Gilbert Paid By W. Shepherd from the 1ˢᵗ Augˢᵗ Last at The Rate £60, Yʳ To The 1ˢᵗ March	40
	£227, 10

Surpulas Money Collected By William Snow, and William Barton Paid into William Shepherds hands	28, ...
Fines in Shepherds hands..........................	11,
ditto of William Snow a Fine for not Meeting the Commissioners Paid William Shepherd for the Use of the Poor..	10,
	£ 49,

Easter Monday 31ˢᵗ March 1777	
The Charge of the Parish brought Forward........	£227, 10
Robert Cox accᵗ for Board Docᵗ Wood's Childs, 6 Mᵒ.	30,
	£257, 10
Paid By W. Shepherd, £25, 10	
Deduct the Money Paid into Wm Shepherds Hands As The Other Side.	49,
	£208, 10
Pay William Jones as Allowed Last Easter, Paid By W. Shepherd..	20,
	£228, 10,
Pay Mary McCleroy for the Support of her Family Paid by W Shepherd..............................	30,
Carried Below....................................	£258, 10,

The Ball⁸ Parochal Money in Capᵗ Whites Hands
Brought Forward.......................... £ 9,
ditto in William Wilson's................... 27,

_____

£36,

To Pay William Wilson, As Regʳ & Sexton.......... £ 10,
ditto for Cleaning & Burning Round the Parsonage 20/   1,

_____

£ 11,

Deduct this Sum Out of the Parochal Money
In William Wilson's Hands, The Ball⁸.............. £ 16,
Jannet Campbell a Poor Girl at Richard Rennalds
This Day Taken On the Parish—
The Parish Asses⁴ at the Undermentioned Rates to
Raise this Sum.................................. £258, 10
    As a Standing Fund...........................£ 20,

_____

£278, 10

    Slaves at 1/3 pʳ head & Land pʳ Cᵗ 1/3, Money at
Int⁸ 7½ & Faculty at 7½ pʳ Cᵗ
Amᵗ Braught from above.........................£258, 10
Add the funirall Expence of Benjamin Gilbert Paid
By Wᵐ Shepherd to Geo. White....................   9,

_____

£267, 10

Deduct for Sundrys Sold By Geo. White the
Property of Benjamin Gilbert Setled with W. Shepherd £ 30, 3, 1
Poor Tax, Recᵈ By William Shepherd and Paid as
above... £258, 18, 1
Ditto Recd By John Futhy, And Paid as above...... 60,

_____

£318, 18, 1

Then Proceed to Election of Parish officers When the Undermentioned Ware Elected

Richard Green ⎫ C. W.	William Pawling ⎫
Fraˢ Green ⎭	Anthony White
	William Shepheard
	Anthʸ White Junʳ ⎬ Vestry
Regʳ William Wilson	William Barton
Sexton Thoˢ North	John McDowell
	William Wilson ⎭

Overseers { Fra⁸ Britton
              Alex M⁰Crea
              Isaac Macheau

This 27ᵗʰ Sepʳ 1777 Mett at the Parish Church

Richard Green } C. W.   Anthony White   }
Fra⁸ Green   }   John M⁰dowell   }
                          William Barton } Vestry
                          William Pawling }
                          William Wilson }

Complaint Made That The Widow Hughes A Poor Woman Liveing Near The Church was a Starving She and Cheldren Agreed this Day That the Wardens Take the Two Bigest Children and Put Them Out Apprentices in Creditable houses, and that the Widow Go to Work to Maintain herself & Young Child as she is verry Able & A Great deel of Spinning offerd her

Easter Monday Apˡˡ 20ᵗʰ 1778

Present

Richard Green } C.   Anth⁷ White   }
Fra⁸ Green   } Wardens   Wᵐ Pawling   }
                          Wᵐ Shepherd   }
                          Anth⁷ White Junʳ   } Vestry
                          Wᵐ Barton   }
                          John M⁰Dowell   }
                          Wᵐ Wilson   }

Richard Rennels Acc⁺ for Board &c Jane Campbell }
10 Months & 20 days at £5 M⁰ .... } £53, 6, 8
Mary Williams Acc⁺ for Board &c of Margaret Spencer 80,
Charles Wilson ditto for Board &c for Jacob Otner.... 60,
Hannah Cails ditto for Board &c for Michael Carey... 80,
allowed Mʳˢ M⁰Cleroy for the Support of her family... 50,
allowed Wᵐ Jones to assist him in his Support........ 40,
Two Parochal Orders Given W. Wilson for This & Last

Yr £80. .... 383, 6,8
To Pay William Wilson as Regʳ £5, Standing Fund
To Pay Tho⁸ North Sexton £5. 20,

£383, 6, 8

The Parish asses^t at 1/3 p^r head 0 1/3 p^r hund. Acres Land
Money at Int 7½ p^r hundred pound & Faculty
To Raise the Above Am^t
Then Proceeded to Election, When the Under Mentioned Persons
ware Elected as Parish Officers

C. Wardens { James Snow   Richard Green
            { George Stellings   Anth^y White
                                  William Barton
                                  John McDowell   } Vestry
                                  Fra^s Green
                                  William Shepherd
      Thos North Reg^r &   Thos North
          Sexton
      Benjamin Duke
      William Gambell } Overseers
      Thos Potts

Easter Monday April 5th 1779

                         Present
                              Anthony White Junr
Geo Stelling   C. Warden   William Barton
                              Richard Green   } Vestry
                              William Shepard
                              Francis Green

Mary Williams Acc^t for Board &c of Marg^t Spencer... £160,
Charles Wilsons d^o d^o Jacob Otner.................. 120,
Thos McCullough d^o d^o Mich^l Carey............... 175,
Allow^d William Jones to assist him in his Support..... 60,
                                                         ————
                                                         £515,

A Petition in Regard of Margaret Martin was given in this day
it is desired the Church Wardens to Write to her Brother John
McKelvaine & his son informing them if they does not Maintain
her himself She will be taken away from them & Boarded at their
Expence, agreeable to a Law provided For that Acc^t

The Parish assest at 1/3 p^r head & 1/3 p^r hun^d Acres Land Money
at Interest 7½ p^r Hundred Pound & Faculty the Same for Every
hundred pound

Then Proceeded to Election When the Undermentioned Persons where Elected as parish officers

Will: Davidson } C. Wardens

Will: Grace

Will: Shepard ⎫
Francis Green ⎪
Richard Green ⎪
James Snow ⎬ Vestry
A. White Junr ⎪
Jn° McDowell ⎪
Thos North ⎭

Thos North Register & Sexton }

Will: Hamilton ⎫
Jn° Potts ⎬ Overseers
Paul Macheau ⎭

Att a Meeting of the Vestry 20th of May 1779

Present

John McDowell ⎫
Richd Green ⎪
Francis Green ⎬ Vestry
Anth^y White ⎪
Thos North ⎭

William Grace ⎫
William Davidson ⎬ Church Wardens

Agreed that Margeret Marten shud be allowed £10, pounds p^r Week for hir Maintanence & Cloathing at the Expence of John McNight hir Son

[End of second part of Parish Records found in Book 1756–1779]

PAPERS LOOSE IN THE REGISTER OF PRINCE FREDERICKS PARISH BOOK—UNDATED.

Cash Paid Capt White for R^d Smith..............	£ 30
ditto Moses Britton.........................	40
ditto William Bruce.........................	3, 10
ditto Elezabeth Scott.......................	65, 10, 71/2
ditto Capt White for Smith....................	30
ditto John McDowell.........................	4, 2,
ditto Mary Williams.........................	72, 17, 9
ditto Moses Britton.........................	40,
	£286, —, 41/2
ditto to Mary Williams.......................	71, 11, 71/2
	£337, 13

James M^cpherson
Thos Woodd } Ch. Wardens   40,
36, 8, 6

John Godfrey
Bartley Clark
Wm Green Senr
Anth^y White Junr } Vestry   3, 11, 6
Willm Wilson
John Burns
John Glen Senr

Reg^t
    William Wilson
Sexⁿ
    Danl MeGinny

Dr Mr Henry Bossard Junior In Account Current With Prince Fredricks Parish

1764 To this Amount of Poor Tax Received for the Use of the Poor..................... }	102, 14, 6
To Cash Received of the Communacants...	5, 2

To Cash Received of the Parochall Order..   20,

To Cash Received of Bartley Clarke Being ⎱
Surpleluss Money in his Hands......... ⎰   36, 8, 6

To this Amount of Poor Tax.............   186, 4, 4

To Cash of Francis Britton, he Collected...   17, 14, 3

To Cash of John Ervin, he Collected......   36, 19,

To this Sum as appears he received by his ⎱
List from Sundry Persons.............. ⎰   9, 8, 3 1/2

                               414. 10, 10 1/2

1766   C^r

By this Sum Paid to Anthony
White......................30,

By this Sum Paid to Moses Britton 40,

By this Sum Paid to William ⎱
   Wilson the New Warden, ⎰ 5, 2,
   Being the Communion Mon..

By this Sum Paid John Wagenfeld 5,

By this Sum Paid James Lane.....5,

By this Sum Paid William Barton 5,   90, 2

By this Sum Paid William Bruce. 3, 10

1767   By this Sum Paid Elezabeth Scott 65, 10, 7 1/2

By this Sum Paid Anthony White 30,

By this Sum Paid Jn° McDowl..   4, 2

By this Sum Paid Mary Williams 72, 17, 9

By this Sum Paid Anthony White   5,

By this Sum Paid Moses Britton 25, 15

By this Sum Paid Mary Williams 71, 11, 7 1/2   278, 07—

                                   368–9—

By a Ballance in favour Prince Fredericks
Parish, due from Henry Bossard p^r Book.... 46 –1–10 1/2

1770 Mr Henry Bossard Junr To Prince Frederick
Parish.................................... £414–10–10 1/2

Aug 27 To A Ballance due to Parish £46–1–10

The Church Wardens of Prince Fredricks Praish to
Aaron Baker Dr,
1769
March 14 To 5 Days Attendance on Tho^{mas} Sewellon
              of the Poor of Said Parish when on his Death
              Bed @ 10/............................. £2, 10,
              To Sheet 40/ A Coffin 50/ Burying 50/.....   7,
                                                       ──────────
                                                       £9, 10

Revd Mr Villette from England 1771 It appears after a Request
to live in Geo Town, & officiate at Prince frederick Ch, Returned
to England 1772.

Mr William Barton,   Dr
1775   to Robert Davidson
February 4 To a Large Pair of Window Shutters for   £
              Black River Church, taking them to the Spot
              and Putting in &c.........................   9

Rec^d 17th Ap^{ll} 1775 of Capt Anth^y White The Sum of Nine pounds
in full of this Acc^t
                                        Robt Davidson

William Shepard
          To Prince Fredricks Parish Dr
1776   As Warden for the Year 1776
Apr^l 8   To Cash Rec^d from the Board Commissioner^s⎫ 6.......
              being part of Fines from the Roads......⎭
Aug. 5   To ditto ditto............................   5.......
   1777
March 31   To Cash Rec^d of the Vestry..........   38,........
   1778
Ap^l 20   To Cash Rec^d of Sundries pr Bill Ren^d
              for ther Poor Tax for Said Year 1776.... 159, 15, 3 3/4
                                                       ──────────────
                                                       £208, 15, 33/4
          To Rec^d Geo White for Sund^s sold
          belong. to Est. Benj. Gilbert............   30, 3, 1
                                                       ──────────────
                                                       238, 18, 43/4

1777   Cr
March 31   By Paid M^rs McKelroy p^r rec^t........   £30,
           ditto Robert Cox, pr ditto £25, 10,

316, 10	238.18.13/4
298, 18, 1, 3/4	60,

[A fragment]   17, 11, 101/4   298, 18,13/4

A Request forwarded to Charleston, to request the Lecturer of
St Philip's to Preach in Prince Frederick Parish
[A fragment]

State of South Carolina formerly Prinče George's Parish,
To the Church Wardens of this Parish
This is to Certifie that We the Subscribers do know that Margret
Marten is redueced to Want and Poverty by Reason of the disorder
of the Polsey & is uncapable of doing aneything for hir Sealf, &
now Stands much in Need of Sum Sisteance from the publick as a
Parishener as She has been aliver in this State upward of thirty
Years & has been of good behaver & of good repetion in the Nebour-
hood, whare She lived So it is to be hoped you will take it in to
Consideration the deplorable state She is now in given under our
handes this twenty first day of January 1778
                    James McCollough
                    Andrew Patterson
                    John Jones
                    William Scott
                    William Cooper
                    James Daniel
                    George McCutehin
                    John Scott,
                    Thos McConnell
                    Alex^r MCra sener
                    Wm Miller
                    William Dobien
                    Wm Hamilton

INDEX

Abner, Mary, 51.
Acadians, The, 141–143.
Allein, Mary, 53.
Allen, Joseph, 4, 5.
    Joseph (b. 1730), 5, 55.
    Susannah, Mrs., 4, 5.
    Susannah (bapt. 1727), 4.
Allston, Hester, Mrs., 6.
    John, 6.
    Mary, Mrs., 47 (2).
    Peter, 47 (2).
    Peter (b. 1770), 47.
    Samuel, 47.
    William, 6.
Andree, John, 100.
Andres, John, 59.
Andrews, John, Rev., 105, 149, 152, 156.
Arrino, John, 56.
Atkins, George, 171.
Atkinson, Anthony, 4, 57 (2), 59, 63–94.
    Elizabeth, 54.
    George (b. 1725), 4, 28, 29, 56, 110–149.
    George (b. 1754), 29.
    Hannah, 28.
    Jane, 57.
    Mary, Mrs., 4, 57 (2).
    Mary (Stuart), Mrs., 28, 29.
    Mary (b. 1750), 28.
Atnor, Sarah, 55.
Avant, Aaron, 4.
    Agnes, 4.
    Ann (Brunston), Mrs., 13.
    Ann (b. 1742), 13.
    Anna, 19.
    Benjamin, 4, 6, 9, 13, 52.
    Benjamin (b. 1736), 6.
    Caleb, 3, 4, 79, 91.
    Francis, 3, 19, 23, 27, 29, 53, 64–124.
    Francis (b. 1752), 29.
    Hannah, Mrs., 3 (5), 58.
    Hannah (b. 1737), 9.
    Hannah (b. 1725), 3.
    Hannah (b. 1749), 27.
    John, 3 (5), 58, 64–104.
    Katherine, 56.

Avant—*Continued.*
    Lydia, 3, 52.
    Mary, Mrs., wife of Benjamin, 4, 6, 9.
    Mary, Mrs., wife of Caleb, 3, 4.
    Persis, 55.
    Rebecca, 3.
    Sarah Wigfall (Thompson), Mrs., 19, 23, 27, 29.
    Sarah Wigfall (b. 1746), 23.
Bail, Joseph, 71.
Baird, Archibald, 147.
Baker, Aaron, 225.
    Elizabeth, 53.
Ball, Bartholomew, 6, 21.
    Bartholomew (b. 1736), 6.
    Edward, 21.
    Elizabeth, Mrs., 6, 21.
    Elizabeth (b. 1723), 11, 53.
    Mercy, Mrs., 11.
    Robert, 11.
    Stephen, 54.
Ballantine, Catherine, 12.
    Eleoner, Mrs., 12.
    William, 12.
Barns, John, 28.
    Mary, Mrs., 28.
    Mary (b. 1752), 28.
Barton, Elizabeth, Mrs., 7.
    Esther, 49.
    Hannah, 29.
    Hester, 16.
    Honora (Bonnell), Mrs., 13.
    Honora (b. 1742), 13.
    Jane, Mrs., 48 (2), 49 (4).
    Jane (b. 1784), 49.
    John, 7, 13, 52, 82, 92.
    John (b. 1736), 7.
    Joanna, 8.
    Mary, Mrs., wife of William, 8, 10, 16, 25, 29, 45.
    Mary Ann, 49.
    Sarah, Mrs., wife of William, 49.
    Sarah (b. 1741), 10.
    Sarah (b. 1775), 48.
    Sarah (b. 1776), 48.
    William, 8, 10, 16, 25, 29, 45, 108–225.
    William (b. 1781), 4 9(2).

Brown—*Continued*.
Alpheus, 44.
Catherine, 41.
Elizabeth, 5, 52.
Frances, 5, 54.
Geofry, 41 (3), 55.
Godfrey, 55.
Hannah, Mrs., 6, 50.
Hannah (b. 1727), 6, 54.
Hannah (b. 1748), 25.
Hester, Mrs., 13, 17, 23, 25.
Hester (b. 1741), 13.
Hester (b. 1746), 23.
James, 6.
James (b. 1728), 23.
James (Capt.), 57.
Jane, 17.
John, 79–92.
Jonathan, 5 (2), 6, 55, 65, 67, 68.
Jonathan (b. 1731), 6.
Margaret, Mrs., 5 (2), 6.
Martha, 47.
Mary (b. 1746), 23.
Mary, Mrs., 23 (2), 25, 58, 158, 163.
Messer, 41.
Moses, sen., 198, 207, 212.
Rachel (Burkitt), Mrs., 41 (3).
Rebecca (b. 1746), 41.
Rebecca, 52.
Samuel, 23.
Sarah, Mrs., wife of Samuel, 23.
Sarah, Mrs., wife of Abraham, 44 (3).
Sarah (b. 1747), 25.
Thomas, 211.
William, 13, 17, 23, 25, 58.
Zacheus, 44.
Bruce, Ann, 52.
William, 185, 189, 223, 224.
Brunson, Abigail, 4, 55.
Ann, 52.
Anne, Mrs., 4, 57.
Benjamin, 25.
John, 4, 53, 57.
John, jun., 25.
Mary, Mrs., 25.
Bryan, John, 55, 56, 167.
Buckel (Buckells)
Abraham, 34.
Elizabeth, Mrs. 34.
Mary, 34 (b. 1753).
Mary, 55.
Buckholts, Elizabeth, 7, 51.
Bull, William, Gov., 185.

Burdell, Elisabeth, 26.
John, 54.
Margaret (Wright), Mrs., 26.
Mary (Lieubray), Mrs., 17, 24.
Sarah, 17.
Thomas, 17, 24, 26, 53.
Thomas (b. 1746), 24.
Burkitt (Burkett), Mary, 56.
Rachel, 55.
Burnett, Andrew, Dr., 142, 179, 181, 185.
Burns, John, 195–223.
Burrows, George, 198.
Burtley, Margaret, 8.
Richard, 8 (2).
Sarah, Mrs., 8 (2).
Sarah (b. 1735), 8.
Burton, Jacob, 174.
Butler, Abigail (Mrs.), 1, 4 (2), 50.
Bartholomew, 2.
Christopher, 1, 4(2).
Christopher (b. 1734), 1.
Edward, 2.
Edward, 52.
Henrietta, 4.
Mary, Mrs., 2.
Samuel, Capt., 4, 127, 130.
Buxton, Ann, Mrs., 31, 37.
George, 37.
Samuel, jun., 31, 37.
Sarah, 31.

Cails, Hannah, 220.
Cain, Ann (Power), Mrs., 8, 10, 11, 23.
Hannah, 11.
John, 8, 10, 11, 23, 51.
John (b. 1738), 8.
Mary Hannah, 23.
Sarah, 10.
Campbell, Anne, Mrs., 56.
Alexander, 31 (2).
Dougal, 111.
James, 56.
Jannet, 219, 220.
John, 31.
Mary, 31.
Priscilla, Mrs., 31 (2).
Cansor, Mr., 208.
Cantey, Ann, Mrs., 13 (3).
Elizabeth, Mrs. 39 (3), 51.
George, 39.
Jane, 13.
John, 38 (2).

Jones—*Continued.*
  Priscilla, 34.
  Richard, 35.
  Sarah, Mrs., 37.
  Susanna, 34.
  Thaieth (?), 37.
  William, 216–221.
Jordan, Abraham, 136.
  Margaret, 136.
Joulee, James, 46.
  Mary, Mrs., 46.
  Mary (b. 1770), 46.
June, Ann, Mrs., 9.
  Elizabeth, 9.
  John, 9, 19, 24, 26, 53.
  John (b. 1744), 19.
  Katharine, 26.
  Lucretia (Kennel), Mrs., 19, 24, 26.
  Peter, 24.

Karwon (Kerwon) Crafton, 51, 58, 89–92.
  Mary (Mrs.), 56, 107.
Keaton, Hannah, Mrs., 37 (2).
  John, 37 (2).
  Mary, 37.
  Sarah, 37.
Keble (Keeble), Elizabeth, 53.
  Kary, 56.
Keen, Andrew, 9.
  Elizabeth (Pelleo) Mrs., 9.
  Elizabeth (b. 1742), 19.
  John, 9, 51, 86.
  Martha, Mrs., 51.
  Mary, Mrs., 19.
  Thomas, 19.
Keightly, Jane, Mrs., 27, 33.
  John, 27, 33, 56.
  Mary, 33.
  Peter, 27.
Keith, Alexander (Rev.), 26, 27, 45, 56, 168.
  Benjamin, 47 (3).
  Benjamin (b. 1772), 47.
  James, 47.
  Sarah, Mrs., 47 (3).
  William, 47.
Kelly, Agnes, 12.
  Agnes, (b. 1752), 32.
  Elizabeth, Mrs., 32.
  John, 12, 32.
  Mary, 56.
Kemp, Elizabeth (Mrs.), wife of William, 7, 11.
  Elizabeth, Mrs., wife of John, 44 (2).

Kemp—*Continued.*
  Elizabeth (b. 1761), 44.
  John, 44 (2).
  John (b. 1756), 44.
  Sarah, 7.
  Stephen, 11.
  William, 7, 11.
Kennedy, Bryan, 23, 28.
  Bryan (b. 1749), 28.
  Mary, Mrs., 23, 28.
  Mary (b. 1740), 23.
  James, 23.
  Richard, 23.
Kennel, Lucy (Lucretia), 53.
Kerr, Isaac, 52.
Killy, Emme, Mrs., 40 (2).
  Gerrald, 40.
  Kizziah, 40.
  William, 40 (2).
King, Anna, 142.
  Charles, 10, 14.
  Elisabeth, 56.
  James, 54, 59, 109.
  Jasper, 93–109.
  John, Dr., 110, 111.
  Mary, Mrs., 10, 14, 54.
  Mary Anna 57.
  Priscilla, 10.
  Richard, 179, 182, 183.
  Sarah Berrisford, 14.
Knee, Elinor, Mrs., 31.
  Elizabeth, 31.
  John, 31.
Knight, Ann, 32.
  Catherine, Mrs., 32 (2).
  James, 32 (2).
  James (b. 1751), 32.
  John, 32.
  Sarah, Mrs., 32.
  Thomas James, 32.
Knox, Janet, 52.
  John, 214.
  William (Rev.), 50 (3).
Kolp, Tinman, 51.

Labruce, Hannah, 54.
Lacey, Jonathan, 20.
  Sarah, Mrs., 20.
  William, 20.
Lake, Philip, 97.
Landon, Thomas, 76.
Lane, Christopher, 33.
  Drury, 33, 174.
  Elizabeth, 19.
  Hannah, 28.
  Hester, 42.

McCortry, Robert, 213.
    William, 196, 215.
McCrea, Alexander, sen., 220, 226.
McCullough, James, 226.
    Thomas, 221.
McCully, Mr. (Rev.), 50.
McCutchin, George, 226.
McDaniel, Ann, 51.
    Daniel, 18, 21.
    Daniel, 52.
    John, 56.
    Mary, 56.
    Mary, Mrs., 18, 21.
    Susannah, 18, 21.
McDonald, Adam, 198.
    Daniel, 146.
    Elizabeth, Mrs., 32 (2).
    James, Capt., 130.
    John, 32 (2), 127, 146, 147, 151.
    William, 32, 149, 155.
    Zachariah, 32.
McDowell, Andrew, 187.
    Ann, Mrs., 46.
    Fargus, 47.
    John, 14, 19, 145–190, 213–224.
    John (b. 1742), 14.
    John (b. 1767), 46.
    Lucretia, Mrs., 14, 19.
    Susannah, Mrs., 47.
    William, 19, 46, 47.
    Mrs., 209, 211.
McElroy, Mary, 209–226.
McGee, Elizabeth, Mrs., 15.
    Peter, 15.
    William, 15, 206, 207, 209.
McGinney, Ann, 8.
    Catherine, 51.
    Daniel, 42, (2), 43, 44, 146–223.
    Elizabeth, 42.
    James, 42.
    Mary, 51.
    Richard, 43.
    Susanna, Mrs., 42 (2), 43, 44.
    Thomas, 44.
McGregor, Margaret, 207.
McIlvaine, John, 221.
McIver, Mr., 101.
    Mrs., 184.
McKants James, 52.
McKinney, Benjamin, 40 (2).
    Christian, 40.
    Mary, Mrs., 40 (2).
    Michael, 40.
McKenet, Daniel, 205.
McKleveney, Rebecca, 51.

McKnight, John, 222.
McLendan, (McClanden), Dennis, 36 (3).
    Enoch, 36.
    Francis, 36.
    Isaac, 30.
    Jacob, 30 (2).
    Jamima, 30.
    Joel Jesse, 37.
    Joil, 37.
    Martha, Mrs., wife of Jacob, 30 (2).
    Martha, Mrs., wife of Dennis, 36 (3).
    Thamar, Mrs., 37.
    Zilpha Girk (?), 36.
McPahaphy, Mary, 39.
    Oliver, 39 (2).
    Phibi, Mrs., 39 (2).
    Sarah, 39.
McPherson, Daniel, 14, 59.
    Elias, 27, 200–206.
    Elisabeth (Brown), Mrs., 14, 19, 24, 27, 58.
    James, 14, 19, 24, 27, 52, 58, 59, 122–223.
    James (b. 1747), 24.
    Jannet, 19.
McRea, Alexander, 146, 220, 226.
    John, 204.
Metcalfe, Ann, 13.
    Sarah, Mrs., 13.
    William, 13, 51.
Michael, Frances, Mrs., 32.
    George, 32.
    John, 32.
    Massey, 32.
    Moses, 32.
    Sarah, Mrs., 32.
Michau, Abraham, 17 (3).
    Abraham, jun. (b. 1723), 13, 17 (2), 18 (4), 27, 42, 146, 158, 188.
    Abraham (b. 1753), 42.
    Charlotte, Mrs., 17 (3), 18 (4).
    Daniel, 18.
    Hester, 17.
    Isaac, 220.
    Julian, 17.
    Lydia, Mrs., 13, 17.
    Lydia (b. 1738), 18.
    Noah, 18.
    Paul, 18, 191, 193, 217, 222.
    Peter, 17, 196.
    Sarah, Mrs., 42.

www.ingramcontent.com/pod-product-compliance
Lightning Source LLC
Chambersburg PA
CBHW021857020426
42334CB00013B/372